Fighting *for* Your Empty Nest Marriage

David H. Arp
Claudia S. Arp
Scott M. Stanley
Howard J. Markman
Susan L. Blumberg

Fighting *for* Your Empty Nest Marriage

Reinventing Your Relationship
When the Kids Leave Home

JOSSEY-BASS
A Wiley Company
San Francisco

2114 0430

Jossey-Bass books and products are available through most bookstores. To contact Jossey-Bass directly, call (888) 378-2537, fax to (800) 605-2665, or visit our website at www.josseybass.com.

Substantial discounts on bulk quantities of Jossey-Bass books are available to corporations, professional associations, and other organizations. For details and discount information, contact the special sales department at Jossey-Bass.

Manufactured in the United States of America on Lyons Falls Turin Book. This paper is acid-free and 100 percent totally chlorine-free.

Library of Congress Cataloging-in-Publication Data
Fighting *for* your empty nest marriage / David H. Arp . . . [et al.].
    p. cm. — (The Jossey-Bass psychology series)
Includes bibliographical references and index.
    ISBN 0-7879-5222-2 (alk. paper)
  1. Marriage. 2. Empty nesters. 3. Empty nesters—Psychology.
4. Man-woman relationships. 5. Parent and adult child. I. Arp, Dave. II. Series.
    HQ734 .F434 2000
    306.81—dc21
                                        00-009169

FIRST EDITION
HB *Printing*   10 9 8 7 6 5 4 3 2 1

Contents

Part IV: Feathering Your Own Empty Nest

Acknowledgments

From Scott, Howard, and Susan

The PREP approach, as described in this book, is built on foundations provided by many other contributors to the fields of behavioral marital therapy, psychoeducational approaches to marriage and family relationships, and the general field of personal relationships. There are numerous researchers and theorists in the field whose work has been extremely important to us, including John Gottman, Clifford Notarius, Don Baucom, Neil Jacobson, Robert Weiss, Gayla Margolin, Andy Christensen, Frank Floyd, Danielle Julian, Mari Clements, Kristin Lindahl, Kurt Hahlweg, Bernard Guerney, Kim Halford, Steven Beach, Dan O'Leary, Amy Holtzwoth-Monroe, Ted Jacob, Jill Hooley, Caryl Rusbult, Tom Bradbury, Mike Johnson, Steven Duck, Janice Levine, Cas Schaap, Ted Huston, Gerald Patterson, Pat Noller, Frank Fincham, Sherrod Miller, and Norm Epstein.

Over the years, we have been assisted by a set of colleagues and research associates as we have developed, evaluated, and disseminated the approach that underlies this book. We are especially grateful for our friendships and the ability to have collaborated with these people in various ways: Savanna McCain, Daniel Trathen, Milt Bryan, Pam Jordan, and Bill Coffin. These are wonderful people who care deeply about helping couples.

We also express our strongly felt appreciation to Lisa LaViolette Hoyer, Amy LaViolette Galloway, Wendy Cowperthwaite, Donna

Jackson, Nancy Montgomery, Chris Saiz, Ragnar Storaasli, Naomi Rather, Mary Jo Renick, Pat Burton, Brigit Van Widenfelt, Holly Johnson, Audie Novak, Hal Lewis, Karen Jamieson-Darr, Paul Howes, Joyce Emde, Matt Johnson, Doug Leber, Wayne Duncan, Deb Butte, Natalie Jenkins, Veronica Johnson, Shelle Kraft, Lydia Prado, Michelle Bobulinski, Laurie Tonelli, Michelle St. Peters, Allan Cordova, Antonio Olmos, Sarah Whitton, Natalie Monarch, and Tom Wilkens.

We also cannot thank enough the staff at PREP, Inc. for their ongoing support. They help us keep going. Natalie Jenkins has been particularly helpful, not only in making PREP run but in providing detailed, insightful feedback about this manuscript. We also greatly appreciate the support and aid of Phyllis Lemons, Janelle Miller, and Glenda Roslund. A more talented and kind group you could not find.

Some of the key research studies that underlie material in this book have been supported by the University of Denver, the National Institute of Mental Health, and the National Science Foundation. We are grateful for the support from these institutions, which has enabled us to develop the research basis for the program presented in this book.

Finally, we want to express our deep sense of appreciation for the couples and families who have shared their lives with us in our various research projects. Over the years, these couples have opened their hearts and their relationships to our interviewers and video cameras. They have shared their struggles and successes, and we hope that the knowledge presented in this book represents some small compensation to these couples, without whom the book could never have been written. We would also like to acknowledge the role that our clients and seminar participants have played in shaping the ideas and case histories presented in the book. We have disguised the identities of the couples in the vignettes presented here through the use of composites and detail changes. Nevertheless, the stories told by many couples over the years are often so strikingly similar that the themes in the case histories we present will speak to a variety of people. We can all learn from each other.

From David and Claudia

We wish to express our gratitude and thanks to all the people who participated in our Second Half of Marriage and Empty Nest surveys. We appreciate your willingness to share the inside of your marriage, both your failures and your successes. We also want to acknowledge Vera Mace, with her late husband, David Mace, for their life work in helping marriages succeed and for their encouragement, friendship, and input in our lives and marriage over the years. To Scott Bolinder (publisher) and Sandy Vander Zicht (editor) of our book *The Second Half of Marriage* (Zondervan, 1996), we express our thanks for your friendship and for your encouragement and cooperation in our participation in this joint writing project with PREP.

From All Five of Us

Our editor at Jossey-Bass, Alan Rinzler, has been a wonderful friend and enthusiastic supporter for many years now. We are blessed to know him and work with him. He has been a major contributor to the quality of this book and the others in this series. He has pushed us in our goal to make this book as effective as possible for couples. We thank Alan and his staff at Jossey-Bass for their support and expertise during this process.

Diane Sollee was enthusiastic about this joint project all along the way. We wish to acknowledge her for her national efforts to put marriage education on the map and for letting the cat out of the bag that people are aging and so are their marriages!

Before You Begin

A Personal Note from David and Claudia Arp

The phone rang. An attorney from New York City was on the line. "My wife says she doesn't love me anymore—that our marriage is boring and now that our last daughter is leaving for college, she wants out. I had no idea my wife was so unhappy. Is there something you can do to fix my marriage?" Not an isolated incident. Today's version of "You've Got Mail" includes a cry for help from a wife whose husband of twenty-five years just walked out. Daily, spouses are faced with the reality that if their empty nest marriages are going to make it, they will have to fight for them!

No one warns us of the crises ahead. Most books on marriage deal with the first half of the relationship, not the second. Yet in divorce courts across the country, long-term marriages are breaking up in record numbers. Judging from the cries for help and other indicators that long-term marriages are in trouble, the future promises no relief.

Even though statistically the future of your marriage may be at risk, the good news is that you don't have to become a divorce statistic! Actually your marriage in the second half of life can be far more rewarding and enjoyable than in the first half. But one thing is for certain: the predictable passage of time will usher in the empty nest years.

We want to help you navigate them successfully. In the chapters that follow, we show you how to prepare for the next stage of your relationship. We'll teach you new skills that will help you successfully "fight" for your empty nest marriage. We are convinced that you can build a more fulfilling relationship than was ever possible during your active parenting years. We're writing, in part, from personal experience.

OUR OWN STORY

It was over a decade ago when Domino's Pizza® called us. A concerned voice on the other end asked if we were OK—it had been weeks since we'd ordered pizza!

Dave assured him that all was fine. Actually we were overdosing on lima beans, broccoli, and brussels sprouts—all the vegetables our youngest child, Jonathan, hated. Why the change in menu? Several weeks ago we had dropped Jonathan off at college. Now we could eat what we wanted to eat and when we wanted to eat it. Now our time belonged to us. No longer was Claudia the family air traffic controller. No more junior tennis tournaments or soccer practices. No more impromptu teenage parties. Our house—and the kitchen—was ours again, and menu planning once again became delightful.

Please don't misunderstand us. We love our three sons and enjoyed the active parenting years—well, most of them—yet our initial reaction to the empty nest was relief. Parenting three adolescent boys had not been easy—but with a few good parenting principles, a sense of humor, God's grace, and over twenty years of forced labor, we made it through the teenage years.

Now was *our* turn to enjoy life! After all, we were once again in control of our home, our schedules, and ourselves—or so we thought! Wrong. It didn't take long to realize that transitioning to the empty nest wasn't the breeze it first appeared to be; instead, it was more of a tornado. Our family's typical hectic and crisis-filled rhythm was disrupted, our responsibilities and roles turned upside down.

After bingeing on vegetables, we struggled with just eating regular meals. Without Jonathan's hungry demands, we would find ourselves working and doing other things until nine or ten at night and suddenly realizing we had not eaten dinner. Our late-night Frosted Mini-Wheats® gourmet dinners threatened to become an empty nest tradition.

Changing roles also confused the landscape. I (Claudia) had been more involved with our children and running our home than Dave had been. Now was my time to do what I wanted to do with my life—but what was that? I still remember a conversation we had the first year of our empty nest. In the middle of fitness-walking around our block, Dave shocked me by saying, "Claudia, for the first half of our marriage, we've lived wherever I've needed to be professionally. For the second half, let's live wherever you want to be."

That was quite impressive, but the problem was that I didn't know where I wanted to be—or exactly who I was. I knew I was a writer. And I knew I had enjoyed the occasional times we had traveled and spoken together during the active parenting years. But what now? Suddenly I realized that all those things I had delayed until the kids left home were possibilities. Children had definitely moderated my workaholic tendencies. So with my urging, we accepted too many writing projects, speaking engagements, and seminars, which left us with little time and energy for each other.

Sitting over coffee at our breakfast table one morning, we agreed something had to give. We realized we needed help; we needed to regroup, refocus, and refresh our own relationship. So to help us retool our marriage, we decided to research this passage into the empty nest and beyond. That day we began what turned out to be a ten-year journey, and during those ten years we have learned how to reinvent our own relationship, how to refocus on each other, and how to renegotiate and resolve issues in new and fresh ways that reenergized our own marriage.

OUR SURVEY ON THE EMPTY NEST

Our research included conducting a national survey of long-term marriages; it took us to the very heart and soul of many empty nest marriages (and brought us into contact with our coauthors for this book).

Through the kaleidoscope of over six hundred written survey responses, we saw many unique marriages. Some were beautiful to behold: healthy, loving, warm relationships. Others were distressing: hurting, bitter, isolated, and lonely. Most were somewhere on the continuum between ecstasy and despair. The reality of how hard relationships are to maintain was our constant companion, but one of our most encouraging discoveries was that couples who successfully make it through the empty nest passage are the ones that successfully learn how to fight for their marriage. Read what two couples wrote about the best aspects of their marriages in the empty nest: "The freedom to think of ourselves and each other again. A new beginning at goal setting and tapping back into our senses of what it is we enjoy doing, now that our time is our own again. The joy of a son well launched and of the expanding family. . . . Knowing each other well. Beginning to reach out to others rather than being totally focused on our family."

"In contrast to our previous marriage, we can communicate no matter how severe the issue. Our issues are no less complicated in our present marriage—some blended-family issues are even more complicated. But we can communicate on them, and that's the biggest and most essential difference from our previous marriages. We like each other—that helps a lot. We get angry with each other, etc., but no matter what happens I can look at my wife and say, 'You know, I really do like that woman.' We also have similar values and religious orientations, similar personalities, etc."

We draw on this research—including input from an updated survey with nearly five hundred marriage educators, counselors, clergy, and researchers—and on twenty years of research conducted by our coauthors on what makes marriages work. Together with our coauthors, we will teach you some very powerful strategies for making the second half of your marriage your better half.

OUR COAUTHORS: SCOTT STANLEY, HOWARD MARKMAN, AND SUSAN BLUMBERG

Our coauthors, Scott Stanley, Howard Markman, and Susan Blumberg, are internationally known for their research on the prevention of marital distress and divorce. Along with other researchers worldwide, they have been engaged in groundbreaking research on how couples can develop and preserve a lasting love. Their years of university-based research were the source for their book *Fighting for Your Marriage*. Many of the core concepts from that book are based on their program for couples called PREP (the Prevention and Relationship Enhancement Program). The best of the strategies and techniques from PREP are included here because, for so many couples, they work, and work well. What follows is a summary—written by Howard, Scott, and Susan—about PREP and their work.

WHAT IS PREP?

Based on twenty years of marital research, the PREP approach focuses on specific attitudes and ways of acting that can make a powerful difference in your marriage over time. This book will help you apply those powerful strategies in your marriage at this crucial time of transition in your life. PREP incorporates principles derived from couples research done in the United States and around the world. For example, there is a great deal of evidence that compared to happier couples, couples who are not doing as well in their marriages show a major difference in their ability to handle conflict. Such findings have led us to develop a number of very specific strategies couples can use to handle issues more constructively.

These strategies we will teach you here. But this book is not just about communication and conflict. We will also focus on such topics as commitment, forgiveness, spiritual intimacy, friendship, sensuality, and fun—each with special application to you who are moving into or are already in the empty nest phase of life together.

Much of the research underlying key points and strategies in this book has been conducted at the University of Denver. Some of this research has been supported by the National Institute of Mental Health through grants awarded to Howard Markman and Scott Stanley. A careful analysis of years of research, comparing couples who are having significant problems to couples who are happy together and solidly committed, resulted in PREP and, now, many of the suggestions in this book.

Among the kinds of studies we or other researchers have conducted over the years are long-term studies looking at which couples thrive, which fail, and which limp along in misery for years. In these kinds of studies, we and other researchers have learned about specific risk factors; we will warn you about these factors and teach you ways to protect your marriage from them into the years to come. Knowing more about how marriages fall apart gives us a much clearer idea of where couples should focus their attention to make their marriage all it can be. *In this book, we focus on things that are changeable, things you can really do something about in order to experience greater peace and openness in your marriage.*

One of the things we are most delighted about in writing this book for empty nest couples is our collaboration with David and Claudia Arp. Not only have they themselves been going through this empty nest time of life; they have also collected wonderful data on the issues and dynamics many empty nest couples deal with in this time of transition and opportunity. The Arps bring knowledge, fresh insights, and a wonderful style of communication to this work. Furthermore, they are internationally known for their other materials and Marriage Alive seminars in the area of helping couples have great marriages. We hope you will benefit from the combination of our work and theirs in bringing this material to you.

HOW ARE THINGS GOING FOR YOU?

The following quiz has been developed from numerous marriage studies, both by us at the University of Denver and by many marital researchers around the world. It can help you get a rough sense of how you are doing on some key dimensions. It certainly doesn't cover everything that's important, but it does address key patterns that studies show are related to how a marriage will do over time. Don't panic if you mark several statements as "true" for your relationship. You can use them as a guide to areas to work on in your marriage. In Part Two of this book, we go into more detail about how to deal with the "true" answers. Everyone would occasionally answer "true" to some of these statements, but a persistent pattern of yes answers over time can be a warning signal that your relationship needs help—and you'll want to begin taking steps to turn things around. Or you may find that you answer "false" to most of these statements. In that case, you should approach what we have to teach you as a matter of prevention. In other words, take the time to learn the kinds of strategies that can keep your marriage on track and growing over the years to come.

Respond to the following statements on your own; do not work on them with your partner.

1. Little arguments escalate into ugly fights with accusations, criticisms, name calling, or bringing up past hurts.

2. My partner criticizes or belittles my opinions, feelings, or desires.

3. My partner seems to view my words or actions more negatively than I mean them to be.

4. When we have a problem to solve, it is as though we are on opposite teams.

5. I hold back from telling my partner what I really think and feel.

6. I think seriously about what it would be like to date or marry someone else.

7. I feel lonely in this relationship.

8. When we argue, one of us withdraws—that is, doesn't want to talk about it anymore or leaves the scene.

9. I am fearful about what our future together will be like.

As you read this book, you will understand not only why your responses to these statements are important but also what you can do to build and maintain a great marriage that brings delight to both of you.

HOW TO GET THE MOST OUT OF THIS BOOK

We (all the authors) believe that creating and maintaining a good relationship are largely skills, like any other skills, and that you can learn these skills together as a couple if you are motivated to do so. Furthermore, we believe that transitional periods in life—such as when you are moving into the stage of life during which your life together is more and more about the two of you, and less focused on raising your children—are the ideal times to make changes that can improve your future together.

We'll introduce a number of very effective skills for handling conflict and disagreements. We'll also suggest strategies for building and maintaining friendship, commitment, and spiritual intimacy. Some of what we cover are very specific skills that you can learn. Like any new skills, these become easier with practice. (To help you learn the skills and put them into practice, there are exercises at the end of each of the chapters.) With regard to each skill or principle, we'll also tell you about the underlying theory and research so you understand why it works. You will find that these techniques are not really difficult to understand, but *they will take work to master*. We believe it will be worth your effort to make what you learn here a part of your relationship.

OFF WE GO

Because we (the Arps) have been on our empty nest journey for the past decade, we take the lead in sharing our personal experiences with you. Then in each chapter, with our coauthors, we help you chart your own course for the future.

Won't you join us in this fight? In the following pages, we give you the tools to help you fight *for* your empty nest marriage. You can learn to surmount the unique challenges this stage presents. The second half of your marriage—the empty nest years—can be a time of incredible fulfillment no matter what challenges you have faced before. You can work toward a more personal, satisfying, and fulfilling union than you experienced during the active parenting years—especially if you're willing to fight for it! So let us welcome you to the second half of your marriage. You *can* make the rest the best!

Fighting *for* Your Empty Nest Marriage

Part I

Understanding Your
Empty Nest Marriage

1

Meet the Second Marriage
of Your Marriage

Each fall, colleges across the country fill the freshman dormitories with new students all set to begin their college careers. Other high school graduates, all ready to enter the job market, move into apartments and condos with their friends, while still yet others join the army, air force, navy, or marines to be all they can be. Still other young adults do not leave home, at least not for some time, but live very independent lives, mostly using their parents' home as a place to sleep but little else. What do the parents of all these adult children have in common? They are entering the second half of marriage.

WHAT IS THE SECOND
HALF OF MARRIAGE?

Because a lot of empty nesters really don't have a truly empty nest, we prefer the term *second half of marriage*. How can you know if you are approaching the second half or are already in it? Check out the symptoms:

- You begin to see some light at the end of the tunnel, and it doesn't spotlight your role as parents; you realize your active parenting years are coming to a close.

- Suddenly your arms aren't long enough to hold the newspaper you are trying to read.

- Your own parents are aging and may be experiencing health problems.

- You just got your invitation to join AARP.

- The golden oldies radio station is playing your song.

- You start losing hair where you don't want to lose it and start growing hair where you don't want it.

- That extra ten pounds threatens to became a permanent resident.

- You repeat yourself.

- You repeat yourself.

IS THIS BOOK FOR YOU?

Traditionally, we think of the empty nest family as one in which some or all of the children have left home to begin their own journeys through life. Couples in this category have usually been married twenty-plus years, and often the wife has not regularly worked outside the home, or the husband will be retiring and spending more time at home. Actually the empty nest syndrome starts at different times for different couples. Some couples are so overwhelmed with the teenage years that they don't even see the next stage coming until the last child leaves home or gets married. Others begin talking about it when the first college catalogue appears in their mailbox.

Today, many couples reaching the second half of their marriage find that their nest is filled (or refilled) with all sorts of unexpected visitors, such as toddlers or preschoolers or both. (Maybe they started their family late, or they may be raising a grandchild.) Their nest might also include teenagers, an adult child, or an elderly parent who is experiencing health problems and needs extra care. These situations may be harder to deal with if you have had a period of time with just you and your partner at home. You've started to adjust to an empty nest and now have to readjust to sharing your home and facing increased complications.

We wrote this book not only for those of you who are entering the "traditional" empty nest with the first or last kid leaving home but also for those of you in the more complicated situations, such as the blended marriage, perhaps with both spouses having their own sets of adult or almost adult children. Perhaps you are in a new marriage with no kids but are in the second half of life. Or maybe you have survived the initial transition into the empty nest but need a marriage tune-up. So whether you are a newlywed or have been married twenty, thirty, forty or more years, if you want to keep improving your marriage, this book is written for you.

YOUR PATH TO THE SECOND HALF

As you can see, a marriage in the second half of life is far more complex than a mom and dad with no kids at home. But whatever your unique situation, we believe the sooner you begin to prepare for the empty nest (even if it *never* empties!), the smoother the transition you will make to this new and challenging stage of life.

Although the first emotion many new empty nesters feel is relief, life can become confusing. For many couples, it is almost as though they are in a new marriage. But like a new marriage, the empty nest marriage can take several different paths. Consider the following couples' experiences. They reflect three different paths: (1) drifting into the empty nest without much thought or awareness, (2) charging into the empty nest with celebration, and (3) crashing into the empty nest and the crises of transition.

Joe and Nancy

"Our twin daughters were the spark plugs that kept our family lively," Nancy told us. "When they left for college, everything changed. It was so quiet. Actually I had looked forward to a little peace and quiet, but it seemed so weird to be just the two of us again—like we really didn't know each other any more. I began to realize that our marriage was stagnant. We had little in common, few things to talk about. It's not that either of us had intentionally ignored the other, but with the demands of two very active and social children, over the years, we had drifted apart."

Joe added, "I didn't have a clue as to what to do, so I reacted by spending more time at work and more time with my golf buddies."

"I felt so alone," Nancy continued. "I was disoriented. My major focus in life was the girls. Now they were gone, and so was my job. No more college applications to help with or track meets to attend. No more impromptu teenage parties. I realized my own personal interests were limited. No wonder Joe didn't want to spend time at home. I was boring. And I was bored. Wasn't the empty nest supposed to be more fun than this?"

Frances and Albert

"Have you seen the commercial on television, where the mom is upstairs redecorating her son's room before he gets out of the driveway?" Albert asked. "Well, that was Frances! It wasn't that we didn't love our kids, but parenting three adolescent boys had not been a joyride—it was more like forced labor! When they left we were ready to party."

Frances continued, "While we did have some adjustments to make, entering the empty nest was not a crisis time for us. Actually, I had the most adjusting to do. I'd always wanted to pursue a graduate degree, so now was my time. Albert was supportive, so I cut back on my hours at work and enrolled in the MBA program at our local university."

"I was glad Frances got accepted into the grad school, and I wanted to encourage her in anyway I could," Albert said.

Frances, smiling at Albert, added, "And now when the boys come home for visits, we enjoy them—but we aren't that sad when they leave again."

Hank and Susan

"When our kids left home, we didn't know each other," Hank told us when we met them at a neighborhood party, "and we came close to divorcing. Previously our lives revolved around our children and their activities. We had few conflicts, but when the kids left home there was a vacuum. We had nothing in common. It was a crisis time in our marriage. Susan became more assertive. I didn't know what was happening!"

"For years my identity was my role as a mother," Susan went on. "Now I had a whole new world to discover."

Hank added, "I was experiencing some health problems and wanted to slow down and spend more time at home, but Susan seemed driven to start her own interior decorating business. We were on different tracks. It was scary."

"But you made it," I (Dave) commented. "We've been observing you all evening, and you like each other and seem to have a close relationship. What happened?"

Hank responded, "We had to rebuild our marriage. In some ways it was like starting all over again. We had to get reacquainted. We rarely talked about "us," so we had to learn how to communicate and how to work through issues. We were both amazed how little we really knew about each other and how hard it was to change. But now we're enjoying one another's company again. It's like we have a whole new marriage."

Three couples on three different paths. Joe and Nancy drifted into the empty nest. Albert and Frances celebrated it, and Hank and Susan found the empty nest passage a real time of crisis. With which couple do you most identify? Whatever path you're on now, we can help you get on the path to making the coming years the best years of your life together.

THE EMPTY NEST YEARS
OF YOUR MARRIAGE

As nests empty, couples enter uncharted waters full of the risks and dangers of midlife marriage burnout. Whereas Hank and Susan were able to rechart their course, other couples become divorce statistics.

In the following pages, we share with you some of what we have learned—from our combined research, from other couples, and from our own experience of the last decade in the empty nest. We're convinced that this phase of your life can be the best—but you have to fight for it to be so. Why is the empty nest so challenging? Consider the following points.

The Empty Nest Passage Is a Time of Insecurity

Children are leaving home, and with them they take their energy and vitality. There is more time to be introspective. For the first time, many spouses take a serious look at their marriage. This can be a risky time for spouses who have not maintained a close relationship during the parenting years. Mothers who had chosen to stay home with their children struggle to find their identity. Joyce, our friend who home-schooled her three children, told us as she sent her youngest off to college, "Now I have to decide who I want to be when I grow up."

As we age, a shift also takes place across gender lines. Many men become more nurturing and begin to focus back on the home. They are ready to slow down and enjoy life. Work becomes less important than in previous years. At the same time, women can become more focused, more assertive, and independent. Now it's their time to go out and make an impact on the world—especially if they, like Joyce, dedicated the first half of their marriage to nurturing and parenting their children. These changes are developmental and occur across different cultures; if they are not managed well, they can threaten the health of any marriage. One husband, married thirty years, wrote in the survey that he was fearful "that we will stop talking and pursuing each other for an honest level of intimacy."

But changes handled wisely can enhance a second-half marriage. Couples can move closer to each other and may actually have more in common than during the active parenting years.

The Term *Empty Nest* Is Misleading

The "empty nest" is not always empty. For instance, Gail Sheehy, in her book *New Passages* (1995), reports that of unmarried American men between the ages of twenty-five and thirty-four, more than one-third are still living at home. Also, many adult children return home—often bringing a spouse, grandchildren, or both with them.

"Really, we never had an empty nest," Jennifer told us. "My widowed mother lived with us in her own apartment in our home for twenty-five years. One son left home, lived on his own for a while, and then returned to live with us. A year ago my mother died at ninety-two, and my son, his wife, and their baby moved into my mom's apartment. Consequently, we've never experienced an empty nest."

In addition, at this stage of life, many couples are in their second marriages with his children, her children, and younger children from the present marriage. Blended families add to the ambiguity of this life stage. Even in a "non-empty nest," the dynamics change when the children become young adults. It's definitely a new season of marriage.

More Couples Are Reaching the Empty Nest Stage, and the Divorce Rate for Empty Nest Marriages Is Accelerating

Conventional wisdom indicates that many couples stay together while children are the focus of the relationship; when the children leave home, so do the reasons for staying in the relationship. Long-term marriages are breaking up in record numbers. According to the National Center of Health Statistics, although divorce in the United States declined 1.4 percent from 1981 to 1991, divorce among couples married thirty years or longer increased 16 percent. A wife, married twenty-two years, wrote in the Arps' survey, "When our children leave (#1) and if my husband's anger and critical spirit remain (#2), then #3 is inevitable. It seems hopeless—will you please pray for us?"

People Are Living Longer, Making the Empty Nest a Major Stage of Marriage

Today it is not unusual to hear about couples celebrating their six-tieth or seventieth wedding anniversary. People are living far longer than in previous generations. Now the empty nest years may be the biggest chunk of your marriage. In the past, couples married, raised their families, and then died. Now people are living longer, and the possibility of a really long term marriage is the norm instead of the exception. Perhaps more people are calling their marriage quits because they don't want to face the next forty or fifty years in a less than satisfying marriage. The glue that held them together (the children) is gone, and these couples simply don't know how to stick together. One coauthor, Scott Stanley, noted in his book *The Heart of Commitment* (1998) that couples who stay together long term either stick or become stuck. Decisions you make at the beginning of the empty nest phase have a lot to do with what path you will be on in the years ahead. This book is about helping you to stick.

Resources to Help Couples Through the Empty Nest Passage Are Limited

Most marriage books, resources, and seminars are focused on pre- and early marriage or on marriage with children. When we (David and Claudia) hit the empty nest phase a decade ago, we were incredu-lous to discover how few resources even mentioned marriage in the empty nest—thus our decision to research it ourselves.

RESURVEYING EMPTY NEST ISSUES

Since we researched and wrote our book *The Second Half of Marriage* (1996), we conducted an additional survey and found once again that the issues in a marriage remain basically the same over the years. Issues and problems in marriage cause you neither success nor failure; it's how you deal with them that makes a difference, especially in the empty nest. When you are no longer meeting the demands of active parenting, issues will resurface and perhaps loom larger on the landscape of your marriage. So what are those major issues you'll take with you into the empty nest?

Consider the top ten issues in our empty nest survey, number one being the most severe problem area, number two, the next most severe problem, and so on:

Top Issues in the Empty Nest Years

1. Conflict
2. Communication
3. Sex
4. Health
5. Fun
6. Recreation
7. Money
8. Aging parents
9. Retirement planning
10. Children

The top three issues in the empty nest—conflict, communication, and sex—are also among the major problem areas for younger couples. People take their issues along as they transition through the different seasons of a marriage. We observed no overall gender differences that were very strong. However, females tended to say communication was more of a problem than did males, and males tended to say that sex was more of a problem than females reported. (Are you surprised?)

At this stage of life, money issues are not rated as high as for younger couples, but health issues are rated higher. The fact that fun and recreation are rated so high indicates that perhaps couples are having trouble figuring out what to do together that's enjoyable for both or finding fun things that both will take time out for. For years their shared recreational activities may have been centered around their children, and now they don't know what to do to have fun together.

How would you rank these issues in your marriage? Think about your relationship: with which issues do you struggle the most? You may want to take the same survey we give to our couples as an in-depth way to look at issues and discuss them with your partner. It is the second exercise at the end of this chapter. After you complete the survey, you may want to compare your rankings with the mean score of the empty nesters we surveyed. But first let's look at the challenges that all long-term marriages face.

CHALLENGING YOURSELVES FOR THE SECOND HALF

Through the findings of our surveys as well as the research of our colleagues and coauthors at the University of Denver, we have identified the major challenges facing couples who want to make a successful transition into the empty nest and beyond. The good news from our combined research is that for those of you who hang together through the empty nest transition, marital satisfaction can begin to rise again and stay that way if you risk growing in your relationship. But if you do not grow, the bond between the two of you will likely weaken slowly but surely in the years to come.

The second half of marriage gives you the opportunity to reinvent your marriage, to make midcourse adjustments, and to reconnect with one another in a more meaningful way. Long-term marriages have staying power because they are held together from within. Competent couples invest time and energy in building and maintaining a positive relationship with each other.

The Eight Challenges of the Empty Nest

In our book *The Second Half of Marriage*, we listed the following eight challenges to those entering the empty nest years. We are convinced that if you work on these eight challenges, your marriage will be enriched. If you do not surmount these challenges, then your empty nest marriage will not be as fulfilling as it could be. Check and see how many of these challenges you are facing right now.

Let Go of Past Marital Disappointments, Forgive Each Other, and Commit to Making the Rest of Your Marriage the Best

Are you willing to let go of unmet expectations and unrealistic dreams? What about that missed promotion—for either you or your spouse? Can you give up your dream for a condo by the ski slopes? Or maybe you are realizing that your kid is never going to be a Rhodes scholar or professional baseball player. Can you accept those extra pounds? Those gray hairs—or the lack of hair? Your mate's irritating little habits don't seem to be disappearing; can you accept them?

Giving up lost dreams and dealing with each other's imperfections are positive steps toward forgiving past hurts and moving on in your marriage. Holding on to marital grudges and disappointments will only prevent you from moving on in your relationship and developing a new, more loving marriage.

Create a Marriage That Is Partner Focused Rather Than Child Focused

Too often when the children leave the nest, couples move from a child-focused marriage to an activity-focused marriage. Community or church activities may now take up the time and energy formerly devoted to their children. Unfortunately, excessive activities may buffer the couple from making their marriage a true partnership. How can you make the transition to a partner-focused relationship?

In the second half of marriage, the dynamics of your relationship change. Roles and functions that previously worked are no longer relevant. Without children as distractions, you have the opportunity to refocus and redefine your marriage. Marriage in the second half can be more personal and more fulfilling as you focus on the couple relationship and not on children.

Maintain an Effective Communication System That Allows You to Express Your Deepest Feelings, Joys, and Concerns

You may find the communication patterns that seemed to work during the first half of your marriage to be inadequate and lacking in the second half. With the children absent, there may be more silent spaces between you, with less to say to each other. You may ask yourself, "We made it this far, why is it now so difficult to have a really personal conversation?" A husband, married thirty-four years, wrote of his "hope for a renewal of the kind of communication experienced during courtship."

When you begin to talk about really personal matters, it's easy to feel threatened. Midlife is a time when it is vitally important to develop interpersonal competence—the ability to converse on a personal level by sharing your deepest feelings, joys, and concerns. Successful couples are able to find a proper balance between intimacy and autonomy, and this is critical for healthy relationships in the second half of marriage.

Use Anger and Conflict in a Creative Way to Build Your Relationship

Love and anger can both be used to build your marriage, but you must process your anger in an appropriate way and develop a proper balance that allows you to express your concerns in the context of a loving relationship. A healthy marriage is a safe place to resolve honest conflict and process anger. The reason this challenge is so critical to long-term marriages is that in most conflict situations, the issue itself is often not the greatest problem. As we mentioned earlier, it is how you deal with the issues you face that is most crucial. A wife, married forty-one years, found the best aspect of her marriage to be "unity—we have the same goals and objectives. We are two individuals with very different interests. We learned to accommodate each other." This illustrates that working on your relationship communication can be effective. She wrote later in the survey that she looked forward to "unknown adventures" in the future, sending a message of the strength and growth this couple has experienced.

For most couples, the issues that cause conflict stay pretty much the same year in and year out. But, as we will describe later in the book, certain patterns of negative interaction are deadly for your marriage. We challenge you to learn to face your more difficult issues in a whole new manner that allows you to grow closer in the years ahead.

Build a Deeper Friendship and Enjoy Your Spouse

At this stage of marriage, you can deepen your friendship and become close companions. One advantage of a long-term marriage is being more familiar and comfortable with each other. You know you aren't perfect, so you can relax and enjoy each other. What are you doing to build your friendship with your spouse? Are you taking care of your health and pacing yourself for the second half? What are you doing to stretch your boundaries and prevent boredom? The second half of marriage is a great time to develop "couple friends." How can you put more fun in your marriage and use humor to diminish the effects of an already too serious world? Friendship and fun in marriage—especially in the second half—is serious business!

Renew Romance and Restore a Pleasurable Sexual Relationship

Many assume that as people grow older they lose interest in sex. Research shows otherwise. Our survey results suggest that sexual satisfaction actually increases rather than decreases with number of years married. As couples enter the second half of marriage it is important for them to protect their privacy, cherish their love relationship, and renew romance, while also acknowledging the inevitable changes in their bodies. The quality of one's love life is not so much a matter of performance as it is a function of the quality of relationship. A husband, married thirty years, wrote of the best in his marriage: "We enjoy each other. We like to do similar activities. We are good friends. We are in good health and exercise. We enjoy good healthy sex; we do know how to party and celebrate life." What more could anyone ask for?

Adjust to Changing Roles with Aging Parents and Adult Children

Just as you need to release your children into adulthood, you need to reconnect with them on an adult level. At the same time, you need to balance relationships with your own parents. If your parents did not successfully meet this challenge in their own marriage, it may be more difficult for you. Whatever your situation, the relationships with your elderly parents and your adult children definitely have an effect on your marriage. Understanding and accepting what is realistic in your own family relationships is very important. You can't go back and change your past family history, but what you do in the future is your choice and decision. You can choose to forge better relationships with those loved ones on both sides of the generational seesaw.

Evaluate Where You Are on Your Spiritual Pilgrimage

Couples reading this book will come from many different perspectives about faith, religion, and belief systems. Regardless of your particular beliefs and whether or not the two of you share them, this is a very important time of life to draw together in this area. Research has confirmed that most people, as they age, get more religious. Researchers speculate that this is because people think more about "what it all means" as they get closer to death. Or, as one gentleman put it in a PREP workshop years ago, "they are getting wiser with age." You may have noticed this tendency to "get wiser" in your own life. Our challenge to you is rather simple: to consider this time of transition as a great opportunity for the two of you to talk more openly and regularly about how you view life at this point— what it means, what matters, where it all heads, and what core beliefs you share in your marriage.

The Marriage Journey

Marital success comes through daily struggles. Marriage is made up of the daily grind; the little things, such as making unselfish choices and forgiving each other, help build a healthy marriage. If taken in good faith, little steps can turn the tide. But it helps to have a plan.

You can take the initiative to improve your relationship with your spouse and master the challenges of the empty nest, but remember that real growth involves more than knowledge. You must transform that knowledge into experience. Then you can make the rest of your marriage the best. The following chapters give you the tools to surmount these challenges.

PREPARING FOR THE EMPTY NEST WITH THIS BOOK

In Part One, we'll walk you through the first step of preparing. You need to evaluate where you are right now in your relationship. Taking stock of your relationship as it is now will help you accept each other as a package deal, forgive each other, and refocus on your marriage.

In Part Two, you'll learn how to develop your own coping system— it will be your key to communicating and to handling conflict in the empty nest. We will look at patterns to avoid as well as habits to develop, such as the Speaker-Listener Technique. You will learn how to talk things out—even when you disagree. We'll introduce the critical distinction between issues and events and show you how that concept will help you stay on course and open the door for continued growth and intimacy in your relationship. You'll be able to solve problems more effectively when you learn how to fight fair— especially if you follow our ground rules.

In Part Three, we look more specifically at empty nest issues. One of the biggest challenges is dealing with unmet or unrealistic expectations. Some things are just not going to change or happen in this lifetime. To move on in your relationship, you must accept your unique situation.

We look at the huge role that commitment plays in an empty nest marriage as well as the importance of core beliefs and how to focus on developing spiritual intimacy for this stage of marriage.

Relating to young adult children and older aging parents is a huge challenge. The key is to make your marriage the anchor relationship. Let your marriage be the relational tie that binds you together, so that together you can weather those inevitable family storms that surface from time to time.

In Part Four, we look at ways to enhance your empty nest. This season of marriage holds great challenges as well as great rewards. From our survey, we discovered that empty nesters may be the best lovers and may attain the highest level of sexual satisfaction. A key to enhancing your marriage is simply having fun and building your friendship. We are convinced you can keep your relationship strong and that a successful empty nest marriage may be your greatest reward for the years you spent raising your family.

*

Now let's get started. It is time to take stock of the second marriage of your marriage by working through the exercises.

In Chapter Two, we guide you in discovering the refreshing, restorative power of being willing to forgive each other and to commit to making the rest of your marriage the best!

EXERCISES

Taking Stock of Your Marriage

These questions are designed to help couples think carefully about the issues in their relationships in preparation for discussion about these issues. Consider the following questions about your marriage. You may want to discuss one or more of them with your spouse after you answer them individually, in writing if you wish.

1. What are the major transitions you are presently facing? (First or last child leaving the nest? Changing roles? Relating to new in-laws? Grandchildren?)

2. What do you want your marriage to look like when you are in your eighties?

3. What are your financial goals? Educational plans? Retirement plans?

4. How is your health and physical fitness? Do you need to make any changes?

5. What do you do just for fun?

Second Half of Marriage Survey

Again, each of you may think about these issues individually and discuss them later as a couple. Keep your written answers to refer to later in the book (Chapter Seven). To complete the survey, please make two copies of the issues inventory on the next page; each of you should complete it on your own.

Issues Inventory

Consider the following list of issues. Please rate how much of a problem each area currently is in your relationship by writing in a number from 0 (not a problem at all) to 10 (a severe problem). For example, if money is a slight problem in your relationship, you might enter a 2 or 3 next to Money. If money is not a problem, you would enter a 0, and if money is a severe problem, you would enter 10. If you wish to add other areas that aren't included, please do so in the blank spaces provided. Now rate each area on a separate scale of 0 (not a problem) to 10 (a severe problem):

____ Money	____ In-laws
____ Recreation	____ Communication
____ Conflict resolution	____ Friends
____ Extended family	____ Aging parents
____ Careers	____ Alcohol and/or drugs
____ Sex	____ Children
____ Grandchildren	____ Religion
____ Retirement planning	____ Health and physical fitness
____ Household responsibilities	____ Ministry and community service activities
____ Friendship with spouse	____ Fun and leisure activities
____ Other _____	____ Other _____

Briefly answer the following questions:

What are the best aspects of your marriage?

What are the areas that cause the greatest stress in your marriage?

What do you fear the most about your marriage in the future?

What are you looking forward to in your marriage in the future?

2

Letting Go and Moving On

For us (Dave and Claudia), entering the empty nest was a benchmark in our lives. Some things changed forever. For instance, from this time on we would catalogue our lives as B.C. (before children left) and A.C. (after children left). Faced with so many life changes as we entered the empty nest passage, we did what we often do—we made a list. Making our list was a reality check and was the first step in letting go of some unrealistic expectations; frankly, some weren't that unrealistic, they just would not be fulfilled in this lifetime!

On our lists we wrote down the things we would never do again and things that would never change. For instance, we would never have a daughter. (Three daughters-in-law and two granddaughters help compensate, but our nuclear family will always be four guys and a gal.) We would never ride across the Swiss Alps on a motorcycle. We would never have completely healthy backs again. We would always struggle to keep our weight under control and our office neat and tidy.

Obviously, our list also included disappointments with each other: Dave will always sneak ice cream at night, forget to call when he is running late, and hum in his sleep; Claudia will always take on too many commitments, leave the gas tank empty, and buy low-fat, flavorless snacks. Even though this list may sound negative, writing it was an important part of the process of accepting each other.

At this stage of our marriage we realized we needed to view our little individual idiosyncratic behaviors as endearing traits instead of irritations. Making our lists helped us do just that.

You may also want to make your list. Now is the time to let go and acknowledge things that are not going to change, such as a partner's personality traits that irritate, or that you or your spouse are not going to make a lot of money, or that your partner is putting on weight and no longer the beautiful hot thing you married. Maybe you need to accept that you don't share political or religious beliefs or that your partner will always be reluctant to talk about emotional issues, such as dealing with aging parents.

As the years go by, our "we'll never do" list gets longer, but one thing we continue to try to do is to accept each other as the imperfect people we are. One of the wonderful perks of this time of life is that we do know each other so well. We know our faults and imperfections—yet we still love each other. A real key to a successful empty nest marriage is being willing to accept each other as a package deal. The good comes with the bad. Realizing that your spouse will never change those little irritating quirks in his or her personality is a step forward in building a long-term successful marriage.

THE OIL OF FORGIVENESS

Acceptance opens the door to forgiveness and to moving on in your relationship. We have found that forgiveness is the oil that lubricates our love relationship—and it's an oil we need for the daily irritations as well as for the larger issues that come up from time to time.

One benefit of the empty nest is that you have more time to talk and to invest in your relationship, but it isn't always easy to transition from being a family to being two. In the active parenting years, children buffer and often short-circuit in-depth conversations. Unexpressed hurts and misunderstandings fester beneath the surface and may never really be addressed. Instead they become buried in the hustle and bustle of family life. Then the last child leaves the nest, and it seems that a bomb explodes. You wonder what happened.

Charlie and Karen

We (Dave and Claudia) were leading a Second Half of Marriage seminar when a man named Charlie spoke up. "I don't know what happened. I thought our relationship was fine—then when our kids left home, Karen started blowing her top like an active volcano. We never argued that much. I had no idea she was upset with me. What's a guy like me to do with this?"

"I'm not sure what happened either," Karen said. "I was so involved with the kids. Charlie was always at work. We were like two ships that occasionally passed in the night. Then when the kids left, there was time to be a couple again, and I was clueless as to how to do that. I began to evaluate our marriage, and suddenly it seemed all the hurts and unresolved issues of the past two decades came crashing down on me. I just see his faults—things I don't like. We both just turned fifty. We could be married another thirty years. I'm not sure I want to continue this marriage unless something changes fast."

Can you identify with Charlie and Karen? Do you know couples whose relationship seemed to crumble when the kids left home? When a long-term marriage falls apart, most of the time it isn't because of a one-time event or a major crisis. More likely it is the culmination of the little things that have built up over the years—often years of neglect. Spouses keep waiting for each other to change, but they don't change, and then they begin to realize that change is not on the horizon.

Disappointments, hurts, and unresolved issues can fester like a wound on an injured cat. When a cat is wounded and bleeding, sometimes the surface heals over, but the injury continues to fester under the skin. The same thing can happen in a marriage. Lack of forgiveness, unresolved issues, sins of omission and commission, missed expectations, unfulfilled dreams—all can fester beneath the skin of a marriage and then suddenly break through to the surface. This is especially likely to occur as couples transition into the empty nest. A wife, married thirty-five years, responding to the survey wrote that what she feared the most about her marriage in the future was "that it won't ever change and we'll never again have the 'couple' sense we had early on; or, that if he someday changes, I won't care any longer about it." Sometimes the effect of years of neglecting your marriage is suddenly apparent when it is just the two of you at home.

Not all is gloom and doom. As negative as the beginning of this chapter may sound, letting go of past hurts and disappointments is actually the key to moving on and restoring and revitalizing your marriage for the second half. You can begin again, but first you must be willing to deal with and let go of past disappointments, missed dreams, and unfulfilled expectations, and forgive each other. Like us, you may want to make your own list.

Over the years of a marriage, many things can cause minor or major hurts: put-downs, avoidance, negative interpretations, abusive comments, forgetting something important, making decisions without regard for the needs of the partner, affairs, addictions, impoliteness, and so on. Probably both you and your partner have committed "sins of omission and commission" over the course of your marriage. Minor infractions are normal, and it's important to expect them to happen—even or especially in the empty nest. It's far more valuable to learn how to move on at these times than to expect them not to happen at all. For some couples, more significant "sins" will be committed as well. These couples will need to work harder to put the events in the past. The more significant the issues or events that caused harm, the more likely it is that you'll need some of the specific steps we'll recommend in Part Two of this book.

Let's look at two couples facing the empty nest who both need to practice forgiveness as they face this critical marital passage. We call this "making forgiveness happen." Please note that the infractions are very different—one is minor and current, one is major and buried in the past—and they have very different implications.

Meet the Dillards

Beth and Jack Dillard met each other in a divorce recovery support group and later married. Each was married once before. Each had custody of the children from their first marriages. They found they had much in common, including a desire to marry again.

There's been nothing remarkable about their marriage and blended family except that they have done a great job. They've handled the myriad stresses of bringing two sets of kids together. They have survived the adolescent years, which had its share of ups and downs. Now that the last kid is leaving the nest, they look forward to focusing on each other. Actually, this will be the first time in their whole relationship that kids have not been a major factor. For Beth and Jack, this should be a real treat.

Billy, Jack's youngest child, was in the middle of graduation activities. He had excelled academically and was being honored at an awards luncheon by Jack's Rotary Club. He was proud of Billy and wanted Beth to share this moment with him. After all, she had been a great stepmom to Billy, and he knew it would mean a lot to Billy to have her there. Jack asked Beth to attend the luncheon, and she said she'd be glad to come. At the luncheon, he saved a place for her at the front table, right beside him. But she never showed up.

What happened? Beth became distracted on the big day and completely forgot about the luncheon. While she was deep in a project with a client, Jack was at the luncheon alone with Billy and feeling very embarrassed. Beth totally forgot the luncheon! Jack was also a little bit worried, as it was unlike Beth to miss anything. Here were his peers honoring his son, and his wife, the stepmom, fails to show up without explanation. If it had been her daughter, Karen, Beth for sure would have showed up! So he fumed and made the best of the embarrassment, telling his friends that "she must have had an emergency at work."

As soon as Jack walked in the door that evening, Beth realized that she had forgotten the luncheon:

BETH: *(distressed)* Oh no! Jack, I just remembered—

JACK: *(cutting her off)* Where were you? I have never been so embarrassed. I really wanted you there. Billy wanted you there.

BETH: I know, I know. I'm so sorry. I wanted to be there with you and with Billy.

JACK: So where were you? I tried calling.

BETH: I was with a client, and we worked straight through lunch. I completely forget the Rotary luncheon. I feel terrible.

JACK: So do I. I didn't know what to tell people, so I made something up about you having an emergency at work. It made me uneasy too—now that Billy is leaving, are you going to leave too? It's silly, but I know the empty nest is going to change things, and I want us to change together.

BETH: Please forgive me, dear. I lost it. I've been so stressed out with work, Billy's graduation activities, and just the culmination of dealing with teenagers. I know things are going to be different, but I'm sort of looking forward to being alone with you. Is that so bad?

Although Jack was let down by Beth, it should not be hard for him to forgive her. Now consider a very different example.

Meet the Larkins

Kim and Jon met and married in college. Their rocky marriage, which included an earlier affair, survived the pre–empty nest years. The affair took place ten years ago when Jon became involved with Joy, his secretary. When Kim discovered Jon's infidelity, the affair had already ended—his secretary had quit and moved to another town—but to this day, the hurt she experienced remains. Since then, she has had difficulty really trusting Jon, and when he is late coming home, she often lets her imagination run wild.

During the parenting years, Kim was a great mom and threw herself into her two children's activities. She was a loyal supporter at most school events and often volunteered at the local high school. Their two children lived at home all the way through college—delaying a true empty nest—but in the past six months, both children married and moved out of state. Kim and Jon were thrust into the empty nest unaware of the trauma ahead.

At first the quiet evenings were a welcome respite. But soon they discovered that quiet can be uncomfortable. Old issues began to surface. One evening, Jon was an hour late getting home to dinner, with no phone call or explanation. At dinner, Kim exploded.

KIM: *(agitated)* Now just where were you? Why didn't you call? Why, I wouldn't be surprised if Joy wasn't back in town!

JON: *(disgusted)* Where did *that* come from? I suppose you're going to hold that over my head for the rest of my life! Gee, Kim, that was years ago!

KIM: *(even more agitated)* Well, where were you?

JON: *(getting more angry)* Hey, I'm not on trial here. Haven't we already worked through this one?

Gridlock. Old hurts resurface. This evening may prove to be quiet, but it won't be peaceful or productive. Choices made years ago flavor their initiation into the empty nest. Lack of trust has corroded their love relationship. Issues unresolved and disappointments not dealt with cloud their marital skies. Now that the couple is suddenly without buffers and with fewer activities, old issues resurface that should have been dealt with, forgiven, and put behind them long ago. Routine conflicts become more intense. Now that the kids were gone, Kim wondered if it wouldn't just be easier to divorce and have a fresh start with her life. She had already decided that she might never trust Jon again, not fully.

What do you think? Should she forgive, and what does it mean to forgive in this situation? And what about Jon? If he wants to work at earning back Kim's trust, he must accept responsibility for his contribution to the problem and make a commitment never to repeat the offending behavior. Let's take a closer look at what it means to forgive.

WHAT IS (AND ISN'T) FORGIVENESS?

Forgiveness is a decision to give up your perceived or actual right to get even with, or hold in debt, someone who has wronged you. Webster's *New World Dictionary* says it this way: "1. to give up resentment against or the desire to punish; . . . 2. to give up all claim to punish; . . . 3. to cancel or remit (a debt)." The picture of forgiveness is a canceled debt.

Forgive is a verb. It's active; it's something you must decide to do! When one of you fails to forgive, you can't function as a team because one of you is kept "one down" by being indebted to the other.

A lack of forgiveness is the ultimate in scorekeeping, with the message being "You are way behind on my scorecard, and I don't know if you can catch up." In that context, resentment builds, conflict increases, and, ultimately, hopelessness set in. The real message is that "maybe you can't do enough to make this up." People often walk away from debts they see no hope of paying off.

As we have seen, infractions can be small or large, with the accompanying sense of debt being small or large as well. Beth has a much smaller debt to Jack than Jon has to Kim. Regardless of the size of the debt, the opposite of forgiveness is expressed in statements such as these:

"I'm going to make you pay for what you did."

"You are never going to live this down."

"You owe me. I'm going to get even with you."

"I'll hold this against you for the rest of your life."

"I'll get you for this."

These statements sound harsh, but the sentiments are nevertheless quite relevant for marriage. When you fail to forgive, you act out these kinds of statements, or even state them openly.

What Forgiveness Is Not

We will focus here on some of the most important issues people have raised when we have spoken publicly about forgiveness. These issues usually have more to do with what forgiveness isn't than what it is.

Forgiveness Isn't Forgetting

Maxine, a fifty-five-year-old woman in her second marriage, had been brought up to believe that to forgive meant to forget. She asked us, "It seems so hard to forgive and forget, how can you really do this?"

We said nothing about forgetting in defining forgiveness. You hear the phrase *forgive and forget* so often that the two get equated when they have nothing to do with one another. This is one of the greatest myths about forgiveness. Can you remember a very painful wrong someone has caused in your life, for which you feel you have forgiven that person? We bet you can. We can, too.

Just because you have forgiven—and given up a desire to harm another in return—doesn't mean you have forgotten the event ever happened. Fortunately, when people say "forgive and forget," they usually mean you need to put the infraction in the past. There's value in that, but forgiveness should not be measured in this way. If putting something in the past means you've given up holding the infraction over your partner's head, that's right on.

One misconception related to the "forgive and forget" myth is the belief that if a person still feels pain about what happened, he or she has not really forgiven. You can still feel pain about being hurt in some way yet have fully forgiven the one who harmed you. That's called grief.

Kim Larkin may have actually come to a point years ago of completely forgiving Jon, as we have defined it here. She may have worked through and eliminated her rage and desire to hurt him back. However, even in the best of circumstances, what happened years ago left her with a wound and a grief that will remain for many years and is now resurfacing in the empty nest. It's part of the backdrop of her empty nest marriage, and she will have to continue to deal with it emotionally.

In the case of the Dillards, the way in which Beth hurt Jack is far less severe, with fewer lasting consequences. As it turned out, Jack did forgive her. He didn't dwell on the incident, and he didn't need to grieve about it. However, when he is reminded of it, such as at other Rotary award luncheons, he remembers. He feels a twinge of the humiliation he felt on that day. This doesn't mean he's holding it over Beth or that he's trying to get even. He has forgiven. He just has a painful memory along the road of their marriage.

Forgiveness Isn't Ignoring Responsibility

We commonly hear this question: "But, in forgiving, aren't you saying that the one who did wrong is not responsible for what was done?" This is the second big misunderstanding about forgiveness. When you forgive, you are saying nothing about the responsibility of the one who did wrong. The one who did wrong is responsible for the wrong he or she did, period. Forgiving someone does not absolve that person of responsibility for his or her actions. It does take the relationship out of the mode of one punishing the other, but it shouldn't diminish the responsibility for the wrong done.

In this light, it's important to distinguish between punishment and consequences. Your partner can forgive you—that is, no longer seek to hurt or punish you—but you can still accept and act on the consequences of your behavior. Taking personal responsibility means not repeating or continuing the offending behavior.

*

Let's summarize what we have discussed so far. If you have been wronged by your partner—and if you've made it to the empty nest, we assume you have been wronged many times—it is up to you to forgive or not. Your partner can't do this for you. It's your choice. If you've wronged your partner in some way, it's your job to take responsibility for your actions and, if needed, take steps to see that it doesn't happen again. This approach assumes that the infraction is clear and that you are both humble and mature enough to take responsibility. The key is that if you want your empty nest relationship to move forward, you need to have a plan for forgiving. Even if you don't want to forgive—perhaps because of your own sense of justice—you may still need to do so for the good of your marriage.

The Dillards followed this model in the ideal sense. Beth took complete responsibility for missing the awards luncheon. She apologized and asked Jack to forgive her. He readily forgave her, having no intention of holding it against her. Their relationship was actually strengthened by the way they handled this event. Jack gained respect for Beth in her total acceptance of responsibility. Beth gained respect for Jack in his loving and clear desire to forgive and move on.

Before we move on to specific steps you can take to practice forgiveness, we want to discuss the crucial distinction between forgiveness and restoration in a relationship. What do you do if one partner can't or won't take responsibility? How can you move forward then?

What If You've Been Wronged But Your Partner Won't Take Responsibility?

Forgiveness and restoration usually go hand in hand in a relationship, as in the case of Jack and Beth. Intimacy and openness in their relationship was quickly restored—no barriers were placed in the way. Each handled their own responsibility without complication. When partners do this, restoration will naturally follow. By *restoration* we mean that the relationship is repaired for intimacy and connection.

But what do you do if you've been wronged in some way and your partner takes no responsibility? Do you allow there to be restoration in your relationship?

Whether or not you both agree on the nature of the infraction or mistake, you can still move ahead and forgive. It may be hard, but if you don't, you and the relationship will suffer added damage. In fact, there's good reason to believe that when you hang on to resentment and bitterness, you put yourself at risk for psychological and physical problems such as depression, rage, ulcers, and high blood pressure. That's no way to live. Although you probably prefer not to think about it, you are aging, and your body may well have more difficulty handling prolonged stress as you age further. If you are not able to deal effectively with resentments in your marriage, you may even accelerate some of the health problems that are more common to any of us as we age. We believe the healthy thing to do is to do what you can to restore the relationship and move on.

Now for the really difficult case. Suppose it's very clear to you that your partner did something quite wrong and isn't going to take any responsibility. Virtually no one is going to deny that years ago Jon Larkin (described earlier) did something wrong, for example. He had to take responsibility for his own behavior, or their marriage would have never had any chance of moving forward. He was responsible for that action, not Kim.

What About Regaining Trust?

We are often asked how you regain trust when something has terribly damaged it. The question is not so relevant for more minor matters of forgiveness. For example, there is no erosion of trust in the Dillards' incident. But for the Larkins, years ago there was a significant loss of trust.

Whatever the incident, suppose forgiveness proceeds smoothly, and you both want restoration. How do you regain trust? It's not easy, but it is possible. Consider these three key points:

1. *Trust builds slowly over time*. Trust builds as you gain confidence in someone being there for you. Although research shows that people vary in their general trust for others, deep trust comes only from seeing that your partner is there for you over time.

2. *Trust has the greatest chance to be rebuilt when each partner takes appropriate responsibility*. The greatest thing the offender can do is to take full responsibility for his or her actions. If a wife, for example, sees her husband doing all he can do to bring about serious change without her prodding and demanding, her trust will grow. In seeing his effort, she gains confidence that things can get better—not perfect, but really better. It's easier to trust when you can clearly see your partner's dedication to you.

3. *Trust is a decision of the will*. The one offended can also help rebuild trust. For one thing, the offender will need to see that his spouse doesn't plan to hold the offense over his head forever. Can she really forgive? If she reminds him about it, especially during arguments, he won't be able to trust that she really wants him to draw closer and move ahead. If you need to rebuild the trust level in your marriage, the one (or both of you) needing to trust the other more will, at some point, have to decide to take those chances. In taking wise steps forward in trusting, though, trust can grow over time.

NOW IT'S YOUR TURN

In a successful marriage, forgiveness is an ongoing process, and to build and maintain a healthy empty nest marriage you must forgive your partner. But one caution: you can't solve in one day what took years to develop. Long-standing problems take more time to resolve. However, you can begin today. Looking realistically at your own relationship and situation will help you let go of past marital disappointments. You can accept your spouse with his or her faults, realizing that when you married your spouse, it was a package deal!

We'd like to add a word here about the most powerful motivation to forgive. We, as well as many others, have often said that one of the most obvious reasons to forgive others is that it frees you up to move into the future. In other words, even if you don't otherwise like the idea of forgiving your mate, it's good for you to do that— that your life will be improved. We do believe this. However, researchers like Michael McCullough and Everett Worthington, Jr. have been studying forgiveness, and they are finding that when people forgive mostly for the benefit it will bring them, that kind of forgiveness does not last like another kind does. The kind of forgiveness that lasts is that which is motivated by your desire to give a blessing to your mate.

As we go on with what we have to tell you in this book, we will suggest many specific strategies for handling issues well in your relationship. We can think of nothing more powerful, though, than having such an attitude toward forgiving one another as you walk through each day of the rest of your life together. Now, we want to suggest some very specific advice for putting forgiveness into action.

Is there something right now that disappoints you about your spouse? No matter where your hurts fall on the continuum, from little daily irritations to a missed awards luncheon on to serious issues like infidelity, you must make that decision to forgive each other and to move beyond these grievances before you can have a fulfilling marriage into the years ahead.

When one partner is not ready to move on, the relationship can remain stuck in that negative place. A survey respondent wrote of her husband, "He is still into blaming and thinks he is right about everything. He does not realize that everything he says makes people either want to 1) approach you more, 2) avoid you, or 3) attack you. By being critical he pushes people away." He has certainly pushed his wife away, but there is still a seed of hope here, as she expresses her wish that her husband would learn to talk in a way that will bring them together.

Forgiving Your Partner Starts Now!

At the end of Chapter Eight, we help you work through the steps for forgiveness and restoration for more serious issues. If your issues are marriage-threatening, really serious issues, you need professional help. But if your issues are more the little daily irritations, here are five steps suggested in the Arps' book *The Second Half of Marriage* to help you forgive each other right now, accept those little things that irritate, and move on and make your empty nest marriage the best it can be.

Identify Grievances

These are the items on the list you may have rattled off in your own mind a thousand times. Actually write these grievances down. Include everything: from the little things like how your spouse puts the toilet paper on the holder, to more complicated issues that never seem to go away, like disagreeing on how much help and advice to give your adult children. One caution: *do not* show this list to your partner—you may even want to burn it when you are through—but do acknowledge to yourself those little things that continually pop up in your relationship.

Evaluate Your List of Complaints

Take some time alone and reflect on your list. Think about ways you were actively hurt by your partner, but also about ways in which you have been grieved about your mate simply not being all you thought she was or wanted her to be. Which issues can you easily forgive and let go (like habitually forgetting to close the garage door, leaving dirty dishes on the coffee table, or not sharing the remote)? Which issues need some more closure because they still cause you some pain (your mate's refusal to golf with you or unwillingness to accompany you to the symphony)? Which issues need to be discussed because you're still not sure it's time to let them go? (After all, you *both* would benefit from exercising together and eating a more healthy diet.) And which issues will take a serious effort on your part, perhaps even professional intervention, to overcome (a boring or nonexistent love life, an inability to work through conflict about your adult kids, or an unresolved health issue with your aging parents)? Remember, you will have an opportunity to deal with the more serious issues later. For now, let's consider those little grievances that are the flies spoiling your marital soup.

Decide to Forgive

From your list, consider those things that would be the easiest to forgive and let go. Ask yourself if you are willing to forgive your mate and let go of this issue between you. Forgiveness begins with a decision on your part, a simple act of your will. It is not dependent on your partner asking for your forgiveness or even agreeing he or she has done anything wrong. One survey respondent recognized the "need to accept each other where we are." He wrote that he fears the "failure to continue to try to grow" that could result from not letting go of old issues.

Let Go

Think about what would be an appropriate send-off for the easily forgiven irritations on your list. Maybe you will want to burn your list or flush it down the toilet. One wife wrapped her list in a box and gave it to her husband with a note saying, "I promise never to be bothered by these, your previously incredibly irritating but now lovable idiosyncratic behaviors. This is my empty nest gift to you."

For the more serious hurts and disappointments, wait until you have worked through Part Two of this book. Doing so will give you a more solid set of skills and strategies for handling conflict well in your marriage. If you've already worked through some of your pain and disappointments—even if they are small issues—take pride in how far you've journeyed toward improving your relationship for the second half. Surviving marital strife with your relationship intact can only increase your potential for a loving, fulfilling empty nest marriage.

Change Your Responses

You can't change the other person, but you can change how you respond. Now that you've forgiven your partner and put some of the little grievances behind you, how will you respond to these same issues in the future? Most of the time, our reaction to our partner's perceived shortcomings is worse than whatever it was our partner did or did not do. The next time you realize you are getting irritated with your mate, try to turn the situation around by replacing your negative response with loving encouragement for your spouse. Choose to verbalize something positive to your mate each day.

Moving On

Now that you've had a chance to deal with some of the little daily irritations in your relationship, take the next step of feathering your empty nest. You may need to forgive yourself, your children, your parents. Maybe you gave parenting your best shot but still feel you fell short. Maybe your kids didn't turn out to be just who you thought they were going to be. They're not bad people—just not who you pictured they were going to be. Maybe your parents disappointed you—they just weren't the parents or grandparents you would have liked them to be. This is a time of life to let go of unrealistic expectations, disappointment, and unfulfilled dreams and move on if you really want to enjoy the empty nest years.

And what did we (Dave and Claudia) do after we made our list of things that we once had hoped we'd do in life or that would happen to us but that we now realize will never happen? First we acknowledged that there were some things we just had to accept and let go of if we wanted to continue to grow together. Then we looked toward the future and made another list—this one was our "what we *will do* in the empty nest" list. It included those things we chose to do to make the rest of our marriage the best it can be.

We share our list with you in hopes that it will inspire you to make your own "what we *will do*" list for your empty nest.

Things We Will Do in Our Empty Nest

- We will release and let go of our missed dreams and disappointments with each other, with our children, with our parents, and with ourselves.

- We will accept each other as a package deal.

- We will keep on forgiving and asking each other for forgiveness when we blow it.

- We will renew our commitment to each other and to growing together in the second half of our marriage.

✳

As we close this chapter, let us encourage you: do not take your spouse for granted. Be future focused. Keep short accounts with each other—be generous in forgiving and asking each other for forgiveness. Accept your partner as a package deal. Practice patience, compassion, and kindness. Keep dreaming together and let go of your missed dreams and little disappointments. Your future is too bright to carry that baggage into it.

Make a fresh commitment to yourself, to your spouse, and to your marriage. It's time to move on in your marriage. Trust us: you can handle disappointments and unmet expectations. You can reconnect and rebuild your relationship. You can make the empty nest years the best yet.

EXERCISES

As presented in the chapter, here are the steps for practicing forgiveness.

Your Own Private Forgiveness Exercise

As the name of the exercise implies, this is something to do by yourself, not with your partner. Work through the following five steps for forgiving little irritations:

1. Identify grievances

2. Evaluate your list of complaints

3. Decide to forgive

4. Let go

5. Change your responses

Looking Back and Looking Forward

Try to do these steps alone and then together. The goal is to move on and begin your successful transition to the empty next.

1. Make a list of things you will never do or will never do again.

2. Make a list of things you will do in the empty nest.

3

Becoming Partner Focused

As we enter the empty nest, life changes. Communication patterns that worked in the first half, when the children were front and center, no longer work because roles shaped by parenting responsibilities are suddenly irrelevant. The only constant at this time of transition is change, but change can be an opportunity for growth—especially if you refocus and upgrade your marriage relationship.

Crafting a successful empty nest marriage might be compared with learning to fly a jet-engine plane when you have been trained to fly only a prop plane. It's a totally difference experience and requires different skills.

Years ago, when airlines upgraded to jets, the pilots had to be retrained because the jet-engine planes were far more complicated. Just consider what would have happened if the airlines had simply put pilots in the jets and told them to just do their best. Planes would have been crashing all over the place!

This is what is happening to many marriages as they reach the second half. The first half of marriage is like flying a prop plane. Your marriage isn't as complicated as it can be in the second half. In the first half, marriage is more confined by your circumstances—you're parenting your children, establishing your career; therefore, much of life is reactive. Choices are limited. But in the empty nest, you can have a jet marriage—you can fly higher. With fewer constraints and restraints, you can build your marriage the way you want it to be.

That freedom can also be a bit intimidating, because you have to make many decisions that will affect how you now live. For some couples, this is like running and skipping down the beach with carefree abandon. But for others, it's like being on a train coming off the tracks, and the ride can be scary. For still others, it's like being in a jet with no knowledge of how to pilot the thing!

But with some training—whether you identify with the beach, train, or jet analogy, marriage in the empty nest can actually be better and more fulfilling than it was in the demanding parenting years. With the children no longer the major focus, couples can move to a deeper, more personal marriage relationship. Now you have the opportunity to recraft your marriage, to upgrade to a more sophisticated relationship. But like the jet pilots, you need to be retrained. You need to learn new relational skills to succeed in communicating on a deeper level and using conflict constructively. For your empty nest marriage to really work, you need to go from a child-focused to a partnership-focused relationship. Then your marriage can fly high.

When we (Dave and Claudia) hit the empty nest, we made a common mistake: we tried to fly our prop marriage at jet speed! (This is really not very hard to do if you take a typical prop plane and just push it off a high cliff. You can get going very fast, but you can't fly higher.) We filled up the silence and free moments with more work and more activities. After all, we felt guilty if we weren't doing two things at once. We didn't give ourselves a chance to let things settle out, so we went from one stressful situation to another, and our relationship suffered. How much smoother our transition into the empty nest would have been if we had intentionally taken more up-front time to refocus on our marriage and upgrade our marital skills.

WHAT KIND OF MARRIAGE DO YOU WANT?

Would you like to move your marriage into the jet age? It will take some work to refocus on each other and upgrade your relationship. But not all empty nest couples surmount this challenge the same way. From our seminars and our survey, we have observed several patterns of marriage with varying degrees of success in refocusing for the second half. Consider the following three empty nest marriage styles.

The Prop Marriage

This is the couple who never makes the transition from a child-focused marriage to a partner-focused one. They continue to focus their attention on their adult children. This behavior hinders their children's transition into adulthood—which results in more things for the couple to be concerned about. All that family baggage weighs their marriage down. They bump through life in their prop-plane marriage.

When Emily and Dan's only child, Helen, left for college, Emily almost went with her! Daily phone calls and e-mails kept her closely connected to her daughter. When Helen graduated and moved to the West Coast, Emily worried that she would not be able to cope with her job as a computer programmer. Each evening, over the dinner table, the conversation between Emily and Dan centered on their daughter. They used most of their vacation time visiting Helen. When she married, their circle of concern just grew larger and included Helen's new husband and stepdaughter.

Dan, though concerned about his daughter, grew tired of the constant focus on Helen and spent more time at work and less time at home. After several years, Emily and Dan came for counseling. They weren't sure what had happened to their own relationship—they just knew they needed help.

A survey respondent who was facing the empty nest wrote: "Hopefully we will be able to reestablish a good relationship once my daughter is out of college and on her own. Actually we have tried some already this week as we said good-bye to our son who is away in grad school, and our daughter is a half-hour away at college. She will be home periodically. On our twenty-fifth wedding anniversary, we went to a bed-and-breakfast inn and had a good time on one overnight. Even my husband liked it because it was low stress. He worries so much about the future of his job, etc., that we don't enjoy much."

The Two-Jet Marriage

This is the couple who has made the transition away from focusing on the children, but the spouses have instead refocused on their jobs and other activities. They are like two jets on different flights but sharing the same hanger.

"I hardly notice it when Allen is out of town," Dora said. "Once when we were both traveling, we accidentally ran into each other at the L.A. airport! Neither knew the other was even in California! We spend less time together than when the kids were home. Sometimes I feel like I don't even know Allen anymore."

A wife, married thirty-four years, wrote in the survey that she fears a "lack of growth in intimacy [because my] husband seems to be more content to get to puttering around and I'm more relational, and he pursues me less and seems boring at times. I get lonely." Another woman, married thirty years, wrote, "We do not scream or cause chaos in our family because we do live parallel lives. . . . [I fear] my husband will die without reconciliation. I fear ultimate abandonment." A husband, married thirty-five years, fears "going separate directions while still living together." An overwhelming number of survey respondents use the words "lonely," "alone," and "separate" to describe their lives in the empty nest years. It is clear that none of these couples expected this to happen, and none are happy with this pattern of living.

The Copiloted Jet Marriage

This is the companionship marriage: the two of you are copiloting your marriage. But don't try to fly a jet without being in close communication and in synch with your copilot, or you will crash! Here are some examples of companionship marriages from the survey:

"We are mostly in agreement about our values and the important things in our relationship. We find it easy to be together, rarely disagree about most issues, and enjoy doing many of the same things."

"The best parts of our marriage are its longevity, having been through a lot together (twenty-three years), being forgiving, listening to new ideas, supporting each other in new ventures and educational opportunities."

"My husband and I both love the Lord and each other. We were both alone many years and so we truly appreciate our companionship. We treat each other with great respect and enjoy the support we give each other." (This respondent, sixty-one, had been married one-and-a-half years.)

Although most couples during the parenting years see their marriage as a partnership, in the empty nest you have the opportunity to become more partner focused—to take down your defenses, open up your inner self, and make yourself more vulnerable to each other. You can build a much more intimate relationship if you choose to upgrade to a copiloted jet marriage.

This kind of intimacy is possible in what Dr. David Mace, marriage education pioneer, in his book *Close Companions* (1982) calls a "companionship marriage." Mace defines it in the following way: "Companionship marriage is a socially registered commitment between a man and a woman, in which they seek to know themselves and each other as far as they are capable of being known, and, through mutual affection and affirmation, help each other to grow and change in order to become the loving and creative persons they are capable of becoming."

One way to nurture your marriage is by continually adjusting to each other and striving to be partner focused. Actually, the survival of a long-term marriage depends on the complex process of mutual adjustment of the two people to each other. A strength of the companionship-partnership marriage model is promoting a strong sense of being part of a couple in each partner. It is critical in the second half of marriage to develop a sense of "we-ness."

By *we-ness* we don't mean some kind of Vulcan mind-meld or the disappearance of one of your identities into the other's. We're talking about two individuals with a clear sense of their own identities, choosing to develop and nurture the "we" part of marriage, such that "we" becomes more important than "I." This couple makes decisions based on what is best for the couple. Here is how coauthor Scott Stanley put it in his book *The Heart of Commitment:*

> Various researchers and theorists have described the formation of commitment as a shift in thinking from what's best for self to what's best for the team. I'm not talking about religious writers, mind you, but secular marital experts who have noted what happens in the development of strong marriages. I have called this sense of oneness *couple identity*. People who are the most comfortable thinking in terms of "we" tend to be the most dedicated and happy in their marriages. That's not just an interesting finding; it flies in the face of the intense emphasis on individualism dominating our world today. Instead of two separate people out for themselves, a marriage that is really sticking tends to have two partners who think and act on what's best for the team.

One survey respondent puts it very clearly: "He is my best friend, we both know that we can trust each other and that nothing will ever come between us that we can control. I know that he will never be unfaithful to me, and we are always here for each other."

It's in a marriage with a strong sense of "us" and "we" that many wonderful things can happen. When you are a strong team, you will be freer to give fully to one another, you will tend to be less competitive about who is doing what, and you will have far fewer power and control dynamics than couples who are trying to have a great marriage without developing the "us" part of it.

✳

We do need to express one caution. In a companion-partnership marriage, couples have higher expectations for their marriage relationship. Their quest for intimacy leads to a degree of closeness that at the same time can generate conflict. A companionship marriage is more complicated and much more work, but it is worth the effort!

So how can you begin to build a partner-focused marriage? We have two suggestions: first, apply some first aid to your tired-out marriage; second, take an empty nest marriage checkup. These two steps will help you upgrade your marriage and create a more partner-focused relationship.

FIRST AID FOR NEW EMPTY NESTERS

Refocusing on your relationship is a long-term process, but a few minor adjustments in the beginning can make it go more smoothly. Here are some first-aid tips for starting out right.

Don't Immediately Fill Up All Your Time

On this topic, as we (Dave and Claudia) have already shared, we speak from experience. All the things we had postponed until the empty nest years we tried to do the first six months! We didn't give ourselves enough down time to recover from parenting three adolescent boys or to chart out together in what direction we wanted our marriage to grow. The result? Our marriage became a lower priority than it was even before we were in the empty nest. (Ironically, this happened while we were trying to help other couples enrich their marriages!) When we realized what was happening, we were alarmed. Here's why.

Before the nest empties, marriage is by necessity child focused. After all, good parents focus on their family. Too many kids struggle today because of parental neglect, so for parents to focus on their children's needs is good and admirable. But when the kids leave and spouses fill up the empty spaces with all sorts of other activities that do not directly relate to their marriage, the marriage is weakened even more.

Why? With kids in the house, you can rationalize that even if the marriage takes a bit of a back seat, it is for a worthy cause. But if after the kids leave you fill all the time with stuff, you can't look at that and conclude that it's a worthy cause like the shared job of parenting. The result? You begin to drift further apart. Previously, you had the kids in common. Now that emphasis is gone, and you're just as busy or busier but without a common focus. At this point, many couples grow apart and wonder what's left to fight for.

Slow Down and Get Some Rest

The first step in refocusing is to slow down. If you are like we were, you're exhausted. So take a nap. Go to bed tonight at 8 P.M. Now is not the time to Lysol the whole house, start that kitchen renovation project, or take on that extra project at work. Just stop and rest. You will never be able to focus on your partner until your life comes back into focus. One woman in our survey is looking forward to the transition to empty nest status to see what her spouse will really be like, as he has always been "driven and married to his work."

I (Claudia) have "empty nest eyes"—they just don't see as well as they used to. When I'm straining to see something on the horizon, I often find myself closing my eyes for a few seconds, letting them take a break. Then I look again, and usually my vision is somewhat better. Use the same principle for the initial adjustment to the empty nest: give yourself a break.

Resist Making Immediate Changes

Until you have more perspective, don't make any major changes. Realize that things are changing and that you can and will change with them—but you need to take it slowly. We see it time and again. Spouses who are disappointed with their marriage bolt right out of the relationship as soon as the last kid leaves the nest. Others may immediately sign up for every class offered in the local adult education program or decide this is the time for a major career change.

Acknowledge That This Is a Time of Transition

It's beneficial even just to say to each other, "Things *are* changing in our marriage." Change can bring out our insecurities that are festering below the surface. He may be concerned that she won't stay in the marriage once the children are gone. She may fear that he will find someone younger and more attractive than she is and, without the constraint of parenting responsibilities, leave her. Acknowledging change does not mean you have to figure everything out right now, but by acknowledging it you will be able to better manage the changes up ahead.

One of the really great things about transition times in life is that, although they are stressful, they give you a chance to redefine who you are and where you are headed. You can only do this, though, if you slow down enough to ponder your future. We encourage you to see this phase of your life together as a wonderful opportunity to take the controls of your marriage into your hands and decide where you want to head in your future together.

Celebrate

You made it to the empty nest. Celebrate. Although it is not at all uncommon to become aware of some sense of loss and regret at this time of life, you can counter any of those sentiments by promoting a strong sense of celebration for where you have come and of excitement about your future. So go have some fun together. Have a date. How long has it been since you did something just for yourself? Just for your marriage? Take a twenty-four-hour getaway with no agenda except to have some fun. If you like to hike, take an afternoon off and go on a hike together. If you like to cook gourmet (or country, or whatever) have a dinner date and prepare all those vegetables and other dishes your kids hated but you really enjoy. In Part Four we give you more suggestions for enhancing the fun in your empty nest, but for now, choose one thing you can do together just to relax and celebrate: "We made it through the active parenting years!"

Don't Fear the Silence

When the kids leave, they take their laughter, music, and general chatter. A quiet evening may seem too quiet. It may take some time for your ears to adjust, and it may be awkward at first, but don't let the silence throw you. Don't just turn up the television to fill the space. It's all right not to talk all the time. Acknowledge that "it sure is quiet around here." We remember how odd it seemed when we could actually sit by the fire and read our favorite book or magazine with *our* music playing in the background! Actually, we were so tired we kept falling asleep!

EVALUATE YOUR MARRIAGE

Once you've had a chance to de-stress and get a little sleep, you can move on to the second step in refocusing your marriage and take an empty nest checkup.

Just what is an empty nest checkup? It is a time of focusing on your marriage for the purpose of evaluating how you are doing in your marriage and of making midcourse adjustments for the health of your relationship. Just as you go to the doctor for physicals or to the dentist for six-month checkups, you also need to have regular marriage checkups. And as you enter the second half, you may find you *really* need one, as we (the Arps) did.

Dave and Claudia Arp

"Dave, things just can't continue like this!" Claudia said, looking at Dave with bloodshot eyes as they had their morning coffee. The fallout from the adolescent years and our overextended fall schedule was adversely affecting our marriage. We were just as tired and worn out as when our home was filled with adolescents, and we were both feeling a little insecure.

We knew we needed to make some changes, but we didn't know exactly where to start. One month later we were leading a Marriage

Alive seminar in the Washington, D.C., area, so after the seminar we took a week off and went to New England. For years we had talked about taking an empty nest trip, and here was our chance. We knew we needed to really talk, and a week alone would give us some much-needed uninterrupted time together to check up on our own marriage. We have alluded to one liability of working in marriage education: it's somewhat easy to teach the principles to others—the hard part is to live them out oneself—so here was our chance.

The first couple of days, we hit a few outlet malls, took some long walks, and slept. No agenda. But we knew this week had an important purpose. So once we were somewhat rejuvenated, we began to talk about our relationship. What were our assets? What strengths did we have going for us in our relationship? Our communication was usually good. We both could laugh a lot of things off and tried not to take life too seriously. Our love life needed some work, but it had survived the years of parenting three adolescent boys. We talked about those things we had in common: our love of family, our treasuring of friends, our values and beliefs—our shared faith in God gives us a lot of spiritual intimacy—and our enjoyment of many of the same interests.

Looking at the positives of our relationship was very affirming, but we also had to consider our liabilities—those things that weren't so great. We didn't have as much patience with each other as when we were younger, and at times we took each other for granted. More than once we had been guilty of promoting dating when our own dating habit had fallen by the wayside. We both tend to take on too much. We have a saying at the Arp house: whatever it is we want to do, "It'll only take ten minutes!" Of course, that ten minutes may take two hours. When we overcommit our time, we stress out and tend to react negatively to each other. Dave likes to avoid issues. His philosophy is, Just wait—most things will work themselves out. Claudia is a confronter. Why wait till tomorrow to deal with something that can be dealt with today? So you can imagine how we lock horns.

Also, we didn't always agree on how to deal with our kids. Dave tended to be more laid back, whereas Claudia wanted more structure. We also had different opinions about how to relate to our parents, and from time to time this created some tension. Claudia came from a closer-knit family whose expectations of us were different from those of Dave's parents.

Our working together in marriage and family education was both an asset and a liability. It was hard to draw boundary lines. After all, if we were working on a manuscript on marriage, couldn't we rationalize that we were also working on our relationship at the same time? Writing about parenting also put extra pressure on us as a family, and that influenced our marriage as well.

Speaking of parenting, all of a sudden our roles were changing. Without the day-to-day parenting responsibilities that I (Claudia) had concentrated on, our roles were less defined. Actually, they were turned upside down. Just how much of my identity was tied to my "mom" role? How would the loss of this major responsibility affect our relationship? Would I "meddle" more in the day-to-day details of Marriage Alive, which traditionally had been more Dave's responsibility? How would we balance all of this?

As we talked, we realized we had some work to do but also that we had a lot going for us. Once we were willing to address troublesome issues and say, "This is crummy—not what I want it to be. Let's work on it," we were able to move on and set some goals for working on our relationship. Whereas we had a relatively easy checkup and an excellent prognosis for positive change, other couples find it more difficult to refocus, and the process of reinventing our marriage—if they are really serious about it—may take years. Consider our friends John and Sarah McCracken.

John and Sarah McCracken

John, a forty-nine-year-old successful surgeon, had his life all mapped out—his practice, his golf, and his family. Sarah, forty-seven, was a dedicated mother and community leader. She seemed focused and settled in her life as well, but when the youngest of their three children left home, John and Sarah were unprepared for the changes and challenges ahead of them. Their marriage during the first half had been fine, but due to their professional choices they had more money than time to invest in their marriage.

Sarah told us, "We made it through the first twenty-five years of our marriage with a comfortable but rather distant relationship. While we didn't have a lot of closeness, I always considered our marriage above average. So when our youngest daughter, Claire, left for college, it was a real change for me. I was out of a job!"

John continued, "It wasn't only Sarah who was out of pocket. Claire was a piano player, and I can't tell you how much I missed hearing her play. Our house was entirely too quiet. Actually, hearing her play the piano had been therapy for both of us. With Claire away, the lack of depth in my relationship with Sarah became more pronounced. We hit an emotional void, and it took a long time to work through it. We had spent the first half of our marriage raising our family and getting established in my profession. Now I questioned why I was working eighty-hour weeks. The kids were gone. Money—what is it for? Why was I working so hard? We were successful by the world's standards, but something was missing."

Sarah picked up the conversation. "One of the first things we discovered was that the second half of marriage is a very personal stage of life, and neither of us handled the personal side of life very well. In a long discussion together, we were talking about what we wanted most for the rest of our life, and John surprised me by saying, 'Sarah, I want a better marriage!' I was incredulous! Since when did he care so much about marriage? Looking at each other in shock, we began to talk about our marriage, and that was the beginning of really refocusing on each other."

Together, John and Sarah began a journey that would span more than a decade and would lead them to a deeper, more satisfying relationship. Their success is recorded in detail in our book *The Second Half of Marriage* and in a letter written just before John retired. Let us share part of it with you:

Dear Claudia and Dave,

In reviewing our thoughts on our forty years of marriage, we asked ourselves what discoveries we felt we'd made, what we'd learned, and how we feel as we close this chapter of our life and begin our adventure into retirement. By far, the biggest discovery was that we should change and can change! At first change was very threatening, but when we became involved and discovered we could, it became very exciting.

Next we had to relearn how to listen to each other. . . . Becoming better listeners, being more honest, more careful, and more companionable, we learned much about ourselves and about each other. Also, learning to work together, we developed more trust and reliance on each other.

Finally, we feel we have reshaped, reworked, and reformed our marriage relationship, in a manner compatible with this stage of life. We look forward to the next chapter of our life together with great optimism and enthusiasm. . . .

Best of friends,

John and Sarah

*

For John and Sarah, change was possible, but it was a lot of work. They had to fight for their marriage! And that's what this book is all about. In Part Two of the book, we help you begin to retool your own marriage. We look at four negative patterns that we all fall into from time to time; if you don't deal with these patterns positively, they can destroy an empty nest marriage. Then we talk about how to talk and really hear what your partner is saying. You can learn how to handle conflict and how to deal with the issues and events in your marriage and life. We spend a whole chapter on problem solving and another on developing relationship ground rules. Basically, we are going to help you develop your own empty nest coping system; you can never expect to *eliminate* challenges and conflict from your life, but the two of you will be better able to handle whatever comes your way.

But marital growth in the empty nest starts with choosing to have a partner-focused marriage. As John and Sarah discovered, it will be a lot of work, but the rewards are worth it. No matter where you are or what challenges you have faced in the past, the empty nest is a great time to reinvent your marriage. There is always hope. You can get some professional help if your problems seem insurmountable, but most couples just need to refocus on each other and upgrade their relational skills. We encourage you to do this now. The longer you wait to make adjustments, the harder it will become. For that matter, sometimes the nest fills up again—but that's an issue we will deal with later!

You can build a more personal and closer relationship in the empty nest. You can actually reinvent your marriage, and you can enjoy your partner more than you ever thought possible. You can have a new, better marriage, with the *same* partner! But to be able to do so, you will have to be deliberate in the choices you make together. Let's get started.

EXERCISES

As we discussed in the chapter, there are three steps to begin the transition to the empty nest. Work together to develop your first-aid list, do your marriage checkup, and identify your marriage style.

Empty Nest First-Aid List

You might want to include things like these:

1. Take a nap

2. Go for a walk.

3. Have a "get lost" date. Take the back roads, get lost, then find your way home.

4. Invest in a swing for two. Use it and talk.

5. Read a book together.

Take a Marriage Checkup

Start by finding a time and place you can be alone for several hours. Maybe you will want to take an afternoon off work. If you have your checkup at home, turn off the television and phone. If you go out for your checkup, choose a quiet place where you can talk and not be interrupted, like a small coffee shop, or take a picnic lunch to a park. Or maybe, like the Arps, you can take a week away to regroup and evaluate the next season of your marriage. Wherever you have your checkup, talk together about the following questions:

1. What are our assets?
2. What are our liabilities?
3. In what ways are our roles changing?

Identify Your Marriage Style

Consider the following empty nest marriage styles. With which do you identify? Which would you like to represent your marriage in the future?

- Prop plane: a child-focused marriage even after the nest is empty

- Two jets sharing the same hangar: a work- or activity-focused marriage

- One jet with two copilots: a partner-focused marriage

Part II

Handling Conflict in the Empty Nest

4

Communication and Conflict

Four Danger Signs

One of the most powerful things you can do to protect your empty nest marriage is to upgrade your communication skills. Over the years, unhealthy communication patterns can become inbred habits. Then when the kids leave, those irritating habits become more pronounced, but by then you're in a rut and don't know how to get out of it.

Consider the case of Butch the dog. Richard and Leslie moved to the lake when their last child was in high school. They were ready for a more relaxed lifestyle, so when they found the home of their dreams, complete with a boat dock, they jumped at the chance to move. They adjusted quite well—it was their dog, Butch, who had problems. Butch, a twelve-year-old Lab, was set in his ways. The move confused him. He didn't like change. So what did Butch do? He circled the house. Round and round he walked until he actually made a rut in their yard. We may chuckle, but when faced with change, isn't that what happens to many empty nest couples? They're in a rut of old patterns and don't know how to break out of them.

In this chapter, we focus on four specific patterns of conflictual interactions that often lead to or reflect marital problems. The patterns we describe here are not the only ones that have been found to predict divorce, but if you understand these four well, you'll understand the fundamentals of what this kind of research has to say. The following are the four danger signs that we will highlight:

1. Escalation

2. Invalidation

3. Withdrawal and avoidance

4. Negative interpretations

Once you understand these patterns, you can learn to prevent them from taking over in your relationship.

SOME RESEARCH FINDINGS

You might be thinking, Why focus on the negative? Even if you are not asking that question, we would like to answer it, because the answer is very important. Researchers from various centers have found that the likelihood of future relationship distress, divorce, or both can be predicted with a surprisingly high degree of accuracy. (Keep in mind that when we talk about research findings, we are always talking about differences that tend to be true, but there are always exceptions, and you could be one.) Some of the factors that increase the likelihood of divorce are a family history of divorce (that is, the divorce of one or both spouses' parents), young age at time of marriage, premarital cohabitation, differences in religious background, and neuroticism (or the tendency to react defensively). There are others, but the most potent predictors of how a couple will do in the future have to do with how the partners interact and how they handle conflict. The danger signs we discuss here have most to do with how you treat one another in the moment-by-moment of life.

We will focus on the negative here because it is very clear that how you treat one another when in conflict can make a huge difference in the quality of your marriage in the years to come. The kinds of negative patterns we describe here can wipe out a great deal of whatever is positive between the two of you. In fact, various researchers, such as John Gottman, and Howard Markman (coauthor) and Cliff Notarius in their book *We Can Work It Out*

(1993), have estimated that one negative interaction can wipe out the effect of five to twenty positive interactions.

In the other chapters in Part Two, we teach you positive strategies for minimizing negative patterns such as those described here. We believe that by changing your patterns, you will give your marriage the greatest chance to fully develop.

ESCALATION: WHAT GOES AROUND COMES AROUND

Escalation occurs when partners respond back and forth negatively to each other, continually upping the ante so that conditions get worse and worse. Negative comments often spiral into increasing anger and frustration. Couples who are happy now and likely to stay that way are less prone to escalation; if they do start to escalate, they are able to stop the negative process before it erupts into a full blown, nasty fight.

Ted, a forty-nine-year-old construction worker, and Cindy, fifty-one, who runs a catering business out of their home, have been married for twenty-eight years. As is true of most couples, many of their arguments are about everyday events:

TED: (*sarcastically*) You'd think you could put the dishes in the dishwasher rather than leave them in the sink.

CINDY: (*equally sarcastically*) Oh, like you always do that!

TED: As a matter of fact, I do.

CINDY: Oh, I forgot just how compulsive you are. You're right, of course!

TED: I don't even know why I've stayed with you all these years. You are so negative.

CINDY: Maybe you shouldn't stay. The last kid is leaving—maybe there's no reason for you to stick around. No one is barring the door.

TED: I'm not really sure why I do stay anymore.

One of the most damaging things about arguments that are escalating out of control is that partners tend to say things that threaten the very lifeblood of their marriage. As frustration and hostility mount, partners often try to hurt each other by hurling verbal (and sometimes even physical) weapons. You can see this pattern in Ted and Cindy's interaction, in which the stakes quickly rise to include threats of ending the relationship. Once very negative comments are made, they are hard to take back, and these reckless words do a lot to damage any sense of oneness and intimacy.

Although partners can say the nastiest things during escalating arguments, such reckless remarks often don't reflect what one generally feels about the other. You may believe that people reveal their "true feelings" in the midst of fierce fights, but we do not believe this is usually the case. Instead, what is said is meant mostly to pierce the other and create a barrier to defend oneself.

In Ted and Cindy's argument, for example, Cindy mentions his being compulsive because she really wants to hit him below the belt. At a tender moment between them, he had shared his concerns about being so driven and told Cindy that growing up he had learned this style to please his father. Although Cindy may have been provoked in this argument, the escalation led to her use of intimate knowledge to win the battle. When escalation leads to the use of intimate knowledge as a weapon, the damage to the future likelihood of tender moments is great. Who is going to share deeper things if the information may be used later when conflict is out of control in the relationship?

You may be thinking, We don't fight like cats and dogs—how does this apply to us? At times, escalation actually can be very subtle. Voices don't have to be raised for you to get into the cycle of returning negative for negative. Yet research shows how even subtle patterns of escalation can lead to distress or divorce in years to come. Consider the following conversation between Thomas and Vivian, a couple of new empty nesters in their late forties, who have just relocated to Colorado and are renting an apartment in Denver while looking for a more permanent home.

THOMAS: Did you get the rent paid on time?
VIVIAN: That's your job.
THOMAS: You were supposed to do it.
VIVIAN: No, you were.
THOMAS: Did it get done?
VIVIAN: No. And I'm not going to, either.
THOMAS: *(muttering)* Great. Just great.

Even though Vivian and Thomas have stuck together over the years, they don't have a very happy marriage. Years of small arguments like this one have taken a toll on their marriage, eroding the positive things they once shared.

It is very important for the future health of your relationship to learn to counteract whatever tendency you have to escalate as a couple. If you don't escalate very much, great! Your goal is to learn to keep things that way. If you do escalate a fair amount, your goal is to recognize it and to stop. Even if you, like Vivian and Thomas, have a long track record of escalation, it is possible to make some changes—even at this late date.

Short-Circuiting Escalation

All couples escalate from time to time, but some couples steer out of the pattern more quickly, and much more positively. Compare Ted and Cindy's argument, earlier, with Reba and Thomas's. Reba, a forty-five-year-old sales manager for a department store, and Thomas, a forty-nine-year-old accountant who works for the Justice Department, have been married twenty-three years.

REBA: *(annoyed)* You left the butter out again.
THOMAS: *(irritated)* Why are little things so important to you? Just put it back.
REBA: *(softening her tone)* Things like that are important to me. Is that so bad?
THOMAS: *(calmer)* I guess not. Sorry I was snotty.

Notice the difference. Like Ted and Cindy's, Thomas and Reba's argument showed escalation, but the couple quickly steered out of it. When escalation sequences are short-circuited, it is usually because one partner backs off and says something to de-escalate the argument, thus breaking the negative cycle. Often this takes the simple humility of choosing to soften one's tone and put down one's shield. For her part, Reba softens her tone rather than getting defensive. For his part, Thomas makes the decision to back off and acknowledge Reba's point of view.

Softening your tone and acknowledging your partner's point of view are powerful tools you can employ to diffuse tension and end escalation. Often that's all it takes. As we go on, we will be teaching you a number of ways to keep escalation in check.

INVALIDATION: PAINFUL PUT-DOWNS

Invalidation is a pattern in which one partner subtly or directly puts down the thoughts, feelings, or character of the other. Let's take a closer look at this pattern, which can take many forms. Here are two other arguments between Ted and Cindy and between Reba and Thomas.

CINDY: *(very angrily)* You missed your doctor's appointment again! You know the doctor told you that you need to slow down and take better care of yourself. You are so irresponsible. I could see you dying and leaving me, just like your father.

TED: *(bruised)* Thanks a lot. You know I am nothing like my father.

CINDY: He was a creep, and so are you.

TED: *(dripping with sarcasm)* I'm sorry. I forgot my good fortune to be married to such a paragon of responsibility. You can't even keep your purse organized.

CINDY: At least I am not so obsessive about stupid little things.

TED: You are so arrogant.

REBA: *(with a tear)* You know, I am really frustrated by the hatchet job Bob did on my evaluation at work. I've been with the company for twenty years!

THOMAS: I don't think he was all that critical. I would be happy to have an evaluation as positive as that from Fred.

REBA: *(with a sigh and turning away)* You don't get it. It upset me.

THOMAS: Yeah, I see that, but I still think you are overreacting.

Both of these dialogues are examples of invalidation, although obviously the first is much more caustic, and hence damaging to the relationship, than the second. With Ted and Cindy, you can feel the *contempt* seeping through. The argument has settled into an attack on character. Although Reba and Thomas do not show the contempt displayed by Ted and Cindy, Thomas is subtly putting down Reba for the way she is feeling. He may even think that he is being constructive or trying to cheer her up by saying, "It's not so bad." Nevertheless, this kind of communication is also invalidating. Reba feels more hurt now because Thomas has said, in effect, that her feelings of sadness and frustration are inappropriate.

Whether it is caustic or subtle, any kind of invalidation sets up barriers in relationships. Invalidation hurts. It leads naturally to covering up who you are and what you think because it's just too risky to do otherwise.

Invalidation also occurs when one partner's contributions to the relationship are ignored or treated as unimportant. One wife responded to the Arps' survey by saying,

My husband has never been one to express himself verbally or physically. I found this to be painful and lonely, especially since I was a stay-at-home mom. Discussions of my feelings, household problems, finances, etc. were met with my spouse's changing of the subject, falling asleep, or leaving to do household chores ("Time was a-wasting," he would say). If there were problems (especially personal ones), I usually handled them alone, to the best of my ability. I also handled

all the finances, home arrangements, and child discipline. Acknowl-
edgments of my accomplishments were seldom made. "I love you"
was thought by my spouse to be empty words—he believed in acting
loving (however, usually not with physical shows of affection).

This wife has experienced invalidation of her entire contribution to her marriage. She also wrote, "The lack of communication
between us of a personal nature has made us acquaintances. . . .
[After he retires and they are forced to spend more time together,] I
will just shrivel up inside." Her comments vividly illustrate the
chilling effect constant invalidation can have on a relationship.
What couple can maintain the ability to be open and intimate
when invalidation is a regular part of their life together?

Preventing Invalidation

In the arguments just described, both couples would have done better if each partner had acknowledged and shown respect for the
viewpoint of the other. Note the difference in how these conversations could have gone.

CINDY: *(very angry)* I am very angry that you missed the doctor
appointment again. I worry about your health and your being
around for me in the future.

TED: *(bruised)* It really upset you, didn't it?

CINDY: You bet. I want to know that you are going to be there for
me, and when you miss an appointment that I am anxious
about, I worry about us.

TED: I understand why it would make you worried when I don't
take care of myself.

REBA: *(with a tear)* You know, I am really frustrated by the hatchet
job Bob did on my evaluation at work.

THOMAS: That must really tick you off.

Reba: Yeah, it does. And I get worried about whether I'll be able to keep this job with all the younger people in the marketplace. What would we do?

Thomas: I didn't know you were so worried about losing your job. Tell me more about how you are feeling.

In these examples, we have replayed the issues but with very different outcomes for both couples. Now there is ownership of feelings, respect for each other's character, and an emphasis on validation. By *validation* we mean that the one raising the concern is respected and heard. You don't have to agree with your partner to validate his or her feelings. Our research shows that invalidation is one of the very best predictors of future problems and divorce but that the amount of *validation* doesn't say as much about the health of a relationship as the amount of *invalidation* does. This doesn't mean that validation is unimportant, but it does clearly mean that stopping invalidation is crucial. Respectful validation happens to be a powerful way to inhibit invalidation when you are trying to stay on the higher road. But it takes discipline, especially when you are really frustrated or angry. In later chapters, we teach you some very effective ways to limit invalidation and enhance validation.

NEGATIVE INTERPRETATIONS: WHEN PERCEPTION IS WORSE THAN REALITY

Negative interpretations occur when one partner consistently believes that the motives of the other are more negative than is really the case. This can be a very destructive pattern in a relationship, and it will make any conflict or disagreement harder to deal with constructively. One wife from the survey calls this her husband's "critical spirit" and talks about how it pervades every aspect of their relationship.

Another couple, Margaret and David, have been married twenty-two years, and they are generally happy with their relationship. Yet their discussions at times have been plagued by a specific negative interpretation. Every December they have had trouble deciding whether to travel to her parents' home for the holidays. Margaret believes that David dislikes her parents, but in fact, he is quite fond of them in his own way. She has this mistaken belief because of a few incidents early in the marriage that David has long forgotten. Here's how a typical discussion around their issue of holiday travel plans goes:

MARGARET: We should start looking into plane tickets to go visit my parents this holiday season.

DAVID: (*thinking about their budget problem*) I was wondering if we can really afford it this year.

MARGARET: (*in anger*) My parents are very important to me. They're getting older, and even if you don't like them, I'm going to go.

DAVID: I would like to go, really I would. I just don't see how we can afford a thousand dollars in plane tickets and pay next semester's college bill for Joey, too.

MARGARET: You can't be honest and admit you just don't want to go, can you? Just admit it. You don't like my parents.

DAVID: There is nothing to admit. I enjoy visiting your parents. I'm thinking about money here, not your parents.

MARGARET: That's a convenient excuse. (*storms out of the room*)

Given that we know David really does like to visit Margaret's parents, can you see how powerful her negative interpretation has become? He cannot penetrate it. What can he say or do to make a difference as long as her belief that he dislikes them is so strong? Even if he goes, she will still believe that he didn't really want to go. If a negative interpretation is strong enough, nothing will change it. In this case, David wants to address the decision they must make from the standpoint of the budget, but Margaret's interpretation will overpower their ability to communicate effectively and come to a decision that makes both of them happy. Fortunately for them, this problem is relatively isolated and not a consistent pattern in their marriage.

When relationships become more distressed, the negative interpretations mount and help create an environment of hopelessness and demoralization. Glenn and Eleanor are a couple who were high school sweethearts, have been married twenty-four years, and have three children, but they have been very unhappy in their marriage for more than seven years—in part due to the corrosive effect of strong negative interpretations. Although there are positive things in their marriage, almost nothing each does is recognized positively by the other, as seen by this recent conversation about parking their car.

GLENN: You left the car out again. Isn't it enough to have teenagers who do that all the time?

ELEANOR: Oh. I guess I forgot to put it in when I came back from Madge's.

GLENN: (with a bit of a sneer) I guess you did. You know how much that irritates me.

ELEANOR: (exasperated) Look, I forgot. Do you think I leave it out just to irritate you?

GLENN: (coldly) Actually, that is exactly what I think. I have told you so many times that I want the car in the garage at night.

ELEANOR: Yes, you have. But I don't leave it out just to tick you off. I just forget.

GLENN: If you cared what I thought about things, you'd remember.

ELEANOR: You know that I put the car in nine times out of ten.

GLENN: More like half the time, and those are the times I leave the garage door up for you.

ELEANOR: Have it your way. It doesn't matter what reality is. You will see it your way.

This may sound like a minor argument, but it is not. It represents a long-standing tendency for Glenn to interpret Eleanor's behavior in the most negative light possible. For the sake of argument, assume that Eleanor is absolutely correct when she says that she simply forgot to put the car in the garage and that this only happens about one in ten times. Glenn sees it differently, especially in his interpretation that she leaves the car out mostly to upset him.

Negative interpretations are a good example of mind reading. You are mind reading when you assume you know what your partner is thinking or why he or she did something. When you mind read positively, it does not tend to cause any harm. But when your mind reading includes negative judgments about the thoughts and motives of the other, you are in real trouble in your marriage—whether or not you openly express the negative interpretation.

So it is very important to be on guard for the tendency to view your spouse harshly. After all, a marriage would be in truly terrible shape if either partner routinely and intentionally did things just to frustrate the other. Much more frequently, the actions of one partner are interpreted negatively and unfairly. This is a sign of a relationship heading for big trouble in the future. Negative interpretations are very destructive, in part because they are very hard to detect and counteract. They easily become woven into the fabric of a relationship, because we all have a very strong tendency toward *confirmation bias,* which is the tendency to look for evidence that confirms what we already think is true about others or situations. In other words, once formed, negative interpretations do not change easily. Even though we can be wrong in our assumptions, we tend to see what we expect to see.

For example, if you believe that your neighbor Bill can never say anything nice to you, then no matter what he actually may say, you will interpret his comments in light of your expectations. He could say, "Gee, you sure did a nice job on that project," and you might think to yourself, "He is only trying to manipulate me; what does he want now?" Supposing that Bill was indeed sincere, your strong assumption will wipe out his good intent. No one is immune from looking for information to confirm his or her expectations about others.

In the example of Glenn and Eleanor, Glenn has the expectation that "Eleanor does not care one bit about anything that is important to me." This assumption colors the good things that do happen. In distressed relationships, there is a tendency for partners to discount the positive things they do see, attributing them to causes such as chance rather than to positive characteristics of the partner. Because of Glenn's negative interpretations, he attributes the times Eleanor does put the car in the garage to his own action of leaving the door open and not to her intention to put it there. She can't win this argument, and as long as Glenn maintains his negative mind-set, they will not be able to come to an acceptable resolution.

Battling Negative Interpretations

We are not advocating some kind of unrealistic "positive thinking"; you can't just sit around and wish that your partner will change truly negative behaviors. You may, however, need to consider that your partner's motives are more positive than you are acknowledging. Negative interpretations are something you have to confront within yourself. Only you can control how you interpret your partner's behavior.

First, you have to ask yourself if you might be being overly negative in your interpretation of things your partner does. Second—and this is hard—you must push yourself to look for evidence that is contrary to the negative interpretation you usually make. For example, if you believe that your partner is uncaring and you generally see most of what he does in that light, you need to look for evidence to the contrary. Does he do things for you that you like? Could it be that he does nice things because he is trying to keep the relationship strong? It's up to you to consider your interpretation of behavior that others might see as obviously positive.

A person in the survey wrote of the stress in her marriage in a way that illustrates both her and her partner's tendency to see each other negatively. She wrote that the cause of greatest stress was the lack of communication, the "confusion that comes because of a lack of understanding or different levels of understanding when communicating," and of her husband's "inability to see 'self' . . . accompanied with no desire to change." As long as she is seeing the marriage through her own layer of negative interpretations, she is certainly not leaving any room for the possibility that her partner may have any positive intentions toward her. She also writes, "My husband has voiced that he doesn't want to lose me, so I feel trapped . . . ," giving a clue that there is more going on here than she is able to express.

As you work through this book and are considering many positive changes in your relationship, make sure you try to give your partner the benefit of the doubt in wanting to make things better. Don't allow inaccurate interpretations to sabotage the work you are trying to accomplish together.

WITHDRAWAL AND AVOIDANCE: HIDE AND SEEK

Withdrawal and *avoidance* are different manifestations of a pattern in which one partner shows an unwillingness to get into or stay with important discussions. Withdrawal can be as obvious as getting up and leaving the room or as subtle as "turning off" or "shutting down" during an argument. The withdrawer often tends to get quiet during an argument or may agree quickly to some suggestion just to end the conversation, with no real intention of following through.

Avoidance reflects the same reluctance to get into certain discussions, with more emphasis on the attempt not to let the conversation happen in the first place. A person prone to avoidance would prefer that the topic not come up and, if it does, may manifest the signs of withdrawal. One husband from the survey reported, "My wife appears to believe it's unhealthy to argue, so disagreements go unresolved, in my opinion." Couples with a partner who avoids discussion end up with two problems: the original issue and the anger and resentment built up by the avoidance.

Let's look at this pattern as played out in a discussion between Caroline, a forty-eight-year-old realtor, and George, a fifty-two-year-old loan officer. Married for twenty-two years, they have a teenage daughter, Cindy, who is a senior in high school. Caroline was concerned that the tension in their relationship was negatively affecting their daughter.

CAROLINE: When are we going to talk about how you are handling your anger?

GEORGE: Can't this wait? I have to get these taxes done.

CAROLINE: I've brought this up at least five times already. No, it can't wait!

GEORGE: *(tensing)* What's to talk about, anyway? It's none of your business.

CAROLINE: *(frustrated and looking right at George)* Cindy is my business. I'm afraid your losing your temper with her is driving a wedge in your relationship with her. She only has one more year at home with us, and your anger is destroying your relationship with her. And you won't do anything to learn to deal better with your anger.

GEORGE: *(turning away, looking out the window)* I love Cindy. There's no problem here. *(leaving the room as he talks)*

CAROLINE: *(very angry now, following George into the next room)* You have to get some help. You can't just stick your head in the sand.

GEORGE: I'm not going to discuss anything with you when you are like this.

CAROLINE: Like what? It doesn't matter if I am calm or frustrated—you won't talk to me about anything important. Cindy is having problems, and you have to face that.

GEORGE: *(quiet, tense, fidgeting)*

CAROLINE: Well?

GEORGE: *(going to closet and grabbing sweater)* I'm going out to have a drink and get some peace and quiet.

CAROLINE: *(voice raised, angry)* Talk to me, now. I'm tired of you leaving when we are talking about something important.

GEORGE: *(looking away from Caroline, walking toward the door)* I'm not talking, you are; actually, you're yelling. See you later.

Many couples do this kind of dance when it comes to dealing with difficult issues. One partner *pursues* dealing with issues (Caroline) and one *avoids* or *withdraws* from dealing with issues (George). Although common, this scenario is very destructive to the relationship. As with the other patterns presented, it does not have to be this dramatic to predict problems to come. It is one of the most powerful predictors of future relationship unhappiness and divorce.

Pursuing and Withdrawing Dynamics: The Gender Dance

The *pursuer* is the one in the relationship who most often brings issues up for discussion or calls attention to the need to make a decision about something. The *withdrawer* is the person who tends to avoid these discussions or pull away during them. Studies show that men tend to be in the withdrawing role, women in the pursuing role. However, there are many relationships in which this pattern is reversed. In some relationships, the partners switch these roles depending on the topic. Simply reverse the points we make here if the patterns are reversed between the two of you.

Why do men tend to withdraw more? Some say it's because they are less interested in change, and pull away to avoid dealing with the issues. That may be the case for some men, but more of the time, we believe that the one who withdraws tends to do so because it does not feel safe to stay in the argument—meaning that it's not emotionally safe or even that the person fears the conflict will turn physical. (If you have concerns about physical conflict and aggression in your relationship, please see Finding a Counselor When You Need One at the back of this book.)

When this pattern gets going, it tends to be very frustrating for both men and women. When married to men who withdraw, women usually feel shut out, and they begin to feel that their husbands don't care about the relationship. For many women, a lack of talking equals a lack of caring. But that's usually a negative interpretation of what the withdrawer is doing—which has more to do with trying to stop the conflict than not caring about the relationship. Likewise, men often complain that their pursuing wives get upset too much of the time, griping about this or that and picking fights, as if their wives like to fight. That's also a negative interpretation, because what pursuers really want is to stay connected or resolve issues. Those are not negative motives either.

So it is important to learn how to stay out of this pursuer-withdrawer pattern. That will take you working together. Refrain from taking the most negative interpretation of what your partner does when you are doing your dance of conflict. Research by coauthors Scott and Howard suggests that the couples who are the happiest, the most relaxed together, and the most open are those who do the best job of not falling into this pursuer-withdrawer pattern. We will give you some tips here for reducing withdrawal, and as we go on there will be many more strategies to help you avoid these destructive patterns in your marriage.

Avoiding Withdrawal

If you are seeing this pattern in your relationship, keep in mind that it will likely get worse in the empty nest if you allow it to continue. That is because as pursuers push more, withdrawers withdraw more. And as withdrawers pull back, pursuers push harder. Furthermore, when issues are important, it should be obvious that trying to avoid dealing with them will only lead to damaging consequences. You can't stick your head in the sand and pretend important or bothersome problems are not really there. For some couples, children-related issues may bring the couple together temporarily, which interrupts the cycle. In the empty nest, the pursuer-withdrawal pattern may return with full force.

In the case of withdrawal and avoidance, the first, best step you can take right now is to realize that you are not independent of one another. Your actions cause reactions, and vice versa. For this reason, you will have much greater success if you are working together to change or prevent the kinds of negative patterns discussed here. Withdrawers are not likely to reduce avoidance unless pursuers pursue less, or at least pursue more constructively. Pursuers are going to find it hard to cut back on pursuing unless withdrawers deal more directly with the issues at hand.

In your marriage, you need to keep the lines of communication open, but do so in such a way that neither feels the urge to withdraw. We will get much more specific on how to combat these patterns in the next few chapters. For now, try to agree that if you are having trouble with pursuit and withdrawal, you will work together to change the pattern.

HOW POSITIVE FEELINGS ERODE IN MARRIAGE: THE LONG-TERM EFFECT OF NEGATIVE PATTERNS

Contrary to popular belief, positives in marriage do not slowly fade away for no reason in particular. We believe that the chief reason that marriages fail at alarmingly high rates is that couples handle conflict poorly, as evidenced by such patterns as those described in this chapter. Over time, these patterns steadily erode all the good things in the relationship.

For example, when a couple routinely escalates as issues arise, both partners may come to the conclusion that it is just as easy not to talk at all. After all, talking leads to fighting, right? Or, as issues arise, the partners become more concerned with getting their own way, and invalidation becomes a weapon easily taken in hand. Over time, no issue seems safe.

Not only do many couples deal with issues poorly; they also may not set aside time to discuss them or come to any agreement about how they will handle them. Even in what starts out as the best of marriages, these factors can lead to growing distance and a lack of confidence in the relationship. Remember George and Caroline, earlier in this chapter. Although they are a genuinely caring couple, their inability to discuss tough issues—in this case, George's anger—has caused a rift that will widen and perhaps destroy the marriage if nothing is done.

Many older couples in Marriage Alive seminars bring up the issues of "parallel lives" or living as "married singles"; the two partners have simply developed separate lives filled with activities and relationships in order to avoid touching on difficult issues with each other. This is certainly an extreme example of one way negative patterns cause erosion in marriages. Real intimacy and a sense of connection may die out, and many couples settle for frustrated loneliness and isolation. If you want to keep your relationship strong or renew one that is lagging, you must learn to counteract destructive patterns such as those we have described. Fortunately, you can do this. You can prevent the erosion of happiness in your relationship for the years to come.

*

In this chapter, we described four patterns in handling conflict that predict future marital discord and divorce. We made the point that certain patterns of dealing with conflict are particularly destructive in a relationship. How can couples manage their tendencies toward destructive patterns and limit the damage that is caused by them? In Chapter Eight we will suggest a specific set of agreed-on rules and strategies for handling conflict and difficult issues in your relationship.

Keep in mind that most couples show some of these patterns to some degree. In the Preface, you took a short relationship quiz to see how your relationship stands on these issues. Go back and look at the questions to which you answered "true." Whether or not you currently show some of these patterns is not as important as deciding to do something to protect your relationship from them. The exercises that follow are a first step toward protecting your relationship from these patterns.

In the next chapter, we focus on how to incorporate a simple set of tools and strategies into your talking together as a couple. The Speaker-Listener Technique addresses the destructive communication patterns we've described and provides a structure for safe, effective communication.

EXERCISES

The exercises for this chapter ask you to see whether the patterns we have discussed are present in your relationship. Please take a pad of paper and write your answers to these questions independently from your partner. When you have finished, we suggest you share your perceptions. However, if doing so raises conflict, put off further discussion of your answers until you have learned in the next few chapters more about how to talk safely on tough topics.

Before getting into specific questions about the four negative patterns, consider the following one about your overall impression of how you handle conflict together: When you have a disagreement or argument, what typically happens? In answering this question, think about the four patterns.

Escalation

Escalation occurs when one of you says or does something negative, the other responds with something negative, and off you go into a real battle. Escalation is an example of the snowball effect; you can get increasingly angry and hostile as the argument continues.

1. How often do you think you escalate as a couple?
2. Do you get hostile with each other during escalation?
3. What or who usually brings an end to the fight?
4. When angry, does one or the other of you sometimes threaten to end the relationship?

5. How do you feel when you are escalating as a couple? Do you feel tense, anxious, scared, angry, or something else?

Invalidation

Invalidation occurs when you subtly or directly put down the thoughts, feelings, actions, or worth of your partner. This is different from simply disagreeing with your partner or not liking something he or she has done. Invalidation includes an element of belittling or disregarding what is important to your partner, either out of insensitivity or outright contempt.

1. Do you often feel invalidated in your relationship? When and how does this happen?

2. What is the effect on you?

3. Do you often invalidate your partner? When and how does this happen?

4. What do you think the effect is on him or her? On the relationship? What are you trying to accomplish when you do this? Is this what happens?

Negative Interpretations

Negative interpretations occur when you interpret your spouse's behavior much more negatively than he or she intended. It is critical that you open yourself to seeing the possibility that your view of your partner could be unfair in some areas. These questions will help you reflect on this.

1. Can you think of some areas in which you consistently see your partner's behavior as negative?

2. Do you really think that your negative view of your partner's behavior is justified?

3. Are there some areas in which you have a negative interpretation but are open to considering that you may be missing
evidence to the contrary?

4. List two or so issues for which you are willing to push yourself
to look for the possibility that your partner has more positive
motivations than you have been thinking he or she has. Next,
look for the evidence that is contrary to your interpretation.

Withdrawal and Avoidance

As discussed previously, men and women often deal quite differently
with conflict in relationships. Most often, women are more prone
to pursue and men are more prone to withdraw from discussion of
issues in the relationship.

1. Is one of you more likely to be in the pursuer role? Is one of
you more likely to be in the withdrawer role?

2. How does the withdrawer usually withdraw? How does the
pursuer usually pursue? What happens then?

3. When are you most likely to fall into this pattern as a couple?
Are there particular issues or situations that bring out this
pattern?

4. How are you affected by this pattern?

5. For some couples, both tend to pursue or withdraw. Is that
true for your relationship? Why do you think this happens?

Sometimes, considering questions like the ones in these exercises can cause anxiety or sadness, as you reflect on where your relationship stands at this point. Although it may not be pleasant to
think about negative patterns, we believe it will help you as you
move ahead in this book and learn constructive ways to keep your
marriage strong.

5

Talking It Out
The Speaker-Listener Technique

When the kids leave home, communication between the two of you can get more complicated. One reason is that you have more time to talk to each other, and many couples, once the children leave home, have fewer things to talk about. Others don't know how to handle the extra talk. As one survey respondent put it, "He finally gets a chance to talk, and so now it seems like he talks too much." Major issues with teenagers are no longer on the front burner. Now you have time to start a conversation or argument and time to continue it or even finish it. If your ability to talk about sensitive matters has become rusty—or if it never was all that good in the first place—the difficulties the two of you have talking about the important themes of your life together can threaten the quality of your marriage.

We assume you really want to communicate well. Most couples do, but many have never learned to communicate well when it counts most: when a disagreement or a vulnerable topic is at hand. What makes matters more difficult for some empty nest couples is the absence of the children in the home. That is because children can act as buffers in the interaction between the two of you. When tensions occur in a relationship, spouses can always talk about—or to—the kids. Other issues that cause stress often remain below the surface. When the kids leave home, they take the buffers with them.

Anne and Ben found out about such changes the hard way. As she noted to us, "I used to wonder why so many people divorced after thirty years of marriage. Then our last child left home, and we learned this isn't an easy time in life. We were used to talking in sound bites. For the first time, we had time to finish a conversation and even finish an argument. My husband, Ben, was terrified!"

Whether or not your children's leaving has a big effect on your communication patterns, this is a great time of life to learn how to communicate better. As you learned in Chapter Four, handling conflict well is critical to a successful long-term marriage. And communicating well is critical to handling conflict. There are two key issues we focus on in this chapter: making it clear and making it safe.

MAKING IT CLEAR: THE PROBLEM OF FILTERS

Have you ever noticed that what you are trying to say to your partner can be very different from what he or she hears? You may say something you think is harmless, and suddenly your spouse is mad at you. Or you may ask a question such as "What do you want for dinner?" and your partner starts complaining about you not doing your share of the work.

We have all experienced the frustration of being misunderstood. You think you are being clear, but your partner just doesn't seem to "get it." Or you are sure you know what she said yesterday, and today she says something that seems completely different.

Like the rest of us, Mary and Bob can relate to this common problem. They hit the empty nest last year and are still readjusting their roles and responsibilities. Mary has just gone back to work full-time as a reservation agent for an airline, and Bob is an accountant for a major firm. Their jobs leave them exhausted at the end of each day. With kids no longer at home, they can usually crash when they get home.

One Thursday night, Bob was home first and read the paper while waiting for Mary. He was thinking, "I sure am wiped. I bet she is, too. I'd really like to go out to eat and just relax with Mary tonight." Good idea, right? This is what happened with his idea (what they are thinking or hearing is in parentheses):

BOB: *(He's thinking he'd like to go out to dinner with Mary, as she comes in the door.)* What should we do for dinner tonight?

MARY: *(She hears "When will dinner be ready?")* Why is it always my job to make dinner? I work as hard as you do.

BOB: *(He hears her response as an attack and thinks, "Why is she always so negative?")* It is not always your job to make dinner. I made dinner once last week!

MARY: *(The negative cycle continues, as Mary tends to feel she does everything around the house.)* Bringing home hamburgers and fries is not making dinner, Bob.

BOB: *(With frustration mounting, Bob gives up.)* Just forget it. I didn't want to go out with you anyway.

MARY: *(Confused, Mary can't remember him saying anything about going out.)* You never said anything about wanting to go out.

BOB: *(feeling really angry)* Yes I did! I asked you where you wanted to go out to dinner, and you got really nasty.

MARY: I got nasty? You never said anything about going out.

BOB: Did too!

MARY: You're never wrong, are you?

Sound familiar? You can see where things went wrong for them this evening. Bob had a great idea, a positive idea, yet conflict blew out the evening. Bob was not as clear as he could have been in telling Mary what he was thinking. This left a lot of room for interpretation, and interpret Mary did. She assumed that he was asking—no, telling—her to get dinner on the table as she walked in the door.

This kind of miscommunication is all too common; it happens in relationships all the time. Many of the biggest arguments couples have together begin with the failure of one partner to understand what the other partner is saying, leading to anger. What gets in the way? *Filters*.

Filters change what goes through them. A furnace filter takes dust and dirt out of the air. A filter on a camera lens alters the properties of the light passing through it. A coffee filter lets the flavor through and leaves the gunk behind. As with any other filter, what goes into our "communication filters" is different than what comes out. When what you say (or what you intended to say) is not the same as what your partner heard, then a filter is at work.

We all have many kinds of filters packed into our heads. They affect what we hear, what we say, and how we interpret things. They are influenced by how we are feeling, what we think, and what we have experienced in our life, our family and cultural backgrounds, and so on.

Empty nest couples are especially vulnerable to filters. Years of pent-up resentments affect the way spouses look at things. Couples who put all their eggs in the parenting basket look at life through a "child focus." Roles that worked for so many years change, adding to their frustration levels. Spouses in second marriages may assume that their new partner will see things the same way as the previous partner. No wonder that when the children leave home, communication becomes more difficult. Let's look at five types of filters that can affect couples as they struggle for clear communication:

1. Inattention
2. Emotional states
3. Beliefs and expectations
4. Differences in style
5. Self-protection

Inattention

A very basic kind of filter has to do with whether you have the attention of the person with whom you are trying to speak. Both external and internal factors can affect attention. External factors are such things as noisy kids, a hearing problem, a bad phone line, or the background noise at a party. Internal factors affecting attention include feeling tired, thinking about something else, feeling bored, mentally forming a rebuttal, and the like. The key is to make sure you have your partner's attention and to give your attention when it really counts most. For important talks, find a quiet place if you can, and don't answer the phone. Make it easier to pay attention to one another, and try not to assume that your partner is ready to listen right now just because you are ready to talk. Ask.

Emotional States

Emotional states or moods become filters that affect communication. For example, a number of studies demonstrate that we tend to give people more benefit of the doubt when we are in a good mood and less when in a bad mood. If you are in a bad mood, you are more likely to perceive whatever your partner says or does more negatively, no matter how positive he or she is trying to be. Have you noticed that sometimes, when your spouse is in a bad mood, you get jumped on no matter how nicely you say something?

The best defense against the damage these kinds of filters can cause in your relationship is to acknowledge the filter when you are aware that one is operating.

Here is an example. Paula had a stressful day at work. She just got home. It's dinnertime, and she's in the kitchen cooking macaroni. Jeremy just got home, too. He's sitting in his favorite easy chair reading the mail.

JEREMY: This bill for the phone company got missed again. We better get this paid.

PAULA: (*snapping with anger*) I'm not the one who forgot it. Can't you see I have my hands full? Do something helpful.

JEREMY: I'm sorry. I should have seen you were busy. Rough day?

PAULA: Yes. I had a very frustrating day. I don't mean to snap at you, but I've had it up to here. If I am touchy, it's not really anything you've done.

JEREMY: Maybe we can talk about it some after dinner.

PAULA: Thanks.

Without using the term *filter*, Jeremy and Paula are acknowledging one is there. Paula had a bad day and is on edge. They could have let this conversation escalate into an argument, but Jeremy had the good sense to see he had raised an issue at the wrong time. He decided not to get defensive, and chose to become gentle with Paula in her frustration. Paula responded by telling Jeremy, in essence, that she had a filter going: her bad mood. Knowing this helped him be less defensive in reaction to her mood. It is very important not to use the presence of a filter as an excuse for treating your partner badly.

Many kinds of emotional filters can exist in any one person. If you are angry, worried, sad, or upset about anything, it can color your interpretation of and response to what your partner says. Jeremy's response was helpful because it opened the door for Paula to clarify her emotional filter and allowed them to de-escalate and be clear with one another.

Beliefs and Expectations

Many very important filters arise from how you think and what you expect in your relationship. As we mentioned in Chapter Four, research and experience tell us that people tend to see what they expect to see in others and situations. You are not immune to the tendency to look for or hear in others what you are expecting. This kind of expectation becomes a filter that distorts communication. Studies show that expectations not only affect what we perceive but can influence the actual behavior of others. For example, if you believe that someone is an extrovert, she is more likely to sound like an extrovert when talking with you, even if she is normally introverted. We "pull" behavior from others that is consistent with what we expect.

This next example shows how difficult it can be to get around mental filters. Alex and Helen are a couple who came to one of our workshops. They were having problems deciding what to do for fun when they had free time. Their daughter, Jessica, who was a single mom, and her two-year-old son, Jason, lived with them. Helen and

Alex did all they could to help out with their grandson. Free time without Jessica and Jason was very valuable to them. But they rarely got their act together to get out and do something, so both were frustrated. This conversation was typical for them. Note how both acted as if they could read the mind of the other:

ALEX: *(He really wants to go bowling but thinks that Helen is not interested in going out and doing anything fun together.)* We have some free time tonight. Jessica gets off work early and will be here to take care of Jason. I wonder if we should try to do something.

HELEN: *(She's thinking that she would like to get out, but hears the tentativeness in his voice and thinks he really does not want to go out.)* Oh, I don't know. What do you think?

ALEX: Well, we could go bowling, but it could be league night, and we might not get in anyway. Maybe we should just stay in and watch *Home Improvement*.

HELEN: *(She's thinking "Aha, that's what he really wants to do.")* That's sounds good to me. Why don't we make some popcorn and watch some tube?

ALEX: *(He's disappointed, thinking "I knew it. She really doesn't want to make the effort to get out and do something fun.")* Yeah, OK.

In this conversation, there was no escalation, invalidation, or withdrawal. Nevertheless, Helen and Alex did not communicate well due to the belief and expectation filters involved. Alex's belief that Helen does not like to go out colored the entire conversation— so much so that the way he asked her to go out led her to think that he wanted to stay in. He "knew" that she really did not want to go, which constitutes mind reading. The kind of mind reading that damages marriages most is the kind that includes a negative assumption about what the other is thinking or feeling. Such mind reading is a specific form of negative interpretation.

From Alex's perspective, they stayed in once again because that is what she wanted. His mental filter pulled the conversation in this direction and become a self-fulfilling prophecy. Helen also did a

good deal of mind reading. In this conversation, she assumed that
Alex really wanted to stay in, and participated in a distorted conversation in which neither said what they wanted. If they had been
able to communicate clearly, without any filters, they would have
concluded that both wanted to get out and probably would have
tried the bowling idea.

Differences in Style

Everyone has a different style of communicating, and different styles
can lead to filtering. Perhaps one of you is much more expressive
and one of you more reserved. You may have some trouble understanding each other because you use such different styles.

Styles are determined by many influences, including culture,
gender, and upbringing. Sometimes, style differences rooted in family backgrounds can cause great misunderstandings, becoming powerful filters that distort communication.

Sue and Ted came from very different families. His family has
always been very expressive of all manner of emotion. They tend to
show great intensity when emotional. It's just their way. Sue's family has always been more reserved. For Sue, a slight rise in voice
could mean great anger in her family, whereas it would hardly be
noticed in Ted's. In many conversations, therefore, Sue would overestimate the intensity of Ted's feelings, and Ted would underesti-
mate Sue's feelings. Here is an example:

TED: What did it cost to get the muffler fixed?

SUE: Four hundred and twenty-eight bucks.

TED: (intense, getting red quickly) What? How could they possibly
charge that much? That's outrageous.

SUE: (lashing out) I wish you could stop yelling at me! I've told you
over and over that I cannot listen to you when you are yelling!

TED: I am not yelling at you. I just can't believe that it could cost
that much.

SUE: Why can't we have a quiet conversation like other people?
My sister and brother-in-law never yell at each other.

TED: They don't talk about anything, either. Look, four hundred and twenty-eight dollars is too much to pay; that's all I'm reacting to.

SUE: Why don't you take the car in next time? I'm tired of being yelled at for things like this.

TED: Honey, look. I'm not upset at you. I'm upset at them. And you know I can get pretty hot, but I'm not trying to say you did anything wrong.

SUE: (*calming down*) Well, it seems that way sometimes.

TED: Well, I'm not upset at you. Let me give that place a call. Where's the number?

Sue and Ted are caught up in a misunderstanding based on differences in style. You would think that after so many years of marriage they would understand each other a little better, but at least they did a great job of not allowing things to escalate. As in preceding examples in which the conversation got back on track, one partner figured out that there was a filter distorting the intended message and took corrective action. Here, Ted forcefully clarifies that he is not mad at Sue.

Being more aware of the effects of your differing styles on your communication can go a long way toward preventing misunderstandings. We recommend that you give some thought to these differences between the two of you.

Self-Protection

This last kind of filter has its origins in the fear of rejection, with which we all struggle in some ways. Basically, we avoid saying what we really want or feel out of fear of rejection. Even something as simple as "Wouldn't you like to go see that new movie with me?" can reflect this. Instead of saying what we want directly ("I'd like to see that new movie; do you want to go?"), we often hide our desire because to speak it more clearly reveals more of who we are—increasing the risk of rejection. This may not matter a lot when it comes to movies, but when it comes to the real day-to-day issues of marriage—such as feelings, desires, and expectations—the tendency can lead to a lot of miscommunication.

Many empty nest couples fear raising old issues to no avail. One woman stated that in her relationship there was "too much old hurt, and [I'm] not willing to trust," making it difficult to speak out directly about anything she may want or feel. For other couples, conflicts from prior relationships are filters that distort what may happen in the new relationship.

Filters and Memory: That's Not What You Heard!

Some of the biggest arguments couples have are about what they actually said in the past. How often have you wished that you had a tape recording of an earlier conversation? This happens to all of us. These differences in memory occur in great measure because of the variety of filters that operate in all relationships. Any of the filters discussed here can lead to differences—and arguments—about what someone actually said or did in the past.

Read again the earlier conversation in this chapter between Bob and Mary. Notice that they ended up arguing about what was actually said at the start of the conversation. Bob truly thinks he asked Mary out to dinner, but what he actually said was vague. Mary truly thinks Bob told her to get dinner on the table, which also is not what he said. Without a tape recording, no amount of convincing would get either one to back off from his or her version of the story.

We recommend two things that can save your relationship from such fruitless arguments about the past. First, don't assume your memory is perfect. Have the humility to accept that it is not. There are countless studies in the field of psychology that show how fragile human memory is, how susceptible memory is to motives and beliefs. Accept that you both have filters and that there is plenty of room for things to be said or heard differently than what was intended.

Second, when you disagree, don't persist in arguments about what was actually said in the past. You will get nowhere. Don't get stuck in the past, even if it was five minutes ago. Shift the topic to what you each think and feel in the present. A lot of times, doing this takes humility, because the fastest path out of arguments about memory is to say something like this: "I'm not sure what I said exactly, but I want to tell you what I meant to say, OK?"

*

We hope you understand how important it is to be aware of filters in your communication with one another. We all have filters. Either we react to them with little awareness, which can cause damage to the relationship, or we learn to look for them when conversations go awry. Try to get in the habit of announcing your filter when you are aware that you might have one. ("I know I'm sensitive about sex, so I may not be real clear in what I'm trying to tell you right now.")

The two most important things about filters are that (1) everyone has them, and (2) they are not intrinsically good or bad. We all have differing moods, levels of attention, and differences in beliefs. We also have differences in experience and upbringing that can result in filters to clear communication. After discussing the importance of safety in your relationship, we will teach you a very effective communication technique for reducing both the effect of filters and the expression of the danger signs in your relationship.

MAKING IT SAFE: THE VALUE OF STRUCTURE

To have a great empty nest marriage, both of you must be able to express your beliefs, concerns, and preferences clearly, without damaging the relationship in the process. The patterns we discussed in Chapter Four can make it unsafe to express your views about what is most important to you—and you can't be deeply connected when it isn't safe to share important thoughts and ideas. People generally do not share openly with anyone, including a spouse, without there being some feeling of safety. Filters compound the problem, making it a wonder that couples can communicate about anything truly important.

Are marriages necessarily safe? No. Most people want the safe haven of a friendly relationship, but many couples just don't get or remain there. By *safe* we do not mean risk-free. If you are going to share what you are concerned with, hurt by, or hoping for, you are going to take risks. There is a direct relationship between risk and reward in much of life. You cannot be accepted deeply without offering something deep for your partner to accept. Conversely, you can take the risk, share deeply, and be rejected. This hurts a lot, because you have chosen to risk a deeper part of yourself in the relationship. But if it goes well, you find a deep, soul-satisfying acceptance of who you are, warts and all.

When you disagree, or think you do, more is at stake and more can go wrong. For your relationship to grow through conflict, instead of being damaged by it, you'll need to work at keeping escalation, invalidation, withdrawal, and negative interpretations out of your communication with your partner.

One way to do this is to use agreed-on strategies and techniques to help you in important conversations. We call this adding structure to your interaction. This is exactly what is done all the time in work and political settings. Consider for a moment what the average session of our U.S. Congress would look like if the members did not agree on the rules for how and when things can be shared. With adequate structure, you can manage conflict with less chance of damage to your relationship. In fact, when you can talk safely about deeper issues, conflicts can become opportunities to grow closer together. When less is at stake or when you are not in conflict, you don't need much structure. Just communicate in whatever way you are most comfortable. But at other times, a bit of structure can get you through without damage and maybe with greater closeness.

THE SPEAKER-LISTENER TECHNIQUE

One wife, when asked in the survey what she feared most about her marriage in the future, wrote, "I dread the prospect of changing thirty years of poor relating. It makes me tired." You can really hear her distress. Possibly though, after reading this far in this book, she may be able to identify some of her filters and negative interpretations that are making communication so difficult for her and her husband. She seems to believe that she will have to do all the hard work and that her partner will not help or be motivated. We often see couples giving up too soon, when we can offer an alternative.

The Speaker-Listener Technique offers couples a safe way of communicating when issues are hot or sensitive or likely to get that way. Any conversation in which you want to enhance clarity and safety can benefit from this technique. It's a simple but powerful way to communicate better when you really need to. And it is something most couples can learn quite easily with a little practice. Yes, old dogs (even middle-aged dogs) can learn new tricks. We won't ask you to roll over, but we will ask you to try some new ways to work on issues together.

We have found particular success with the Speaker-Listener Technique because it is so simple and very effective. Most couples seem to really appreciate this technique (though some do not). In our research, we find that couples taking the PREP program overwhelmingly report that learning this technique was very helpful for them. This technique also is a great way to practice better communication habits that can affect how you interact even when you are not trying to use the technique as taught here.

This technique works because you both follow certain rules, which we will now describe. Following such rules adds structure to your conversation, and that structure can make it safer to talk about things. Such structure is not useful for just having a great talk as friends or for day-to-day sharing of basic information, but it can be immensely helpful for making it safe to talk openly when it otherwise might not be.

The most frequent concern that we hear from couples about the technique is that "it's not natural." Yes, that is very true. But all kinds of things you do in life that are beneficial to you were not natural when you first learned them. Besides, as we have observed, what many couples "naturally" do when they disagree or when they talk about something sensitive looks more like the four danger signs than great communication. So try something unnatural for a change. You just might like it. Also, if you practice, you will truly find that the unnaturalness of the technique goes away with time. What follows are what we mean by rules for the Speaker-Listener Technique. After you learn and practice these rules, you may find ways you want to tweak them to work best in your relationship.

Rules for Both of You

1. *The Speaker has the floor.* Use a real object to designate the "floor." When giving seminars, we hand out pieces of linoleum or carpet for couples to use as the floor. You can use anything, though: the TV remote, a piece of paper, a paperback book. If you do not have the floor, you are the Listener. Speaker and Listener follow the rules for each role.

2. *Share the floor.* You share the floor over the course of a conversation. One person has it to start and may say a number of things. At some point you switch roles and continue as the floor changes hands.

3. *No problem solving.* When using this technique, you are going to focus on having good discussions, not on trying prematurely to come to solutions.

4. *Focus on one issue at a time.* Although sometimes a number of issues are linked, it is wise to try to focus on one key issue at a time in order to really understand each other.

Rules for the Speaker

1. *Speak for yourself. Don't try to be a mind reader.* Talk about your thoughts, feelings, and concerns, not your perceptions of the Listener's point of view or motives. Try to use "I" statements, and talk about your own point of view. "I think you're a jerk" is not an "I" statement. "I was upset when you forgot our date," is an "I" statement.

2. *Don't go on and on.* You will have plenty of opportunity to say all you need to say. To help the Listener listen actively, it will be very important to keep what you say to manageable pieces. If you

are in the habit of giving monologues, remember that having the floor protects you from interruption; you can afford to pause to be sure your partner understands you.

3. *Stop and let the Listener paraphrase*. After saying a bit, stop and allow the Listener to paraphrase what you just said. If the paraphrase was not quite accurate, you should politely restate what was not heard in the way you intended it to be heard. Your goal is to help the Listener hear and understand your point of view.

Rules for the Listener

1. *Paraphrase what you hear*. You must paraphrase what the Speaker is saying. Briefly repeat back what you heard the Speaker say, using your own words if you like, and make sure you understand what was said. The key is to show your partner that you are listening and to restate what you heard. If the paraphrase is not quite right (which happens often), the Speaker will gently clarify the point he or she is making. If you truly don't understand some phrase or example, you may ask the Speaker to clarify, but you may not ask questions on any other aspect of the issue unless you have the floor. And remember this: as the Listener, you don't have to agree with or even believe what the Speaker is saying to do your job well. Your mission is to understand what your partner is saying; you will have your turn to convey your opinion or feelings on the matter.

2. *Don't rebut. Focus on the Speaker's message*. While in the Listener role, you may not offer your opinion or thoughts. This is the hardest part of being a good Listener. If you are upset by what your partner says, you need to edit out any response you may want to make, and *pay attention* to what your partner is saying. Wait until you get the floor to make your response. When you are the Listener, your job is to speak only in the service of understanding your partner. Any words or gestures to show your opinion are not allowed, including making faces!

Before showing how the Speaker-Listener Technique works in a conversation, we want to give you some ideas about what good paraphrases can sound like. Suppose your spouse says to you, "I really had a tough day. My boss got on my case about how I handled the arrangements for today's conference. Ugh!" Any of the following might be an excellent paraphrase:

> "Sounds like you had a really tough day."
>
> "So, your boss was critical of how you handled the conference and really got on you about it."
>
> "Bad day, huh?"

Any one of these responses conveys that you have listened and displays what you have understood. A good paraphrase can be short or long, detailed or general. At times, if you are uncertain how to get a paraphrase started, it can help to begin with "What I hear you saying is . . ." Then you fill in what you just heard your partner say. Another way to begin a paraphrase is with the words "Sounds like . . ."

When using the Speaker-Listener Technique, the Speaker is always the one who determines if the Listener's paraphrase was on target. Only the Speaker knows what the intended message was. If the paraphrase was not quite on target, it is very important that the Speaker gently clarify or restate the point—not respond angrily or critically. One more key point: when you are in the Listener role, be sincere in your effort to show you are listening carefully and respectfully. Even when you disagree with the point your partner is making, your goal is to show respect for—and validation of—his or her perspective. That means waiting your turn and not making faces or looking bored. You can disagree completely with your mate on a matter and still show respect. Just wait until you have the floor to make your points.

Using the Speaker-Listener Technique

Here is an example of how this technique can change a conversation that is going nowhere into a real opportunity for communication. Peter and Tessie are in their early fifties, with two kids, one a twenty-year-old still living at home. For years Peter and Tessie have had a problem dealing with issues. Peter consistently avoids discussing problem areas, and if cornered by Tessie, he withdraws by pulling into himself. They know they need to communicate more clearly and safely on tough topics, and have agreed that the structure of the Speaker-Listener Technique can help.

In this case, Peter and Tessie have been locked in the pursuer-withdrawer cycle about the issue of their son Jeremy's living situation. However, they have been practicing the Speaker-Listener Technique and are ready to try something different. Let's see what happens.

TESSIE: I'm really getting tired of Jeremy continuing to live at home without any plans for moving on with his life. We have got to deal with this, now.

PETER: (*not looking up from the TV*) Oh?

TESSIE: (*walking over and standing in front of the TV*) Peter, we can't just leave this situation hanging in the air. I'm getting really pissed about you putting it off.

PETER: (*recognizing this would be a wise time to act constructively and not withdraw*) Time out. I can tell we need to talk, but I have been avoiding it because it seems that talking just leads to fighting. Let's try that Speaker-Listener Technique we've been practicing.

Again, this is not a "normal" way to communicate, but it is a relatively safe way to communicate on difficult issues. Each person will get to talk, each will be heard, and both will show commitment to discussing the problems constructively. When the person who usually withdraws moves constructively toward the pursuer in this manner, the effect on the relationship is often very positive. It attacks the foundation of the pursuer's belief that the withdrawer does not care about the relationship.

The conversation proceeds, with Peter picking up the piece of carpet they use for the floor.

Peter (Speaker): I've also been pretty concerned about Jeremy's selection of roommates if he does move out, and I'm not even sure he's ready to leave home.

Tessie (Listener): You are concerned that he's still living at home, too, but you're not sure he's ready to move out.

Peter (Speaker): Yeah, that's it. He acts pretty young for his age, and I'm not sure how he would do, unless the situation were just right.

Note how Peter acknowledges that Tessie's summary is on the mark, before moving on to another point.

Tessie (Listener): You're worried that he wouldn't hold his own with other roommates, right?

Tessie is not quite sure she has understood Peter's point, so she makes her paraphrase tentative.

Peter (Speaker): Well, partly that's it, but I'm also not sure if he's ready to be away from us. Of course, I don't want him to be too dependent, either.

Note how Peter gently clarifies. He's moving forward in the conversation, rather than backward. In general, whenever you (the Speaker) feel that clarification is needed or when the Listener requests it, use your next statement to restate or expand on what you are trying to get across.

Tessie (Listener): So you are feeling torn about him needing us and needing to be more independent.

Peter (Speaker): That's right. Here, you take the floor. (*He passes the floor to Tessie.*)

As the Speaker now, Tessie validates Peter in the comments he has made.

TESSIE (Speaker): Well, I appreciate what you're saying. Actually, I hadn't realized you had thought this much about it. I was worried that you didn't care about it.

PETER (Listener): Sounds like you're glad to hear that I am concerned.

TESSIE (Speaker): Yes. I agree that this is not an easy decision. If he did move into an apartment, it would have to be just the right place.

PETER (Listener): You're saying that it would have to be just the right living situation for it to work for him.

TESSIE (Speaker): Exactly. I think that it might work if he could find a supportive, mature roommate and an adequate apartment.

Tessie feels good with Peter listening so carefully, and lets him know it.

PETER (Listener): So you would be for it if he found just the right setting.

TESSIE (Speaker): I *might* be; I'm not sure—I feel conflicted—I want him to move out, yet at times I want him to stay.

PETER (Listener): You're not ready to say you would definitely want him to move out, even with a perfect situation.

TESSIE (Speaker): Right. Here, you take the floor again. (*She passes the floor to Peter.*)

As you can tell, Peter and Tessie have been practicing quite a bit. They are both doing an excellent job following the rules and showing concern and respect for each other's viewpoints. Couples can have discussions like this on difficult topics, even when they disagree. The key is to make it safe by showing respect for your partner's thoughts, feelings, and opinions.

For empty nest couples, sometimes issues are hard to deal with because of past negative patterns. The spouses have been traveling the same road together, but over the years, their avoiding the same issues over and over again has created negative ruts. As is true for ruts in a dirt road, just filling in the ruts with more dirt or gravel doesn't work. What is needed is to scrape all the rough places and level out the road. You don't have to get on a different road or build a new road; just do the repair work on the one you're on. Learning the Speaker-Listener Technique will help you repair your own communication road and prevent future negative ruts from developing.

The Advantages of Using the Speaker-Listener Technique

The Speaker-Listener Technique has many advantages over unstructured conversation when discussing difficult issues. Most important, it counteracts the destructive styles of communication described in Chapter Four.

1. *Escalation*. The structure of the technique makes it much harder to get into escalation. In fact, it is nearly impossible to escalate if you both follow the rules and work at showing respect. It is difficult to scream at one another if you have to stop every few sentences and ask for a paraphrase! The momentum of escalation is stopped dead.

2. *Invalidation*. The simple process of paraphrasing intervenes effectively with invalidation because the Speaker gets immediate feedback that he or she was heard. You can enhance the validation by saying "I understand" or "I see what you mean" at the end of a paraphrase or when you get the floor. This does not mean that you agree, just that you can see it from the other person's perspective. Save agreement or disagreement for your turn as Speaker. You do not have to agree with your partner to be a good Listener! One couple in the survey stated, "[We need to be] able to share even more of our innermost thoughts . . . even if we don't agree we want to hear those thoughts."

3. *Pursuit and withdrawal*. For the spouse who tends to withdraw from conversations in which conflict is possible, the structure makes it much safer to remain in the conversation. With a clear sense that

both of you are committed to keeping things from things from getting out of hand, there is less to be anxious about. Conflict is less likely to occur in an unmanageable way.

For the spouse who is usually in the pursuer role, structure in conversations assures that you will be heard and that issues are going to be addressed. Pursuing is less useful or necessary, as the withdrawer feels safer and more willing to address issues. Thus the two of you get closer to a win-win situation and out of hopeless win-lose cycles.

4. *Filters and negative interpretations*. The Speaker-Listener Technique makes it much easier to identify filters as soon as they come up. They will be evident in the paraphrases. The Speaker will have a nonthreatening opportunity to say, "That's not quite what I said. I said. . . . Could you paraphrase again, please?" All manner of filters can be reduced using this technique, especially negative interpretations.

Our research shows that couples benefit from learning to use structure when handling conflict. This makes a great deal of sense. Agreed-on rules like the Speaker-Listener Technique add some degree of predictability, which reduces anxiety and avoidance and helps both partners win rather than lose when dealing with conflict. Instead of fighting each other, you need to work together to fight negative patterns. And there is no better time to change some patterns for the better then when in a life transition. Out with the old and in with the new. You can do it.

Practice Is the Key

Practicing this technique regularly for some time can help all of the communication in your marriage to be better—not just when you are using all the rules of the technique. Our research strongly suggests that practicing such skills for a period of time can result in long-term, positive changes in how you communicate. We also think such practice makes couples more aware of ways to inhibit the danger signs covered in Chapter Four. So even if you don't think you want to communicate this way very often, practicing these kinds of skills can produce big benefits.

If you want to strengthen your marriage and reduce your chances of divorce, learn to move toward each other and deal constructively with those issues that have the potential to drive you apart. We will cover many other important principles in this book, but none is more critical.

*

In Chapter Six, we will look at some other ways conflicts in your relationship can develop and how you can identify and constructively address some complex issues. We'll help you separate trivial events from important relationship issues.

EXERCISES

The Speaker-Listener Technique isn't for everyone, but we have seen a great many couples who end up really appreciating what the structure can do for them, even when they were pretty skeptical early on. It does not work miracles, but it does work well. If it is going to be useful, you have to practice. As when you are learning any new skill, you are likely to be a bit unsure at the start. You need to learn this technique so well *together* that the rules are automatic when you have something really difficult to discuss.

If you were learning to play tennis, you would not try to perfect your backhand at center court in Wimbledon. Instead you would hit backhands against the back wall for hours to get it just right.

When we (Dave and Claudia) moved to Vienna, Austria, in the late 1970s, our assignment was to develop a small-group marriage education program for use in German-speaking countries. But before we could help couples build better marriages, we first had to learn how to speak their language. German is not an easy language to master, and at first it seemed to be an impossibility. We felt awkward and more than a little silly when we would attempt to use the few German words we had acquired. But we stuck with it. To master another language, we had to be willing to make mistakes and take the risk to speak out in German even when we felt insecure. But the more we studied and practiced actually speaking German, the more natural it became. Now when we visit Austria, Germany, or Switzerland, we enjoy being able to understand what others are saying, and though it's a bit rusty now, we enjoy using our German.

Why are we telling you about our language-learning experience? Simply to encourage you. If we can learn German, you can learn to use the Speaker-Listener Technique. Learning to really communicate with each other by sharing the floor will be a lot easier than learning a foreign language. But here is a caution: trying to learn a new skill in a high-stress situation is not advisable. Hence, we suggest you follow the suggestions here to practice the Speaker-Listener Technique.

Starting Out

Practice the Speaker-Listener Technique several times a week for fifteen minutes or so each time. If you do not set aside the time to practice, you will never find this powerful technique very helpful.

For the first week, try the technique only with nonconflictual topics. Talk about anything of interest to either of you: your favorite vacation ever, news, sports, your dreams for the future, concerns you have at work, and so on. Your goal here is not to resolve some problem but to practice new skills. Try not to talk about relationship issues unless you know they are not an area of conflict.

Moving Forward

After you have had three successful practice sessions about nonconflictual topics, choose minor conflict areas to discuss. Sometimes couples are poor at knowing what will and will not trigger a fight. If things get heated on a topic you choose, drop it. (It won't go away, but you can deal with it when you have practiced more together.)

Practice several discussions in which you both exchange some thoughts and feelings on these issues. Don't try to solve problems, just have good discussions. Your goal is to understand each other's point of view as clearly and completely as possible. Problems are sometimes solved in this process because all that was needed was to understand the other person's point of view. That's OK, but don't set out to solve problems or intentionally try for solutions. You are focusing on good discussions right now. You'll learn and practice problem solving in another chapter.

Going Deeper

When you are doing well on the preceding assignment, move up to tougher and tougher issues. As you do, remember to work at sticking to the rules. The technique works if you work at it, and as you become more comfortable with it, you will be able to take full advantage of the other ideas presented in this book.

6

Getting Beneath the Surface

Issues Versus Events

W hen a long-term marriage crumbles, a one-time event is rarely the culprit. Although an event may start the ultimate crash, it's the destructive ways in which many couples handle the little issues over the years that destroy the foundation of the marriage. All couples experience frustrating events, and all couples have difficult issues. In this chapter, we'll help you understand how issues and events are connected and how important it is to deal with them separately. Then we discuss the deeper, often hidden issues that affect relationships.

ISSUES VERSUS EVENTS

As we pointed out in Chapter One, the three major issues that most empty nest couples say cause problems are conflict, communication, and sex. Most other couples list their top three as money, sex, and communication. Other issues empty nest couples commonly struggle with include adult children (and sometimes the grandchildren), in-laws and extended family (especially aging parents), recreation (what to do with time now that the kids are gone), alcohol and drugs, careers, (one career may be winding down, the other gearing up), health issues, housework (previous roles don't work), and retirement planning.

Although these issues are important, we find that they're actually not the things that couples argue about most frequently. Instead, couples argue most often about the small, day-to-day happenings of life—we call them *events*. We want to help you separate out events from issues and then to separate out issues that are more apparent—money, communication, sex, and so on—from the deeper, often hidden, issues that affect your relationship. An example will help you see what we mean.

Mary Sue and Elliot are a couple with big money issues. With two kids in college, finances are tight. One day, Mary Sue came home from work and put the checkbook down on the kitchen counter as she went to the bedroom to change. Elliot got livid when he took a look at the checkbook and saw an entry for $150 made out to a department store. When Mary Sue walked back into the kitchen, tired after a long day at work, she was looking for a hug or a "How was your day?" Instead, the conversation went like this:

ELLIOT: What did you spend that hundred-and-fifty dollars on?
MARY SUE: (*very defensive*) None of your business.
ELLIOT: Of course it's my business! We just decided on a budget, and here you go blowing it.

All of a sudden they were off into a huge argument about money. But it happened in the context of an event—Elliot happening to look and see that Mary Sue spent $150. Events like this are common to all couples. In this case, Mary Sue had actually spent the $150 on a new sweater for Elliot because he had just received an offer for a new job. But that never even came up.

Issues and events work like the geysers in Yellowstone National Park. Underneath the park are caverns of hot water under pressure. The issues in your relationship are like these pressure points. The issues that give you the most trouble contain the greatest amount of heat. The pressure keeps building up when you aren't talking about them in a constructive manner. Then events trigger the eruption.

Many couples, particularly couples in unhappy relationships, only deal with important issues in the context of triggering events. For Mary Sue and Elliot, there is so much negative energy stored up around the issue of money that it's easily triggered. They never sit down and talk about money in a constructive way, but instead argue all the time when checks bounce, college bills come, or other money events happen. They never get anywhere on the big issue because they spend their energy just dealing with the crises of the events. What about you? Do you set aside time to deal with issues before events trigger them?

Another couple, Thomas and Sally, had issues about the intrusion of Thomas's mom on their time together as a couple, but they weren't discussing them. Thomas's dad had died the previous year, leaving his mom alone and lonely. She looked to Thomas and Sally for support and companionship, and sometimes they felt flooded with her phone calls and needs. Also, she would come for extended visits and was in the middle of one right now. One evening, Thomas and Sally went to a baseball game—the first time they'd been out alone for three or four weeks. On the way, Thomas received a phone call from his mother on the cell phone. When the call ended, Sally confronted Thomas.

SALLY: Why do you always let her interfere with our relationship? This is our evening out. Can't we just spend one evening alone?

THOMAS: *(really hot under the collar)* You are the one ruining our evening—blasting me when we're going out to have fun for a change.

SALLY: *(sounding indignant)* Well, I didn't know we were planning on bringing your mother with us.

THOMAS: *(dripping with sarcasm)* Ha, Ha. Real funny, Sal.

Their evening was destroyed. They never even made it to the ballpark. They spent the night arguing about his mother calling and her involvement in their lives.

As in this case, events tend to come up at inopportune times: when you're ready to leave for work, you're coming home from work, you're going to bed, you're out to relax, the kids are around, friends have come over, and so forth. Things come up that disturb you, but these are often the worst times to deal with issues.

How to Deal with Triggering Events

We are suggesting that you edit out the desire to argue about the issue *right then*, when an event triggers it. The key to doing this is saying to yourself, "I don't have to deal with this right now. This isn't the time. We can talk later." There are simply times when dropping the matter for the moment is the wise strategy. This is simple wisdom. In the argument we just described, Sally could have said, "That phone call from your mother really set off an issue for me. We need to sit down and talk about it later." In this way, she could acknowledge the event but leave the issue for a time when the two of them could deal with it more effectively. Likewise, Thomas could have said, "Listen, let's take a time out. I can see you are feeling hurt, but let's wait for a better time to talk about the issue. How about tomorrow after dinner? We could get out of the house and go for a walk while Mom watches *Wheel of Fortune*." If they've been practicing the skills we've presented so far, they could have saved their evening by containing the event so that it didn't trigger the explosive unresolved issues about Thomas's mother and their time together. That's what we mean by separating issues from events, and it's a very wise thing to do.

When an event does come up, you could also try to talk about the issue for a few minutes—agreeing to have a fuller discussion later. You might say, "Let's talk about what just happened for a few moments and then try to move on and have a nice evening together." You can use the Speaker-Listener Technique if you want to do it really well so you both feel heard. Then let it go until later.

Handling Issues Well

One reason people focus on events and let them turn into arguments over issues is that they don't feel that "later" will happen—why wait? Jump in now. You wind up in a marital minefield—the issues being the explosives and the events being the detonators. The effect of being in a minefield is that you become cautious or tense around one another rather than open and relaxed. When you end up mostly feeling anxious around the person who is supposed to be your best friend and support, the effect on your marriage can be devastating. We believe that this dynamic is the hallmark of a marriage headed for the rocks. If this does not sound like you, we want to help you keep things that way. If it does sound like you, it's time for real change.

To avoid the pressure of dealing with issues whenever events trigger them, one of the best things you can do is set aside some time to regularly work on the issues. That means making time, and that means working as a team to deal with issues constructively. Practicing the skills and techniques we teach in this book makes it more likely that you'll handle events better and plan the time to deal with important issues. This way, you maintain control of where, when, and how you deal with the issues.

HIDDEN ISSUES

Most of the time, people can recognize the issues that are triggered by events because they have almost the same content. In the case of Mary Sue and Elliot, his looking at the checkbook started the event, and the issue was money. That's not hard to figure out. But you'll also find yourselves getting caught up in fights around events that don't seem to be attached to any particular issue. Or you find you aren't getting anywhere when talking about particular problems, as if you're spinning your wheels. Often you will think an issue has been resolved, but one or both of you don't follow through on the proposed solution, which indicates that you had addressed the issue only on the surface. These are signs that you aren't getting at the real issues. It's not about money, it's not about careers, it's not about housework, it's not about leaving the toilet seat up—the real issue is deeper and more elusive.

Hidden issues often drive the really frustrating or destructive arguments. For example, Sally and Thomas ended up arguing about his mother and his taking calls from her at any time. But the real issue may have been that Sally felt she was not important to Thomas.

When we say these issues are often hidden, we mean they are usually not being talked about openly or constructively. They are the key issues that often get lost in the flow of the argument. You may be very aware of feeling uncared for, but when certain events come up, that may not be what the two of you talk about, as Sally and Thomas demonstrate. The couple is missing the forest (the hidden issues) for the trees (the events).

To summarize, events are everyday happenings, such as dirty dishes or a check bouncing. Issues are those larger topics, such as money, sex, and in-laws, that all couples must deal with. Hidden issues are the deeper, fundamental issues that can come up for you with any issue or event. In our work with couples, we see several types of hidden issues: hidden issues of control and power, caring, recognition, commitment, integrity, and acceptance. There are surely others, but these six capture a lot of what goes on in relationships. As you will see in Chapter Eleven, because these issues are deeper, they often have a deeper spiritual significance as well.

Control and Power

Spouses' roles change as couples reach the empty nest, and hidden issues of control and power often surface. At the core of these issues are questions of status and power: Who decides who does the chores? Are my needs and desires just as important as my partner's, especially since the kids have left and their wishes don't need to be considered? Is there an inequality here? Is my input important, or are major decisions made without me? Who's really in charge? If these kinds of questions come up, you may be dealing with the hidden issue of control.

Even if there aren't ongoing power struggles between you, these issues can affect your relationship when various decisions come up—even small ones. For example, what happens if one of you really wants to go get pizza, and the other really feels like Chinese food? This is an event without a lot of long-term significance. Nevertheless, if either of you is unyielding in what you want, you can have a lot of conflict over something as simple as cuisine. You can feel that the other is trying to control you or that you need to be in control. A power struggle can result over just about anything, no matter how seemingly trivial.

Whatever the topic or disagreement, control issues are least likely to damage your relationship when the two of you feel that you are a team and that each partner's needs and desires are attended to in decisions you make.

For example, a couple attending one of the Arps' seminars reported ongoing stress around trying to establish new family traditions in their blended family; both partners have adult children from previous marriages. Both wanted to keep their own holiday traditions, and attempts to change the way things were done in a first marriage have led to unintentional conflict in the second.

Some people are motivated to be in control because they're actually hypersensitive about being controlled by others. Usually such a person has experienced a very controlling and powerful authority figure sometime in the past, often a parent, as in the next example.

Harry and Kitty are parents of two daughters, ages twenty-one and twenty-three. All his life, Harry has been a control freak. Harry grew up with a controlling father, so he assumed that if he were really a man, he should be in control of his family. Daily, Harry let his children know he was the ultimate authority in their family.

Kitty, in contrast, is naturally shy and hesitant to say what she really thinks. During the active parenting years, they settled into their respective roles. Harry had the final word. Kitty concentrated on her role as mom and acted as a buffer between Harry and their daughters—especially in the turbulent teenage years.

Harry's big issue was finances, and he controlled the budget. When the kids were still home, this worked well enough. Kitty had a set amount of money each month for food, clothing, and household expenses. She didn't really resent Harry's desire to control everything, but when the last child left for college, she saw no reason to stick to such a rigid budget. Besides, she thought, "the kids have grown up and are on their own; I need to grow up too and make some of my own decisions."

Kitty decided it was time to spruce up their house and one day surprised Harry with a new blue sofa. When Harry came home and saw the sofa, he hit the ceiling. What was wrong with the sofa they had? He hated that color blue. And why did she do this without checking with him first? Kitty resented being treated like one of the kids. She had wanted to surprise him. Why didn't he appreciate her thoughtfulness? Why should she have to check out everything with him anyway? The next day, she went out looking for a job. She would earn her own money—and then she would decorate the house any way she wanted to! This control issue had been there for years but didn't really become that obvious until Kitty triggered it by buying the blue sofa.

It's no accident that in study after study, money is rated the number one problem area for couples in most stages of marriage. So many decisions in our lives revolve around money. If you have significant power or control issues in your marriage, it's likely you struggle a lot with money conflicts. Money in and of itself isn't the deeper issue, but it's an issue that provides many events for triggering the deeper issues.

With Harry and Kitty, the deeper issue was control and power. Kitty was tired of Harry always having to be in control. It might have been better for Harry and Kitty to decide together on getting the new sofa, but Kitty resented Harry making all the financial decisions. The couch triggered a huge conflict that ultimately led them to counseling and to reevaluating their marriage style and choosing to make some changes. They agreed to start making more decisions together. As Harry began to include Kitty in decision making and financial decisions, Kitty felt less controlled and more loving toward Harry. They were a living illustration of the fact that power plays in a marriage destroy the potential for love to grow. But when Harry gave up trying to control Kitty, she responded by loving him more! She felt he must really love her to work on changing such a fundamental part of his personality style.

Every decision you must make together is an opportunity for control issues to be triggered. Working together as a team is the best antidote to the hidden issue of control.

Needing and Caring

A second major arena where we see hidden issues emerge involves caring. The main theme of this issue is the extent to which you feel loved and cared for. Such issues come up when a person feels that his or her important emotional needs aren't being met.

Jill and Nelson married each other after their children were grown. Both first marriages ended in divorce, and in this marriage they repeatedly fight over who should refill the orange juice container. Juice wasn't the real issue fueling their arguments. As it turned out, Nelson had always perceived his previous wife's refilling the juice container as demonstrating her love and caring. Because Jill wouldn't do it, Nelson felt she didn't love him. So he had a caring hidden issue. Refilling the juice container was so important to him that he felt he needed to encourage her to do it. In their arguments about orange juice, he didn't talk about feeling uncared for. Instead he focused on what he saw as Jill's stubbornness.

For her part, Jill was thinking, "Who's he to tell me to make the orange juice? Where does he get off saying I have to do it?" She had a control issue about him trying to force her to behave a certain way. That really wasn't his motive, but she was very sensitive because she had been previously married to a domineering man. Nelson's behavior reminded her of her previous husband, while Nelson felt he needed to be cared for in a certain way. Having an open discussion about their hidden issues brought them closer, and who refilled the orange juice container no longer seemed all that important.

NELSON (Speaker): So for me, it's really not about wanting to control you. I've been so primed by my first wife to connect refilling the OJ with love that I've put this pressure on you to do it to be sure that you love me.

JILL (Listener): *(summarizing)* So for you, the key issue is wanting to know I care, not wanting to control me?

NELSON (Speaker): *(confirming her summary and going on to validate her)* Exactly, and I can see how you'd be feeling controlled without knowing that. *(Nelson passes the floor to Jill.)*

JILL (Speaker): You're right. I've really felt you wanted to control me, and that's a real hot button given what I went through with Joe.

NELSON (Listener): It really did seem to you that I just wanted to control you, and that's an especially sensitive area given what you went through with Joe.

JILL (Speaker): You got it. I want to be your partner, not your servant.

NELSON (Listener): *(capturing what she's saying in his own words)* Sounds like you want us to be a team.

JILL (Speaker): Yep!

As you can see from the tail end of their conversation, learning to talk about their bigger concerns paved the way for greater connection instead of alienation over empty juice containers. This is a clear example of how hard it would be to solve the problem about the event—refilling the orange juice container—unless the partners were communicating well enough to get the hidden issues out in the open. But it's hard to talk about the stuff that makes you feel vulnerable if you can't talk safely! That's the key: to be able to talk constructively about these kinds of deeper issues rather than let them operate as hidden issues in arguments.

Recognition

The third type of hidden issue involves recognition. Does your partner appreciate your activities and accomplishments? Whereas caring issues involve concerns about being cared for or loved, recognition issues are more about feeling valued by your partner for who you are and what you do.

Consider Burt and Chelsea, a couple who owns a business together. Burt is president and treasurer of their corporation, and Chelsea is vice president and secretary. Most of the time, they really enjoy running the business together. Yet one day they were seated at a luncheon where someone asked Burt a question about the company. His quick response was, "I'm the only officer in this company." His wife was sitting right next to him! Chelsea was furious and embarrassed.

We don't know why Burt failed at times to recognize Chelsea's role in the company. Perhaps he has some control issues that are seeping out when he makes such a comment. Perhaps he thinks "I can do it all," and really does disregard her contributions to the company. Whatever his hidden issues, such events will make Chelsea's involvement less and less rewarding. She may slowly pull away from Burt over time. If this couple wants to prevent further damage to their relationship, they had better talk openly about this key issue.

A wife of a church minister complained that he often forgot to tell her of church-related events or other church news, even though she needed to know those things. Her role as preacher's wife seems undervalued in this marriage.

Another common example is that of a couple who has had a pretty traditional division of roles, the woman having taken the major role of day-to-day child care and rearing. For many women, to raise their children has been their key activity and also their primary source of recognition. Now that the kids are gone, either or both partners may fail to make the transition to other ways to value and recognize the contributions of the one who had focused so much for so long on the children. Likewise, many men tell us they feel that their wives don't place much value on their work to bring home income.

Whenever either of you is chronically underrecognized by the other for all you do, there is risk of burnout in the one who is not receiving clear signals of appreciation from the other. How long has it been since you told your partner how much you appreciate the things he or she does?

Another reason this issue tends to surface in the second half of life is that women at this stage tend to become more assertive. During the first half, besides nurturing the children, she probably invested a good bit of energy in encouraging her husband in his career. Even if she had a job outside the home, her interests were divided between work and family. Now it's her time to make an impact on the world. Some women even go back to school to get their MBA or law degree. We know one wife who went to seminary and is now on the staff of a local church.

At the same time, men begin to focus more on home; many realize they have reached the top of their career ladder or as far as they will probably go, and some are even considering early retirement. Now is the time to slow down, play some golf, travel, and have some fun. As they slow down, they want their spouse to appreciate their contribution to the family and focus more on them. It's easy to see how couples at this stage could misunderstand each other's need for recognition.

Commitment

The focus of this fourth hidden issue is on the long-term security of the relationship: "Are you going to stay with me?" One couple we worked with, Alice and Chuck, had huge arguments about separate checking accounts. Whenever the bank statement arrived, he would complain bitterly about her having a separate account.

This problem wasn't so much related to a money or hidden control issue. For Chuck, the hidden issue was commitment. He had been married once before, and his ex-wife had a separate account. She decided to leave him after fifteen years of marriage, which was easier to do because she had saved up several thousand dollars in her account. Now, when the statement for Alice's account would arrive, Chuck would associate it with thoughts that Alice could be planning to leave him. Alice was planning no such thing, but because Chuck rarely talked openly about his fear, Alice wasn't really given the opportunity to alleviate his anxiety by affirming her commitment. The issue kept fueling explosive conflict whenever these events occurred.

When your commitment to one another is secure, it brings a deeper kind of safety to your relationship than that which comes from good communication. This is safety that comes from the lasting promise to be there for one another, to lift one another up in tough times, to cherish each other for a lifetime. One survey couple put it this way: "We feel so secure in our relationship—we know we'll make it through the remaining bumps in the road." When you've had a child-centered marriage for many years, the children's leaving can naturally raise intensely felt issues about commitment. One or both of you may wonder, "Were the kids all that were really keeping us together? What else do we have in common to base our commitment on?"

Do you worry about your partner's long-term commitment to you and the marriage? Have you talked about this openly, or does this issue find indirect expression in the context of events in your relationship? In Part Three of this book, we focus in much more depth on how commitment issues affect relationships.

Integrity

The fifth type of hidden issue relates to integrity. Have you ever noticed how upset you get when your partner questions your intent or motives? These events can spark great fury.

For Byron and Gladys, arguments frequently end up with each being certain they know what the other meant. Most often they're sure that what the other meant was negative. Both are therapists, so you'd think they would know better. They have a serious problem making negative interpretations. Here's a typical example:

GLADYS: You forgot to pick up the dry cleaning.

BYRON: (*feeling a bit indignant*) You didn't ask me to pick it up; you asked me if I was going by there. I told you I wasn't.

GLADYS: (*really angry at what she sees as his lack of caring about what she needs*) You *did* say you'd pick it up, but you just don't care about me.

BYRON: (*feeling thoroughly insulted*) I do care, and I resent you telling me I don't.

Her caring issue is pretty out in the open here, although they are not exactly having a constructive, healing talk about it. But Byron's issue has more to do with integrity. It's not as much in the open, but it's there. He feels insulted at her calling him an uncaring, inconsiderate husband who never thinks about her needs. He feels judged. Each of them winds up feeling invalidated.

As we pointed out earlier in this book, it's not wise to argue about what the other really thinks, feels, or intends. Don't tell your partner what's going on inside, unless you are talking about *your* insides! To do otherwise is guaranteed to trigger the issue of integrity. And most anyone will defend his or her integrity when it's questioned.

Acceptance: The Bottom Line

There seems to be one primary issue that can underlie all the others listed here: the desire for acceptance. Sometimes this is felt more as a fear of rejection, but the fundamental issue is the same. At the deepest level, people are motivated to find acceptance and to avoid rejection in their relationships. This reflects the deep need we all have to be both respected and connected.

The fundamental fear of rejection drives many other hidden issues, and you can see it come up in many ways. For example, some people are afraid that if they act in certain ways, their partner is going to reject them. A lowered sense of self-worth would only make such fears more intense. Perhaps one partner asks for what he or she wants indirectly rather than directly—for example, "Wouldn't you like to make love tonight?" rather than "I would like to make love with you tonight." Their real desires are filtered out because of a fear of rejection.

There are a number of other ways in which people act out their hidden issues around acceptance and rejection. Consider this example about Hector and Louise's problem with his yearly hunting trip.

Hector and Louise have been married for twenty-seven years, and things have gone well for them all along. They have two adult children, ages twenty-two and twenty-five. There are few things they don't handle well. They talk regularly about the more important issues, which keeps things running pretty smoothly. However, there is one problem they've never really handled.

Once a year, every year, Hector goes hunting with his friends for two weeks. The men rent a cabin in the mountains and virtually disappear. The following argument is typical. It was late, and Hector was packing to leave at five in the morning:

LOUISE: I really hate it when you leave for this trip every year. You leave me to handle everything by myself. It's really lonely here by myself.

HECTOR: *(feeling a bit defensive)* You knew when we got married that I did this every year. I did it every year while the kids were growing up, and I plan to do it every year as long as I am alive. I don't know why you have to complain about it now.

LOUISE: *(going on the attack)* I just don't think it's very responsible to leave me alone for two weeks. Something always comes up with one of our parents or the kids.

HECTOR: *(He is thinking, "Why do we have to do this every year? I hate this argument," and getting angry.)* I do a lot for our parents and kids. I just helped Ron with that new car. You need to deal with this better—I'm not about to give this up.

LOUISE: (*angrier herself*) If you cared more about me, you wouldn't have this need to get away from me for two weeks every year.

HECTOR: (*getting up to leave the room, feeling disgusted*) Yeah, you're right. You're always right, *my dear.*

LOUISE: (*yelling out as he walks out*) I hate it when you talk to me like that. You can't treat me like your dad treats your mom; I won't stand for it.

HECTOR: (*shouting from the other room*) I'm not like my father, and you aren't telling me what to do. I'm going, I'll keep going every year, and you might as well just get used to it.

What's really going on here? Hector's getting ready for the trip is the event. They have this same nasty argument every year, usually the night before he leaves. It's as much a part of the tradition as is the trip. Neither likes it, but they haven't found a way to deal with the situation differently.

You can see many of the hidden issues being triggered for Hector and Louise. Deep down, she doesn't feel cared for when these trips come up. She feels lonely when he leaves, and this is hard to handle because she sees him looking forward to being gone. She wonders if he's delighted to get away from her. She feels nearly abandoned—reflecting some commitment issues that also get triggered. Her focus on their adult kids and parents is a smoke screen for her real concerns.

Hector likes to be in control of his life, so that's one hidden issue triggered here. "No one's going to tell me what to do!" Also, as they argue unproductively, an integrity issue comes up. He feels she is calling into question his devotion as a husband. He sees himself as very dedicated to her and just wants this two-week period each year to be with the guys. He doesn't think that's asking a lot.

You can see that underneath it all, acceptance is the most basic hidden issue driving the issues of control, caring, commitment, and integrity in their argument. Neither believes that the other accepts who he or she is. It's not that this is such an unresolved issue for them. After all, they really do have a great relationship, and each generally feels good about the other. Yet the need for acceptance is so deep seated for all of us that it can get triggered by almost any event or issue—if we let it.

In this argument, Louise and Hector aren't talking about the hidden issues in any productive way. The deeper issues aren't totally hidden, but they aren't being dealt with directly and constructively, either. Let's discuss how to do this right.

RECOGNIZING THE SIGNS OF HIDDEN ISSUES

You can't handle hidden issues unless you can identify them. There are four key ways to tell when there may be hidden issues affecting your relationship:

Wheel Spinning

One sign of hidden issues is that you find yourselves talking about some problem over and over again, as though you are spinning your wheels. When an argument starts with you thinking, "Here we go again," you should suspect hidden issues. You never really get anywhere on the problem because you often aren't talking about what really matters—the hidden issue. So you go around and around and get nowhere.

Trivial Triggers

A second clue that there are hidden issues is that trivial events are blown up out of all proportion. The argument between Jill and Nelson described earlier is a great example. The problem with the orange juice container seems like a trivial event, but it triggers horrendous arguments driven by the issues of power and caring.

Most couples struggle with trivial triggers. One that we (Dave and Claudia) deal with is the "battle of the seat belts." We are both big believers in wearing seat belts, but we have different opinions about when to put them on. Claudia always secures her seat belt before turning the ignition key. Dave usually waits until driving out of the driveway or even until he is driving down the street. That pushes Claudia's button!

In the past, Claudia tried everything—even those communication techniques that had worked with their teenagers, such as just saying "seat belt" and waiting for him to react. She even tried manipulation: "Dave, Sophie (our granddaughter) would say, 'Opa. Buckle your seat belt.'" That usually got the seat belt buckled, but it didn't change the habit pattern. Claudia decided Dave was stubborn and that this was one power struggle he was winning. Then one day she actually talked to him about it: "Dave, the reason it's so important to me for you to buckle up is that I'm afraid one day you'll forget to, have a terrible accident, and get splattered all over another car or a telephone pole. I love you so much, I just couldn't bear to lose you. That's why I keep bugging you about it. How about doing this for me as a gift of love?"

Here Claudia is acknowledging two kinds of hidden issues: a caring issue, because she is really worried about Dave's safety, and a power issue, because she realizes the struggle to change this habit has become a power struggle.

Slowly it dawned on Dave how really important this was to Claudia, and he's in the process of developing a new habit of buckling his seat belt before he drives out of the garage. Yes, occasionally he still forgets, but it's no longer an automatic trigger for Claudia, because she knows he is trying to change.

Avoidance

A third sign of hidden issues is that one or both of you are avoiding certain topics or levels of intimacy. It could be that some walls have gone up between you. This often means that there are important, unexpressed issues affecting the relationship. Perhaps it seems too risky to talk directly about feeling unloved or insecure. The trouble is, those concerns have a way of coming up anyway. For too many couples, many issues have been avoided for years, perhaps in the hopes that they would go away or in the natural desire to avoid conflict. Many couples in the second half of marriage report that their greatest stress is "failure to talk about issues we needed to discuss and work through." But if you want to have a deeper, stronger marriage in the years ahead, it is time to change that tendency. However, don't try to deal all at once with a long list of things you may have avoided in the past. That's like trying to swallow a Big Mac in one bite: you'll choke. Move into the issues that you want to address to make the rest of your lives together all they can be, but take it slowly.

Avoidance can be a response to the presence of many hidden issues. For example, we have talked with many couples from different cultural or religious backgrounds who strongly avoid talking about these differences. We think that their avoidance usually reflects concerns about acceptance: Will you accept me fully if we really talk about our different backgrounds? Avoiding such topics not only allows hidden issues to remain hidden but also puts the relationship at greater risk, because these are important differences that can have significant impact on the marriage.

Other common but taboo topics in marriage include issues of sex, weight, and money. There are many such sensitive topics that people avoid dealing with in their relationships out of fear of rejection. What issues do you avoid talking about?

Scorekeeping

A fourth sign of hidden issues in your relationship is that one or both or you start keeping score—that is, a mental list of all the things your partner does wrong or the times your partner has hurt you.

Scorekeeping could mean you are not feeling recognized for what you put into the relationship. It could mean that you are less committed, as we will explain later. It could mean you are feeling controlled and are keeping track of the times your partner has taken advantage of you. Whatever the issue, scorekeeping can be a sign that there are important things not being talked about—just documented.

HANDLING HIDDEN ISSUES

What can you do when you realize hidden issues are affecting your relationship? You can recognize when one may be operating and start talking about it constructively. This will be easier to do if you are cultivating an atmosphere of teamwork using the kinds of techniques we have presented thus far. We strongly recommend using the Speaker-Listener Technique when you are trying to explore such issues.

Deal with the issue in terms of problem discussion, not problem solution. Be aware of any tendency to jump to solutions. In our opinion, the deeper the issue, the less likely that problem solving will be the answer. If you haven't been talking about the real issue, how could your solution address what's really at stake? What you need first and foremost is to hear each other and understand the feelings and concerns. Such validating discussions have the greatest impact on hidden issues because they work directly against the fear of rejection. There is no more powerful form of acceptance than really listening to the thoughts and feelings of your mate. Safe, open talks have real power to overcome this fear.

Remember Dave and Claudia's seat belt problem? This is a great example of how to address hidden issues: no real solution exists besides talking about the issue and learning how your behavior may trigger your partner's hidden issues. Then each of you can take responsibility for behaving in ways that support your partner rather than upset each other.

A DETAILED EXAMPLE

We round out this chapter with a detailed example of how the really important issues will come out if you are communicating clearly and safely.

Simon and Rachel came to one of our workshops. Both worked long hours in the same law firm and had done so for years. They had raised four children together; despite all the strain of Simon's and Rachel's careers, the children had turned out to be wonderful young adults for whom Simon and Rachel shared much pride. However, Rachel had always thought that when the children were all moved out, there would be a renewal of time together in their marriage. But it was not turning out that way at all. When they did have a chance to have time together, Simon was instead spending more and more hours playing golf with his friends. Rachel felt even more alone now that the kids had left, because Simon seemed to be leaving also. Rachel was very upset about this. So, although clearly there were deeper issues operating, what Rachel and Simon argued about a great deal was golf. As we noted earlier, issues around recreation tend to become very pronounced for couples in the empty nest phase of life.

This couple could have argued forever on the level of the *events*—for example, how much golf Simon played—but they made much greater progress when talking about the *issues*, using the Speaker-Listener Technique. This was one of the first few times they used the technique, so you will see that their skills were a little rough around the edges at this point, with some mind reading and less than ideal paraphrasing. Yet they were communicating better than they ever had about the real issues.

We hadn't told the couple to focus on hidden issues, but as you will see, they came out anyway. We find that this happens regularly when couples are doing a good job with the Speaker-Listener Technique.

RACHEL (Speaker): It seems like you spend more time playing golf, these days, than doing anything with me. There are times when you can carve out six hours to play golf, but if it comes down to spending time with me, you're tired and only want to watch sports on television.

SIMON (Listener): So you think I'd rather play golf than be with you?

RACHEL (Speaker): *(with a clear sigh of relief at being heard)* Yeah. I've been wondering if you were even attracted to me anymore, either as a friend or as a lover.

SIMON (Listener): If I'm hearing you right, the really big issue here is that you are no longer sure I want to spend time with you, in any significant way.

RACHEL (Speaker): Thank you. Yes, you've got it.

Rachel was not feeling accepted or cared for by Simon. This issue comes out clearly here, yet in the past when they had argued about the golf, they never got to what was really going on—at least not in a way that drew them closer together. They continued:

SIMON (Listener): Can I have the floor? *(Rachel hands Simon the floor.)*

SIMON (Speaker): I used to really love playing golf, before we had kids. I realize as we talk that, for a long time, I had looked forward to this empty nest thing so I could do more of these kinds of things again.

RACHEL (Listener): So you had planned or hoped for some time that you would be able to play more golf again when the kids all moved out?

SIMON (Speaker): Right. I love to play. But I can see what is bothering you. I can see how you'd wonder if I was interested. I'm sorry I've conveyed the impression that I'm not.

RACHEL (Listener): *(with easing of tension in her face)* You are saying you recognize how this may be affecting me, and you are sorry about that.

SIMON (Speaker): *(in an increasingly tender voice)* Yes, Rachel. I love you. I want to be with you. Please be assured of that. I now realize, though, that I knew I had to carve out time if I were to renew my golfing interest. I had not, and I'm sorry, seen so clearly the same need about making time for you. I thought it would somehow naturally happen.

Rachel (Listener): It was clear to you that you had to carve out time for golf, but you were thinking time for us would just sort of happen, without working so hard to make it happen.

Simon (Speaker): You got it. I think we need to plan some time, very soon, in the next day, to start talking more together about how we can carve out time for us. Let's make this a priority and see what we can bring about. I don't want you to think I do not want to be with you, and making it happen is the only way that I think would really reassure you that this is true.

Rachel (Listener): That sounds wonderful to me. How about we go out to a nice, long, relaxing dinner tomorrow night and brainstorm about ways to build more and more time for us into our lives?

Simon (Speaker): That's a deal.

Simon and Rachel could have argued about golf for the next twenty years, but that would not have addressed Rachel's need. The kind of dialogue illustrated here allowed them to say and hear the more risky things.

✳

Our goal in this chapter has been to give you a way to explore and understand some of the most frustrating happenings in relationships. You can prevent lots of damage by learning to handle events and issues with the time and skill they require. Using the Speaker-Listener Technique to structure your in-depth discussions about the sensitive hidden issues in your relationship will help you move forward.

For all too many couples, the hidden issues never come out. They fester and produce levels of sadness and resentment that eventually destroy the marriage. Your marriage just doesn't have to be that way. When you learn to discuss deeper issues openly and with emphasis on validating each other, what had been generating the greatest conflicts can actually draw you closer together.

In Chapter Seven, we will teach you a structured model for solving problems. As the Speaker-Listener Technique has helped you really hear and validate your partner's deep concerns and feelings, the problem-solving model will add powerful tools for dealing with whatever issues you face as a couple.

EXERCISES

We recommend that you first work through these questions individually, then sit down and talk together about your impressions.

Signs of Hidden Issues

Think through the list of signs that hidden issues may be affecting your relationship. Do you notice that one or more of these signs come up a lot in your relationship? Here they are again. What do you notice?

1. Wheel spinning
2. Trivial triggers
3. Avoidance
4. Scorekeeping

Identifying Hidden Issues

Next, consider which hidden issues might operate most often in your relationship. In addition to the hidden issues listed here, there may be some big issue you would like to add. Consider each issue and the degree to which it seems to affect your relationship negatively. Also, how deeply hidden are these issues in your relationship?

Note whether certain events have triggered or keep triggering the issues. You can list these events on the right-hand side of your list of issues or on a separate piece of paper.

- Power and control

- Caring

- Recognition

- Commitment

- Integrity

- Acceptance

Working Through Hidden Issues

Plan some time together to talk about your observations and thoughts. For most couples, there are certain hidden issues that repeatedly come up. Identifying these can help you draw together as you each learn to handle those issues with care. Also, as you discuss these matters, you have an excellent opportunity to get in some more practice with the Speaker-Listener Technique.

7

Problem Solving

One of the greatest needs of couples in empty nest marriages is to be able to work issues out. Over the years, it is easy to get so used to seeing things "your way" that you can't see the other person's viewpoint. For many couples, problem solving is complicated by feeling a "lack of goals and/or direction (kind of what do we do now?)," as one survey respondent put it. Others feel overwhelmed by the idea of problem solving because they need to identify all over again "what is important and what's not."

In a seminar, Dave and Claudia were talking with a couple, Jesse and Mildred, who reported a very common problem. Jesse said, "I talk to my wife, Mildred, but nothing seems to ring a bell. I try to help her fix whatever is bothering her, and she tells me she's not looking for an answer. I can't figure her out."

Mildred countered, "Jesse, I just want you to be there—to listen to me, to understand; I don't want you to do something. You always want to fix the problem, but sometimes you *are* the problem."

We hear this from so many couples. Many times, all you need is just to discuss an issue such that each of you hears and respects the other. At other times, what you need is to try to solve some specific problem together. This chapter is designed to help you at those times. In the previous chapters, we focused not on solving problems but on the need for clear and safe communication when it counts most. If you're progressing in your ability to talk about issues effectively, you are better prepared for what we'll say about solving problems.

We all want to *solve* problems that affect our relationships. This is natural. But we have held this subject until this point because most couples try to solve problems prematurely—before they have achieved a thorough, mutual understanding of the issues at hand. Understanding, before solving, is crucial for maintaining respect and connection in your relationship. It increases the likelihood that both of you will feel committed to following through on a solution. In this chapter, we present a straightforward approach to problem solving that can help you through those times when you really need practical, workable solutions.

THREE KEY ASSUMPTIONS

Before presenting the specific steps that can help you solve problems effectively in your relationship, we would like to describe three assumptions, all of which have been confirmed by research:

1. All couples have problems.
2. The couples who are best at working through their problems work together as a team, not against each other as adversaries.
3. Most couples rush to find quick solutions; because these quick solutions don't take into account the real concerns of each partner, they do not last.

Let's explore these three points.

All Couples Have Problems

Have you ever wondered why some empty nest couples seem to deal with the challenges of marital life so effectively? For them the transition to the empty nest appears to be a breeze. It's not that they don't have problems—all couples encounter problems—but over time they have learned to deal with them.

Think back over your own marriage. In the early years, problems may have centered around communication, sex, in-laws, and learning how to live together. These issues reflect a core task that couples have early in a marriage: that of establishing boundaries with each other and with those outside the relationship and learning to really communicate and deal with issues.

As the marriage progresses, communication becomes an even greater concern for couples. Then children start coming along, and parenthood brings countless decisions to make and problems to solve. The adolescent years drain your emotional energy and strength— then comes the empty nest. At that stage, problems often center around adult children and aging parents.

Many empty nest couples are just too tired to even think about problem solving, so they focus on their careers, golfing or other hobbies, adult children, grandchildren, and so on. Retirement and health issues often crowd out other concerns. For empty nest couples, communication, conflict, and sex were reported as top areas of concern in the Arps' survey. In other research, money is rated a top problem, no matter what stage the relationship is in. These results also reflect changes in priority as your marriage continues.

The key point here is that although the nature of the problems may change over time, all couples report problems, reflecting that there is a set of core issues all couples have to resolve. Granted, some couples are dealt a more difficult hand in life than others. We also want to point out to you that for most couples, some of their more central problems do not really change all that much over the years. For instance, one is an introvert and the other a full-blown extrovert. That dynamic can present problems that are unlikely to go away, but even in such a case, the partners could come to some agreements about how they can manage their differences better.

You Need to Work Together as a Team

For some couples, their mutual respect and skill combine to produce a powerful sense that they are a team working together to find solutions that will enhance their life together. You have a choice when dealing with a problem: either you will nurture a sense that you are working together against the problem, or you will operate as though you are working against each other. This principle holds with all problems, great or small.

Kyle and Catherine, a couple in their late fifties, attended a marriage seminar under unusual circumstances. They had given the weekend as a gift to their son and daughter-in-law. At the last minute, that couple had to cancel, so Kyle and Catherine, not wanting to waste their money, came instead. The following conversation illustrates that for them, teamwork generally flows naturally. They were talking about how to temporarily help with child care for their newborn grandson, Brent, while their daughter, Rebbie, who is a single mom, works at the local hospital as a pediatric nurse. At the same time, Kyle was looking for a job. Kyle recently lost his job as an executive when his firm merged with another, so he has taken early retirement. He plans to get another job in the near future.

CATHERINE: The biggest concern I have about keeping Brent is that we are going to get sidetracked, and you won't make it a priority to look for a job.

KYLE: What do you mean sidetracked? Rebbie really needs our help. Can't I do a job search from home on the Internet?

CATHERINE: No. That's not going to work because right now it seems that Brent keeps both of us hopping. I'm afraid you'll just procrastinate.

KYLE: I had no idea that you felt that way. Don't you trust me to take the initiative?

CATHERINE: Not without a little prodding.

KYLE: Ouch! That sounds like nagging to me. What can we do to make this work out?

CATHERINE: Well, perhaps for a couple of hours each day I could take Brent and not expect you to help.

KYLE: What about if I try to make some appointments in the morning, when Brent seems to sleep for the longest stretches?

CATHERINE: Would you be willing to take him some in the afternoon so I can get a break? I just don't have the stamina that I had when our kids were little.

KYLE: Sure. We want to help Rebbie, but we also need to take care of us.

CATHERINE: And you need to find employment! We can work on this together.

KYLE: We will.

Notice how Kyle and Catherine are working together. They are listening to each other, and there is a sense of respect and cooperation. This is the way they have learned over the years to approach all kinds of problems—as challenges to be met together.

Contrast the tone of Kyle and Catherine's discussion with that of Christy and Phillip. Christy, the owner of her own dry-cleaning business, and Phillip, a real estate agent, were recently married after some years of living alone, and both have adult children living on their own. The couple has repeated arguments about housework, which generally go like this:

CHRISTY: (calmly) We need to do something about keeping the house looking better. It's such a mess most of the time . . . it's depressing to be here.

PHILLIP: (a bit annoyed) Look, that's your job. My work requires me to be out a lot more than you. I just don't have the time, and you know it! Keeping the place picked up is more your job than mine.

CHRISTY: *(hurt and angered)* Says who? There's a lot more to do than you seem to think. And did you forget that I work, too? Besides, you don't even clean up after yourself!

PHILLIP: I'd do more around here if you could generate more money in your business. You know, when you're home, you spend lots of time watching the tube—you could use your time better.

CHRISTY: *(anger growing)* I need some breaks, but that's not the point. I work just as hard as you outside the home, and you should . . . you need to do more of your share.

PHILLIP: I'm not going to give up my free time just because you aren't using yours well. We had a deal, it's fair, and that's all I have to say.

CHRISTY: What deal?! When did I agree to do all the work around the house?

PHILLIP: You said I wouldn't have to do any more work around here when you began devoting more and more time to your business. That was a deal.

CHRISTY: *(looking him in the eye, very angry)* That was when you used to do a lot more than you do now.

PHILLIP: *(He turns away, indicating the conversation is over for him.)* I don't agree, and I'm not talking about it any more. A deal's a deal.

This discussion ends with Christy more discouraged and Phillip annoyed that she even brought up the problem. There is a definite lack of teamwork. Phillip refuses to accept any role in dealing with this problem. He sees her as someone trying to take something away from him, not as a partner working to make life as good as it can be for both of them. Likewise, Christy sees Phillip as the problem, not as a teammate who is working with her to solve the problem.

All too often, people approach problems as if their partner were the enemy to be conquered. For such couples, problems are approached as if there will be a winner and a loser—and who wants to lose? The good news here is that you don't have to be locked into the cycle of one trying to win at the expense of the other. You can learn how to work as a team.

Don't Rush to Find Solutions

Many well-intended attempts at problem solving fail because couples fail to take the time needed to understand the problem together, thus precluding their working out a solution that both partners can support. If you are deciding which movie to see, not much is at stake in rushing to a solution, except maybe sitting through a boring film. If you are deciding something more important, such as how to parent or how to divide up the household responsibilities, it's critical that you take the time to develop a mutually satisfying solution.

Two major factors propel couples to rush to solutions: time pressure and conflict avoidance.

Time Pressure

Most of us are not all that patient—we want it now. This reflects the hurried pace of our lives. We usually don't take the time to plan what we're doing in our family relationships. The problem is, when it comes to dealing with important issues in families, hasty decisions are often poor decisions. Quick fixes seldom last. You must be committed to spending the time to really hash things out if you are going to make good decisions together.

Conflict Avoidance

This next example is fairly typical in illustrating how, because of the partners' desire to avoid further conflict, a couple can rush to a solution that is destined to fail. Helga and Sebastian have been married twenty-four years, with one child through college and one a senior in high school. Sebastian is an insurance salesman, and Helga works as a nearly full-time volunteer with a local religious charity. They have always had enough money, but things have gotten much tighter with college bills piling up. An issue for Sebastian is Helga's devoting so much time to a job that doesn't pay. The following interaction is typical of their attempts to solve the problem.

SEBASTIAN: *(testy)* I noticed that the Visa® bill was over thirty-six hundred dollars again. I just don't know what we are going to do to keep up. It worries me. I'm doing all I can, but . . .

HELGA: *(gives no indication that she is paying attention to Sebastian)*

SEBASTIAN: *(frustrated)* Did you hear me?

HELGA: Yes. I didn't think we spent that much this time.

SEBASTIAN: How many clothes did Jeanne need, anyway? *(really annoyed now)*

HELGA: *(annoyed, but calm)* Well, we figured she needed one really nice outfit for applying for jobs. I guess we got more extras than I thought, but they were all things she can really use. It's really important to her to look good for interviews. And you know, the sooner she gets a job, the better off our budget will be.

SEBASTIAN: *(settling down a bit)* I can understand, but this kind of thing adds to my worry. *(long pause)* We aren't saving anything at all for retirement, and we aren't getting any younger. If you had some income coming in for all your work, it would help a lot.

HELGA: Why don't we just get rid of that credit card? Then you wouldn't have to worry about it anymore.

SEBASTIAN: We could do that, and also plan to put aside an extra hundred and fifty a month in my retirement plan. That would help a lot to get us going in the right direction. What about a part-time job?

HELGA: I can think about it. What I'm doing seems a lot more important. For now, let's try to get rid of the credit card and save more. That sounds good. Let's try it out.

SEBASTIAN: OK, let's see what happens.

End of discussion. The one good thing about this discussion is that they had it. However, what are the chances that they came to a satisfactory resolution of their money problem? Two months later, nothing was changed, no more was saved, the credit card was still being used, interest was accruing, and they were no closer to working together on the budget.

This example illustrates what couples do all the time: make a quick agreement so as to avoid conflict. Solutions arrived at in this manner rarely last because all the important information is not "on the table." In the case of Sebastian and Helga, they never did address Sebastian's central concern about her volunteer job.

Furthermore, there were no specifics about how their agreement would be implemented. Sebastian and Helga are not generally into quick fixes, but they do tend to rush to solutions at times, because they hate conflict. For Sebastian and Helga, the conversation here is a relatively big fight. Whenever they have a disagreement, both are eager to get back to being nice to one another.

Finding a solution can be a relief when you and your spouse are talking about an issue that causes anxiety. However, when you settle prematurely on a solution, you are likely to pay for the lack of planning with more conflict later.

HOW TO HANDLE PROBLEMS WELL

The approach we take here to solving problems—consistent with the general PREP approach—is structured. In other words, we recommend a specific set of steps that successful problem solvers follow. Similar concepts to those presented here can be found in many books, including *We Can Work It Out* (Notarius & Markman, 1993) and *A Couple's Guide to Communication* (Gottman, Notarius, Gonso, & Markman, 1976).

Although these steps are very straightforward, don't be misled by the simplicity of the approach. You must be creative and flexible, willing to work together, and able to experiment with change. Under these conditions, you'll be able to discover solutions to most of the problems you have to grapple with together.

Following are the steps to handling problems well:

I. Problem Discussion
II. Problem Solution
   A. Agenda setting
   B. Brainstorming
   C. Agreement and compromise
   D. Follow-up

In the next sections, we describe each step, then follow with a detailed example.

Problem Discussion

Problem discussion is critical to handling problems well. In this step, you lay the foundation for the problem solution to come. Although you may not agree about how to solve the problem, a good discussion can lead to a clear sense that you're working together and respecting each other.

Whether the problem is large or small, you should not move on to problem solution until you both understand and feel understood by the other, meaning that you have each expressed your significant feelings and concerns on the topic and that you each believe the other has seen your point of view clearly. This is the best way to prepare for effective problem solving.

We recommend you use the Speaker-Listener Technique for this step. It is best that you place a premium on validation in this problem discussion phase. Problem solution can proceed much more smoothly in an atmosphere of mutual respect.

Sebastian and Helga experienced greater pain and distance because they failed to take the time to discuss the issue before coming to agreement. We have repeatedly seen that when good discussions precede problem solving, problem solving can often go quickly and smoothly, even for difficult issues. When you have put all the relevant facts and feelings on the table, you have laid the foundation for working as a team.

During problem discussion, it is likely that one or both of you may have a specific gripe that you need to express. When this is the case, it is very important that you each present your feelings and concerns constructively. One way to do this is to use what Gottman, Notarius, Gonso, and Markman call an XYZ statement. Using an XYZ statement, you put your gripe or complaint into this format:

"When you do X in situation Y, I feel Z."

When you use an XYZ statement, you are giving your partner usable information: the specific behavior, the context in which it occurs, and how you feel when it happens. This is much preferred to what often happens: a vague description of the problem and an expression of anger and frustration toward your partner.

For example, suppose you had a concern about your partner making a mess at the end of the day. Which of the following statements do you think gives you a better shot at being heard?

"You are such a slob."

"When you drop your pack and jacket on the floor [X] as you come in the door at the end of the day [Y], I feel angry [Z]."

Or suppose you were angry about a comment your spouse made at a party last Saturday night.

"You are so inconsiderate."

"When you said that what I did for work wasn't really that hard [X] to John and Susan at the party last Saturday [Y], I felt very embarrassed [Z]."

Unless you are careful, it is all too easy to fall into a nonspecific attack on your spouse's character. Such statements are guaranteed to cause defensiveness and escalation. XYZ statements are far more constructive. You are identifying a specific behavior in a specific context. The "I feel Z" part requires you to take responsibility for your own feelings. Your partner does not "make" you feel anything in particular—you are in charge of how you feel.

Keep in mind that no one really likes to hear a gripe or criticism, no matter how constructively expressed. But unless you are hiding out in avoidance, there are times when you need to voice your concern, and you need to do it without fostering unneeded conflict. The XYZ format will help you do just that.

Before we turn to problem solution, we want to remind you that in problem discussion, you are really laying the foundation for productive problem solving as a team. So we repeat: *do not move from discussion to solution unless you both agree that the issue or problem in question has been fully discussed.*

In many instances, however, you'll find that after an excellent discussion, there's really no problem solving to be done. Just having a good discussion is enough. In fact, in PREP seminars we often shock couples by announcing that our experience indicates that approximately 80 percent of the issues couples deal with do not really need to be solved, just well discussed. And this may be especially true of couples in the empty nest. Let's face it: there are a number of problems you may deal with that have never been fully resolved, and may never be. That's actually quite normal. Many times, just being fully heard can help you each feel more connected and respected, even where you may disagree.

To couples raised in a culture so oriented to problem solving, the 80 percent figure seems unbelievable. "How can that be?" they ask. It's hard for people to appreciate this point without experiencing the power of good problem discussion that leaves them with what therapists call an "ah-ha!" experience. After such a discussion, there's often nothing left to resolve. That's because most of us want something much more fundamental in our relationships than solutions to problems—we want a friend. And in the empty nest, the friendship factor is even more critical because it's too often been a neglected part of the marriage.

Nevertheless, there are many times when your discussion of problems or issues will naturally lead to the next step: working together to find specific solutions. When you need to come up with a specific solution, the steps of the problem solution phase can help you get there.

Problem Solution

We have found the following steps to work very well for couples, provided that the work of problem discussion has been done.

Agenda Setting

The first step in the problem solution phase is to set the agenda for your work together. The key here is to make it very clear what you are trying to solve *at this time*. Often your discussion will have taken you through many facets of an issue. Now you need to decide what to focus on. The more specific the problem you are tackling now, the better your chances of coming to a workable and satisfying solution. Many problems in marriage seem insurmountable, but they can be cut down to size if you follow these procedures.

For example, you may have had a problem discussion about money, covering a range of issues, such as credit card problems, checkbooks, budgets, and savings. As you can see, the problem area of money can contain many "sub-problem" areas to consider. So take a large problem such as this apart and focus on the more manageable pieces one at a time. It is also wisest to pick an easier piece of a problem to work on at first. For instance, if you're revamping how you handle finances in the empty nest, you might initially decide who should balance the checkbook each month, then deal with budget plans later. Setting the agenda can help in breaking issues down into "doable" pieces that increase the chances that you can achieve a workable solution.

At times, your problem discussion will have focused from start to finish on a specific problem. In this case, you won't have to define the agenda for problem solving. For example, you may be working on the problem of what to do for the holidays—stay home and encourage all your adult children to come to your house, visit your own parents, or visit one of your children and his or her family. There may be no specific smaller piece of such a problem, so you will set the agenda to work on the whole of it.

Brainstorming

As far as we know, the process referred to as brainstorming has been around forever. However, it seems to have been refined and promoted by NASA during the early days of the U.S. space program. NASA needed a way to bring together the many different engineers and scientists who were looking for solutions to the varied problems of space travel. The method worked for NASA and came to be frequently used in business settings. We have found that it works very well for couples, too. There are several rules regarding brainstorming:

- Any idea can be suggested. One of you should write down the ideas.

- Be creative. Suggest whatever comes to mind.

- Don't evaluate the ideas either verbally or nonverbally. (This includes making faces!)

- Have fun with it if you can. This is a time for a sense of humor; all other feelings should be dealt with in problem discussion.

The best thing about this process is that it encourages creativity. If you can edit out your tendency to comment critically on the ideas, you will encourage each other to come up with some great stuff. Wonderful solutions can come from considering the points made during brainstorming. Following these rules helps you resist the tendency to settle prematurely on a solution that isn't the best you can find.

Agreement and Compromise

In this step, the goal is to come up with a *specific* solution or combination of solutions that you both *agree* to try. We emphasize the word *agree* because the solution is not likely to help unless you both agree to try it. We emphasize *specific* because the more specific you are about the solution, the more likely you are to follow through.

Although it is easy to see the value of agreement, some people have trouble with the idea of compromise. We have been criticized for using the term. Obviously, compromise implies giving up something you wanted in order to reach an agreement. To some, compromise sounds more like lose-lose than win-win. But we do mean to emphasize compromise in a positive manner.

Marriage is about teamwork. Two separate individuals may see things differently and may make different decisions. But often the best solution will be a compromise in which neither of you gets everything you wanted, simply because you are not going to have a great marriage if you get your way all the time. The essence of a great marriage is to give regularly to one another, and at times, giving means making the sacrifice of a compromise that benefits the marriage even if it was not all you wanted. We will talk more about this in Chapter Ten, where we discuss commitment.

Follow-Up

Many couples can make an agreement to try a particular solution to a problem. It is just as important to follow up to see how the solution is working out. Following up has two key advantages. First, solutions often need to be tweaked a bit to work in the long term. Second, following up builds accountability. Often we don't get serious about making a change unless we know there is some point of accountability in the near future.

Sometimes there needs to be a lot of follow-up in the problem solution phase. At other times, it's not really necessary. You reach an agreement, and it works out, and nothing more needs to be done.

Some couples choose to be less formal about follow-up, but we think they are taking a risk. Most people are so busy that they don't plan the next step, and then it just doesn't happen. There is an old but true saying: If you fail to plan, you plan to fail.

A DETAILED EXAMPLE: SEBASTIAN AND HELGA

Remember Helga and Sebastian, whom we mentioned earlier in this chapter? It did not take them very long to realize that their problem solving about the credit card, her volunteer work, and their retirement savings was not working. They decided to try the steps we have described here.

First, they set aside the time to work through the steps. Depending on the problem, the problem-solving process may not take a lot of time, but setting aside time specifically for working on the problem is very wise. Let's follow them through the steps:

Problem Discussion

They engage in problem discussion, using the Speaker-Listener Technique.

HELGA (Speaker): I can see that we really do have to try something different. We aren't getting anywhere on our retirement savings.

SEBASTIAN (Listener): You can see we aren't getting anywhere, and you're also concerned.

HELGA (Speaker): (letting Sebastian know he had accurately heard her) Yes. We need to come up with some plan for saving more and for doing something about the credit cards.

SEBASTIAN (Listener): So, you believe we need to save more, and you can see that our credit card spending may be a problem.

HELGA (Speaker): I can also see why you are concerned about my volunteer work—when I could be spending some of that time bringing in some income. But my volunteer work is really important to me. I feel like I'm doing something good in the world.

SEBASTIAN (Listener): Sounds like you can appreciate my concern, but you also want me to know that it's really important to you. It adds a lot of meaning to your life. *(Here, he validates her by listening carefully.)*

HELGA (Speaker): Yeah. That's exactly what I am feeling. Here, you take the floor. *(Helga hands Sebastian the floor.)*

SEBASTIAN (Speaker): I have been anxious about this for a long time. If we don't save more, we are not going to be able to maintain our lifestyle in retirement. It's not all that far away.

HELGA (Listener): You really fear this.

SEBASTIAN (Speaker): Yes, I do. You know how things were for Mom and Dad. I don't want to end up living in a two-room apartment.

HELGA (Listener): You're worried we could end up living that way, too.

SEBASTIAN (Speaker): I'd feel a lot better with about three times as much saved.

HELGA (Listener): Too late now. *(She catches herself interjecting her own opinion.)* Oh, I should paraphrase. You wish we were much further along in our savings than we are.

SEBASTIAN (Speaker): *(This time, he feels he is really getting her attention.)* I sure do. I feel a lot of pressure about it. I really want to work together so we can both be comfortable. *(This lets her know he wants to work as a team.)*

HELGA (Listener): You want us to work together and reduce the pressure, and plan for our future.

SEBASTIAN (Speaker): *(suggesting some alternatives)* Yes. We'd need to spend less to save more. We'd need to use the credit cards more wisely. I think it would make the biggest difference if you could bring in some income.

HELGA (Listener): You feel that to save more we'd need to spend less with the credit cards. More important, you think it's pretty important for me to bring in some money.

SEBASTIAN (Speaker): Yes. I think the income is a bigger problem than the outgo.

HELGA (Listener): Even though we could spend less, you think we may need more income if we want to live at the same level in retirement. Can I have the floor?

SEBASTIAN (Speaker): Exactly! Here's the floor. (*He hands Helga the floor.*)

HELGA (Speaker): (*responding to Sebastian's clarification*) Sometimes I think that you think I'm the only one who overspends.

SEBASTIAN (Listener): You wonder if I think it's your fault for spending too much. Can I have the floor again? (*Helga hands him the floor.*)

SEBASTIAN (Speaker): Actually, I don't think that, but I can see how I could come across that way. (*validating Helga's experience*) I think I overspend less often, but when I do, I do it in bigger chunks.

HELGA (Listener): Nice to hear that. (*validating his comment and feeling good hearing him taking responsibility*) You can see that we both spend too much, just differently. You buy a few big things we may not need, and I buy numerous smaller things.

SEBASTIAN (Speaker): Exactly. We're both to blame, and we can both do better.

HELGA (Listener): We both need to work together. (*They switch the floor again.*)

HELGA (Speaker): I agree that we need to deal with our retirement savings more radically. My biggest fear is losing the work I love so much. It's been the most meaningful thing I've done since the kids got older.

SEBASTIAN (Listener): It's hard to imagine not having that—it's so important to you.

HELGA (Speaker): Yes. I can see why more income would make a big difference, but I would hate to lose what I have at the same time. I really like running those programs for the kids—especially when I see one of them open up.

SEBASTIAN (Listener): You enjoy it, and you are doing something really useful. I can hear how hard it would be for you to give it up.

HELGA (Speaker): Exactly. Maybe there would be some way to deal with this so that I wouldn't lose all of what I'm doing but where I could help us save what we need for retirement at the same time.

SEBASTIAN (Listener): You are wondering if there could be a solution that would meet your needs and our needs at the same time.

HELGA (Speaker): Yes. I want to think up solutions with you.

At this point they discontinue the Speaker-Listener Technique.

SEBASTIAN: OK.

HELGA: So, are we both feeling understood enough to move on to the problem solution steps?

SEBASTIAN: I am, how about you?

HELGA: *(She nods her head, yes.)*

Here they are agreeing together that they have had a good discussion and are ready to try some problem solving. They are consciously turning this corner together to move into the problem solution steps.

Problem Solution

Sebastian and Helga now go through the four steps of problem solution. Note that they do not resume using the Speaker-Listener Technique. Generally, the technique is not helpful when doing the problem solution steps.

Agenda Setting

Here the important thing is for the couple to choose to focus on a specific piece of the whole issue that was discussed. This increases their chances of finding a solution that will really work.

Helga: We should agree on the agenda. We could talk about how to get more into the retirement accounts, but that may not be the place to start. I also think we need a discussion to deal with the issue of how we spend money and the credit cards.

Sebastian: You're right. We are going to need several different stabs at this entire issue. It seems we could break it all down into the need to bring in more and the need to spend less. I don't want to push, but I'd like to focus on the "bring in more" part first, if you don't mind.

Helga: I can handle that. Let's problem-solve on that first, then we can talk later this week about the spending side.

Sebastian: So, we're going to brainstorm about how to boost the income.

Brainstorming

The key here is to generate ideas freely.

Helga: Let's brainstorm. Why don't you write the ideas down? You have a pen handy.

Sebastian: OK. You could get a part-time job.

Helga: I could ask the board of directors about making some of my work into a paid position. I'm practically a full-time staff member, anyway.

Sebastian: We could meet with a financial planner so we could get a better idea of what we really need to bring in. I could also get a second job.

Helga: I could look into part-time jobs that are similar to what I'm already doing, like those programs for kids with only one parent.

Sebastian: You know, Jack and Marla are doing something like that. We could talk to them about what it's about.

Helga: I feel this list is pretty good. Let's talk about what we'll try doing.

Agreement and Compromise

Now the couple sifts through the ideas generated in brainstorming. The key is for them to find an agreement they both can *support*. This could be just one of the brainstorm ideas or a combination.

SEBASTIAN: I like your idea of talking to the board. What could it hurt?

HELGA: I like that too. I also think your idea of seeing a financial planner is good. Otherwise, how do we really know what the target is if I'm going to try to bring in something extra? But I don't think it's realistic for you to work more.

SEBASTIAN: Yeah, I think you're right. What about talking to Marla and Jack about what they're into?

HELGA: I'd like to hold off on that. That could lead them to try and get me involved, and I'm not sure I'm interested.

SEBASTIAN: OK. What about exploring if there are any kinds of part-time jobs where you could be doing something that has meaning for you and make some bucks, too?

HELGA: I'd like to think about that. It'd be a good way to go if they don't have room in the budget where I am now. I sure wouldn't want to do more than half-time, though. I would hate to give up all of what I'm doing now.

SEBASTIAN: And I wouldn't want you to. If you could make a part-time income, I bet we could cut back enough to make it all work.

HELGA: So, how about I talk to the board, you ask Frank about that financial planner they use, and I'll also start looking around at what kinds of part-time jobs there might be.

SEBASTIAN: Great. Let's schedule some time next week to talk about how we are doing in moving toward the solution we need.

HELGA: Agreed.

They set a time to meet, and followed up as planned.

Follow-Up

At the end of the week, Helga and Sebastian met to discuss what they were finding out and what to do next. To Helga's surprise, the board member she talked with seemed eager to try to work out something. In the meantime, she had gone ahead with looking into various part-time jobs that would meet her needs. Sebastian had scheduled a meeting for them with a financial planner for the following week.

In this case, the solution really was a process made up of a series of smaller steps and agreements. Things were moving on an issue that had been a problem between them for a long time, and it felt good to work together and no longer avoid a tough issue.

Later, they went through the steps again and came to a specific agreement about spending less. They decided how much less to spend and agreed to record all the credit card purchases in a check-book register so that they would know how they were doing compared to their target. In contrast to their problem solving about income, which was a process lasting several weeks, this specific solution on spending was implemented right away, with not much tweaking needed.

WHEN IT'S NOT THAT EASY

We wish we could tell you that this model always works as well as it did for Sebastian and Helga, but there are times when it does not. What do you do then? In our experience with couples, there are a few common difficulties that can come up when dealing with problems:

1. *Friction is likely, and discussions can get heated.* If they get so heated that you are resorting to negative behavior, it is time for a Time Out—more on that in Chapter Eight. If you can get back on track by staying with the structure (for example, by using the Speaker-Listener Technique), great. If not, you need a break until you can keep it constructive.

2. *You can get bogged down and frustrated during any segment of the problem solution phase*. If so, it's usually best to cycle back to problem discussion. Simply pick up the floor again and resume your discussion. Getting stuck can mean that you have not talked through some key issues or that one or both of you are not feeling validated in the process. It may mean that one of the six key hidden issues (described in Chapter Six) is acting as a filter and preventing clear communication. It is better to slow down than to continue to press for a solution that may not work.

3. *The best solution you can reach may not always be the best solution for the whole problem*. At times, you should set the agenda just to agree on the next steps needed to get to the best solution. For example, you might brainstorm about the kind of information you need to make your decision.

WHEN THERE IS NO SOLUTION

There are some problems that do not have mutually satisfying solutions. However, we feel strongly that there are far fewer unresolvable problems than couples sometimes think. Nevertheless, suppose you've worked together for some time using the structure we suggest, yet no solution is forthcoming. Either you can let this lack of a solution damage your marriage or you can plan for how to live with the difference. Sometimes couples allow a good marriage to be damaged by insisting there must be a resolution on a specific unresolved conflict. Many couples fear leaving issues unresolved, feeling, as one woman wrote in the survey, that "we will never really understand each other on certain key issues."

Remember what we talked about in Chapter Two about the importance of accepting each other as a package deal. When you give up unrealistic expectations and accept each other as you are today—including your issues with no apparent solutions—you can face the future with great hope and anticipation.

If you have an area that seems unresolvable, you can use the agenda in the problem solution step to protect your marriage from the fallout from that one problem area. You literally "agree to disagree" constructively. This kind of solution comes about through both teamwork and tolerance. You can't always have your spouse be just the way you want him or her to be, but you can work as a team to deal with the differences between you.

*

We have given you a very specific model that will work well to help you preserve and enhance your teamwork in solving the problems that come your way in life. We don't expect most couples to use such a structured approach for minor problems. We do expect that most couples could benefit from this model when dealing with more important matters, especially those that can lead to unproductive conflict. This is yet another way to add more structure when you need it most, to preserve the best in your relationship. You can solve problems in a variety of ways.

In Chapter Eight, we conclude this part of the book, which has focused on handling conflict. We build further on the techniques presented so far to help you prosper in your relationship together. The ground rules we present focus on fitting the skills and strategies you have learned into your life and relationship, and help you take control of the conflict in your relationship so that the conflict cannot take control of you.

EXERCISES

There are three separate assignments for this chapter. First, we want you to practice making XYZ statements. Second, we invite each of you to review your ratings of some common problem areas in your relationship. Third, we ask you to practice the problem-solving model presented in this chapter. No amount of techniques and skills will help you without your practicing them!

XYZ Statements: Constructive Griping

Spend some time thinking about things your partner has done or regularly does that bother you in some way. On you own paper, list your concerns as you normally might state them. Then practice putting your concerns into the XYZ format: "When you do X in situation Y, I feel Z."

Next, repeat the exercise, except list things your partner does that please you. You will find that the XYZ format also works well for giving specific positive feedback—for example, "When you came home the other night with my favorite ice cream, I felt loved." Try sharing some of the positive thoughts with your spouse.

Assessment of Problem Areas

In Chapter One we asked you to rate your relationship issues on a problem inventory, originally developed by Knox (1971) and adapted here for empty nest couples. Please look back at your ratings in order to make a list of low-conflict problems to discuss in the problem-solving exercise next. We include another copy of the inventory on the next page for you to refer to.

Issues Inventory

Consider the following list of issues. Please rate how much of a problem each area currently is in your relationship by writing in a number from 0 (not a problem at all) to 10 (a severe problem). For example, if money is a slight problem in your relationship, you might enter a 2 or 3 next to Money. If money is not a problem, you would enter a 0, and if money is a severe problem, you would enter 10. If you wish to add other areas that aren't included, please do so in the blank spaces provided. Now rate each area on a separate scale of 0 (not a problem) to 10 (a severe problem):

_____ Money
_____ Recreation
_____ Conflict resolution
_____ Extended family
_____ Careers
_____ Sex
_____ Grandchildren
_____ Retirement planning
_____ Household
responsibilities
_____ Friendship with spouse
_____ Other _____

_____ In-laws
_____ Communication
_____ Friends
_____ Aging parents
_____ Alcohol and/or drugs
_____ Children
_____ Religion
_____ Health and physical fitness
_____ Ministry and community
service activities
_____ Fun and leisure activities
_____ Other _____

Practice Problem Solving

To practice the problem-solving model we described in this chapter, it is critical that you follow these instructions carefully. When dealing with real problems in your relationship, the chances of conflict are significant, and we want you to practice in a way that enhances your chances of solidifying these skills.

Set aside time to practice uninterrupted. Thirty minutes or so should be sufficient to get started using the sequence on some of the problems you want to solve.

Look over your problem inventories together. Make a list of those areas in which you both rated the problem as being less serious. These are the problem areas we want you to use to practice the model at the start. Practice with very specific problems and look for very specific solutions. Doing so will boost your skills and help you gain confidence in the model.

We recommend that you set aside time to practice the problem discussion and problem solution sequence several times a week for two or three weeks. If you put in this time, you'll gain skill and confidence in handling problem areas together. Keep this chapter open while you are practicing and refer back to the specific steps of the model.

8

Ground Rules for Handling Conflict

All too often, couples allow conflict to grow, problems to remain unsolved, and intimacy to dissolve, all because they are frightened by the prospect of raising difficult issues and of making things worse. To have a healthy marriage, you need to be able to identify danger signs when conflicts arise and to protect your relationship from negative patterns.

The changes that constitute empty nest syndrome simply intensify the need to get conflict under control. You need to make your marriage a safe place—especially when it comes to dealing with the various conflicts and disagreements that are inevitable in marriage. One key way to create this safety is to have agreed-on rules for protecting your relationship from unproductive conflict. Otherwise the conflicted aspects of your life can damage the really wonderful elements you have together.

Now that you understand some powerful techniques for communicating and solving problems, we will look at six ground rules that can help protect the great parts of your relationship in the years to come. We call these principles *ground rules* to highlight their importance for your marriage. Rather than allowing the difficult issues in your relationship to control you, you can use these rules to help you control the issues.

We end Part Two of the book with this topic for two reasons. First, the ground rules sum up many key points we have made so far.

Second, these rules give you the opportunity to agree on how you want to change the ways in which you communicate and handle conflict together.

In sports, ground rules specify what is allowed and not allowed, what is inbounds and out. To be sure, marriage is not a sport. Further, in using the term ground rules, we don't wish to invoke the image of competition. We just went to a lot of trouble in Chapter Seven to help you find ways to eliminate competitive attitudes and work together as a team. However, when things go downhill for couples, competition is a fact—competition over who will get his or her way. In our experience, these ground rules are powerful tools for helping couples stay on track and work as a team.

GROUND RULE 1: *When conflict is escalating, we will call a Time Out or a Stop Action and either (1) try talking again, using the Speaker-Listener Technique, or (2) agree to talk about the issue later, at a specified time, using the Speaker-Listener Technique.*

If we could get the attention of every empty nest couple and have them all agree to only one change in their relationships, following this ground rule would be our choice. It is that important! This simple rule can really protect and enhance relationships. Why? In general, it counteracts the negative escalation that is so destructive to close relationships, while helping couples work together on important issues.

Why are Time Outs so critical for empty nest marriages? One reason is this: when the kids were present with their needs, chatter, issues, and demands, they provided natural time outs as you put your marital issues aside in order to deal with the children's immediate needs. We have already mentioned how children are buffers. Now consider how they buffer negative escalation. An escalating negative interaction between spouses can be short-circuited when an angry teenager begins to vent his or her own issues. But when your child grows up and leaves home, you're left with all this time together.

When conflict arises and you start down a negative path, you can just keep going and going and going—not good; in fact, it can attack the very foundation of your marriage. At this stage of marriage you need to learn or relearn the skill of taking Time Outs.

One couple who came to a Second Half seminar, Matilda and Willis, shared how since their last child left home, they have incorporated the principle of Time Outs. "We discovered that after our son, Frank, left for the marines, we were arguing more and enjoying each other less," Willis said. "So we made an agreement. When we get on a negative track or just aren't communicating well, either of us can call for ten minutes of silence."

Matilda added, "It usually works, but sometimes we have to add that we won't even look at each other for that ten minutes. We know each other so well that our nonverbal communication can keep us on a negative track without even saying a word, so we're both free to add, 'ten minutes—no eye contact.' At times, we even go in separate rooms!"

Matilda and Willis found what worked for them. You need to do the same. We suggest you not only agree to this ground rule but also use a specific term such as Time Out or Stop Action, which helps you interpret positively what you or your partner is doing. Otherwise, it becomes too easy to interpret what you are doing as avoidance. In fact, calling a Time Out is one of the most positive things either of you can do for your relationship. You are interrupting old, negative behaviors and deciding to do something constructive instead. You might come up with your own unique signal, such as "Red Light" or "Ouch, I feel a pinch." What you want to do is to alert the other that you need time out.

We want you to approach this as something you are doing *together* for the good of your relationship; that is why you need to decide on your own signal. Sure, one of you may use Time Out more than the other, but if you both agree to the rule, you are really doing the Time Outs together. Agreeing to Time Outs is critical. You can't stop escalation without both of you working together when the situation warrants it. Anybody can just walk out, but as we have explained, that just fuels more escalation and later hostility. But when either of you calls Time Out or Red Light, you work together to stop the destructive process right there.

One important hint: you can call Time Out if you realize that you, your partner, or the both of you are getting out of control. Time Out is called on the *communication*, not the person or relationship. Don't simply say "Time Out" and immediately leave the room (unless you have an agreement like Matilda and Willis's)—unilateral actions are usually counterproductive. Instead, say something like "This is getting hot; let's stop the action and talk later, OK?" By including your partner in the process, you are making it mutual and hence de-escalating.

Another key aspect of this ground rule is that you are agreeing to continue the argument—but productively—either right now or in the near future, after a cooling-off period. If you are a pursuer, this feature of the ground rule addresses your concern that Time Outs could be used by a withdrawer to stop discussions about important issues. *This ground rule is designed to stop unproductive arguments, not all dialogue on an issue.* You do need to discuss important issues—just do it in a productive manner. In agreeing to use the Speaker-Listener Technique when you come back to talking about an issue, you are agreeing to deal more effectively with the issue that got out of hand.

This aspect of the ground rule is really important for empty nesters. In the past, you may have gotten in a pattern of seldom getting back to issues that you needed to talk through. Issues got buried, and walls went up. Now that you're beginning to confront those issues and learning to slow down the escalation with Time Outs, you also need to be brave enough to pick them back up using the Speaker-Listener Technique. This is like letting a hot potato cool to the point at which you can pick it up and deal with it.

The Time Out itself can give withdrawers confidence that conflict won't get out of hand. Some withdrawers are even able to tolerate conflict better, knowing they can stop it at any time. Using the Speaker-Listener Technique makes it still safer to deal with the issue that came up, by providing that all-important structure. This ground rule will work without using the Speaker-Listener Technique, but we are convinced that using it is the most effective way to implement this rule. Dee and Loren, a couple from the *Fighting for Your Marriage* videos, likened having this ground rule to having brakes on a car. The rule gives you a way to stop when you need to stop, but at the same time, it gives you the confidence to move forward without fear that you will get going without any way to stop.

When you do decide to talk later, try to set the time right then. Perhaps in an hour, or maybe the next day, would be a good time to talk. If the situation were really heated when you called the Time Out, you may find that you can't talk then even about when you'll come back to the discussion. That's OK. You can set a time after your emotions have calmed down between the two of you.

What follows are two examples of this ground rule being used correctly.

Robert and Paula have been married for twenty-four years and have two sons, both in college. Before learning these techniques, this couple would have frequent, intense arguments that ended with shouting and threats about the future of the relationship. Both came from homes where open, intense conflict was relatively common, so changing their pattern was not easy for them. As you will see, they still escalate rather easily, but now they know how to stop it when the argument gets going.

PAULA: *(annoyed and showing it)* You forgot to get the trash out in time for the garbage man. The cans are already full.

ROBERT: *(also annoyed, looking up from the paper)* It's no big deal. I'll just stuff it all down more.

PAULA: Yeah, right. The trash will be overflowing in the garage by next week.

ROBERT: *(irritated)* What do you want me to do now? I forgot. Just leave it.

PAULA: (very angry now, voice raised) You aren't getting a lot of the things done around here that you are supposed to.

ROBERT: Let's call a Time Out; this isn't getting us anywhere.

PAULA: OK. When can we sit down and talk more about it? After dinner tonight?

ROBERT: OK. As soon as dinner is over.

There is nothing magic here. Calling a Time Out is really very simple, but the effect is potentially powerful for your relationship. This couple used Time Out very effectively to stop an argument that was not going to be productive. Later, they did sit down and talk, using the Speaker-Listener Technique, about Paula's concern that Robert was not meeting his responsibilities at home. Then, using the problem-solving model we presented in Chapter Seven, they were able to come up with some possible ways for the chores to get done.

In this next example, a couple used this ground rule to save an important evening from potential disaster. Warren and Victoria have been married for twenty-six years, and Victoria's mother lives with them. This has added plenty of strain to their marriage. They had decided to take a weekend trip to a cottage in the mountains, to get away and spend a relaxing—perhaps romantic—few days together. They had both been looking forward to this time together for months. This conversation transpired on their first evening, as they got into bed together:

VICTORIA: (feeling romantic and snuggling up to Warren) It's so nice to get away. No distractions. This feels good.

WARREN: (likewise inclined, and beginning to caress her) Yeah, should have done this months ago. It'll be great to have time alone without your mother always around.

VICTORIA: (bristling at the thought) My mother? Why do you have to bring up my mother? You agreed that she could come live with us. It's not easy, but when Dad died, she really didn't have any other place she could go. Can't we just forget her for one weekend?

WARREN: *(anxious and annoyed at himself for spoiling the moment)* I didn't mean for us to talk about her. We have been through that. I just meant—

VICTORIA: *(angry)* You just meant to say that you *really* wish she didn't live with us.

WARREN: Hold on. Stop the Action. I am sorry that I mentioned your mom. Do you want to talk this through now, or set a time for later?

VICTORIA: *(softening)* If we don't talk about it a little bit, I think the rest of the weekend will be a drag.

WARREN: OK, you have the floor. *(He picks up the remote control on the nightstand and hands it to her.)*

VICTORIA (Speaker): I got all tense when you brought up my mom, and I felt like you were blaming me for inviting her to live with us.

WARREN (Listener): So mentioning your mom raised unpleasant feelings, and more so because you felt blamed.

VICTORIA (Speaker): Yes. This whole year since she moved in has been stressful, and I was hoping to get away from it for the weekend.

WARREN (Listener): It's been really hard on you, and you wanted to just forget about it this weekend.

VICTORIA (Speaker): And I wanted us to focus on rediscovering how to be a little bit romantic, like it used to be.

WARREN (Listener): Just you and me making love without a care.

VICTORIA (Speaker): *(feeling really listened to and cared for)* Yes. Your turn. *(She hands Warren the floor.)*

WARREN (Speaker): Boy, do I feel like a turkey. I didn't mean to mess up the moment, though I see how just mentioning your mom affected you.

VICTORIA (Listener): You feel bad that you even mentioned my mom. You did not mean to screw things up between us tonight.

WARREN (Speaker): You got it. And I really don't blame you for her living with us. We made that decision together. It's just that at times I really miss just being with you. I thought that was what the empty nest was all about. And this weekend I was excited that it was just the two of us. That's all I meant.

VICTORIA (Listener): *(with a smile)* You didn't mean to be a turkey.

WARREN (Speaker): *(chuckling back)* That's kind of blunt, but yeah, that's what I'm saying. I think we should just avoid mentioning your mom for the weekend.

VICTORIA (Listener): You think we should make any conversations about Mom off-limits this weekend.

WARREN: Yes! *(He hands Victoria the floor.)*

VICTORIA (Speaker): I agree. OK, where were we? *(tossing the remote on the floor)*

WARREN: *(big smile)* You were calling me a turkey.

VICTORIA: *(playfully)* Oh yeah. Come over here, turkey.

WARREN: *(moving closer to kiss her)* I'm all yours.

Notice how effectively they used the Time Out to stop what could have turned into an awful fight. Victoria was too hurt to just shelve the issue about her mom. She needed to talk right then, and Warren agreed. Doing so helped them diffuse the tension and come back together, and it saved their special weekend.

GROUND RULE 2: *When we are having trouble communicating, we will use the Speaker-Listener Technique.*

We hope you don't need much convincing of the wisdom of this ground rule. The key is to have a way to communicate safely and clearly when you really need to do it well. With this ground rule, you are agreeing to use more structure when you need it. The example of Warren and Victoria shows the value of this principle; however, there are many times when you don't need to call a Time Out but still need to make the transition to a more effective mode of communication. There are other situations in which things have already escalated, and a Time Out might have helped, but you skip right to using the Speaker-Listener Technique. In the next example, Jennifer and Carl used this ground rule to get back on track.

Jennifer and Carl also attended one of our workshops and told us later about this sequence of events. They had been married for seven years, and before they began working on their communication skills had been locked into some unproductive patterns, carried over from their previous marriages. On this occasion, their new skills really made a big difference.

They went out to dinner one evening, and before even ordering, they got into an argument about their friends:

JENNIFER: *(matter-of-factly)* This reminds me. Dick and Barb asked us over for dinner next Saturday. I told them that I thought we could do it.

CARL: *(very angry)* What! How could you tell them we'd go without even asking? You know that I hate being around her.

JENNIFER: *(angry, but speaking in a low, serious tone)* Lower your voice. People are turning to look at us.

CARL: *(just as loud as before and just as angry)* So what? Let them stare. I am sick and tired of you making decisions without talking to me first.

JENNIFER: Don't talk to me like this.

CARL: How 'bout I don't talk to you at all?

At that point, Carl got up, left the restaurant, and went out to the car. He paced a bit, fuming and muttering about how difficult Jennifer could be at times. He got in the car, intending to drive away and leave Jennifer at the restaurant. "Wouldn't that serve her right," he thought. As he cooled off for a moment, he thought better of that idea. He walked back into the restaurant, took his seat across from Jennifer, picked up a menu, and handed it to her, saying, "OK, you have the floor."

This situation might have been a good one for a total Time Out, but instead, Carl decided he wanted to talk this one out right now, productively; Jennifer went with it. They told us they proceeded to have an excellent discussion of the issue. As they passed the menu back and forth, others in the restaurant must have thought they were having a terrible time making up their minds on what to order! Their transition to greater structure took them from what could have been a real meltdown to a victory for their relationship. Experiences like this serve to boost couples' confidence in their ability to work together and keep their relationship strong.

Ground Rule 3: *When using the Speaker-Listener Technique, we will completely separate problem discussion from problem solution.*

As we stated in Chapter Seven, it is critical to keep it clear whether you are discussing a problem or solving a problem at any given time. Too often, couples rush to agree to some solution, and the solution fails. Lots of added problems and hassles come from rushing to agreements without laying the proper foundation of communicating fully with each other about the problem.

Go back to Chapter Five and review the conversation between Tessie and Peter about Jeremy and his college plans. Notice how they had a great discussion but did not seek a specific solution. They each expressed their concerns and were ready to try problem solving on this issue. Let's pick it up from where we left off:

Tessie: I think we're ready for problem solving; what do you think?
Peter: I agree. I'm feeling like we had a good talk and got a lot out on the table. Now working on some solutions would be great.

With these simple comments, they have made the transition from problem discussion to problem solution. They have learned the value of separating the two. Discussion and solution are different processes, and they both work better when you recognize this and act on it.

Ground Rule 4: *We can bring up issues at any time, but the Listener can say, "This is not a good time." If the Listener does not want to talk at that time, he or she takes responsibility for setting up a time to talk in the near future.*

This ground rule accomplishes one very important thing: it ensures that you will not have an important or difficult talk about an issue unless you both agree that the time is right. How often do you begin talking about a key issue in your relationship when your partner is just not ready for it? There is no point in having a discussion about anything important unless you're both ready to talk about it. If while the children were still around you had been in a pattern of avoiding issues, this ground rule will help you feel safe enough to bring emotionally charged (and perhaps buried) issues to the surface. Knowing that you and your partner have the right to say "Not now" will make you more sensitive to each other, and you'll be more motivated to try to understand the other's point of view.

We emphasize this ground rule in appreciation of a fact of life: most couples talk about their most important issues at the worst times—dinnertime, bedtime, when it's time to leave for work or as soon as you walk in the door after work, when one of you is preoccupied with an important project or task—you get the picture. These are times when your spouse may be a captive audience, but you certainly don't have his or her attention. In fact, these are the most stressful times in the life of the average couple—not good times to talk things out.

This ground rule assumes two things: (1) that you each are responsible for knowing when you are capable of discussing something with appropriate attention to what your partner has to say and (2) that you can each respect the other when he or she says, "I can't deal with that right now." There simply is no point in trying to have a discussion if you are both not up for it.

You may ask, "Isn't this just a prescription for avoidance?" That is where the second part of the ground rule comes in. The person who is not up to the discussion takes responsibility for making it happen in the *near* future. This is critical—especially if you are an avoider. Your partner will have a much easier time putting off the conversation if he or she has confidence that you really will follow through. We recommend that when you use this ground rule, you set up a better time within twenty-four to forty-eight hours. Doing so may not always be practical, but it is a good rule of thumb. Here is one example.

Leigh and Clark are a couple with three older adolescents, two still at home. As is typical of many couples with teenagers still in the house, they have little time for talking things out in their marriage, much less sleeping. As a result, they often are alone only at bedtime.

CLARK: I can't believe how Tom wants to talk for hours on the phone at night with that creep of a girlfriend.

LEIGH: She has such a limited vocabulary, you'd think he would be bored to death with her.

CLARK: Speaking of boring things, we need to talk about those life insurance decisions. I know that agent will call back any day.

LEIGH: I know it's important, but I just can't focus right now. I think I could focus about ten minutes on Dave Letterman, and that's about it.

CLARK: Pretty wiped, eh? Me, too. Well, what would be a good time to talk about this?

LEIGH: No guarantee I will be alive, but I think I might have the energy around lunchtime tomorrow. Could you come home for lunch?

CLARK: Sounds good. Let's watch Dave and crash.

It is now Leigh's responsibility to bring the subject up again tomorrow and to make this talk happen. Because their agreement is rather specific, Clark should be able to show up at lunchtime for their talk. They may be too tired and busy for there ever to be a "perfect" time to talk this out, but there are times that are better than others.

As one variation of this ground rule, you may want to come to an agreement that certain times are never good for bringing up important subjects. For example, we have worked with many couples who have agreed that neither will bring up anything significant within thirty minutes of bedtime. These couples decided that at bedtime, they are just too tired and that it is important to be relaxing and winding down.

GROUND RULE 5: *We will have weekly couple meetings.*

Most couples do not set aside a regular time for dealing with key issues and problems. The importance of doing so has been suggested by so many marriage experts over the years that it is almost a cliché. Nevertheless, we want to give you our view on this sage advice handed down probably for centuries.

The advantages of having a weekly meeting time far outweigh any negatives. First, this is a tangible way to place high priority on your marriage by carving out time for its upkeep. We know you are busy. We all are busy. But if you decide that keeping your marriage strong is important, you can find the time to make couple time happen.

Second, following this ground rule ensures that even if there is no other good time to deal with issues and problems in your marriage, you at least have this weekly meeting. You might be surprised at how much you can get done in thirty minutes or so of concentrated attention on an issue. During this meeting, you can talk about the relationship, talk about specific problems, or practice communication skills. That includes using all the skills and techniques we describe in the first two parts of this book.

A third advantage of this ground rule is that having a weekly meeting time takes much of the day-to-day pressure off your relationship. This is especially true if you have gotten tangled at all in the pursuer-withdrawer pattern. If something happens that brings up a gripe for you, it is much easier to delay bringing it up until another time if you know there *will* be another time. Pursuers can relax; you'll have your chance to raise your issue. Withdrawers are encouraged to bring up concerns they have, because you have a meeting for doing just this.

We must debunk one empty nest fallacy: just because the kids are gone doesn't mean you have all the time you need to talk. Every couple can benefit from the structure of a weekly couple meeting.

This format will help you feel comfortable about bringing up issues even if in the past you ignored or buried them. And because you can build a more personal and deeper relationship in the second half of marriage, you may find you have more issues to talk about. Remember, this is marriage maintenance time.

You may be thinking that having a couple meeting is a pretty good idea. But to put this good idea into action, you must be consistent in taking the time to make the meetings happen. You may have the urge to skip the meetings when you are getting along really well. We have heard this repeatedly from couples. Don't succumb to this urge.

Consider Roberto and Margaret, who have set aside Wednesday nights at nine o'clock as a time for their couple meeting. If they are getting along really well during the week and Wednesday night rolls around, each begins to think, "We don't need to meet tonight. No use stirring things up when we are getting along so well." Then one or the other says, "Hey, Hon, let's just skip the meeting tonight, things are going so well."

What Roberto and Margaret came to realize is that things were going so well partly because they were regularly having their meetings. After they canceled a few, they noticed that more conflicts would come up during the week. They had given up their time to deal with issues and had reverted to the uncertainty of dealing with things "if and when." Ultimately they decided that "if and when" was not placing the proper importance on their marriage, and they went back to having the meetings.

If you actually do get to a meeting and have little to deal with, fine. Have a short meeting, but *have a meeting*. Use these meetings to air gripes, have discussions of important issues, plan for key events coming up, or just take stock of how the relationship is going. When there is a specific problem in focus, work through the problem-solving steps presented in Chapter Seven. When there is nothing more pressing, practice some of the skills presented in this book. Take the time and use the time to keep your relationship strong.

GROUND RULE 6: *We will make time for the great things: fun, friendship, and sensuality. We will agree to protect these times from conflict and the need to deal with issues.*

Just as it's important to set aside time to deal with issues in your relationship, it's critical that you protect key times from conflicts over issues. You can't be focusing on issues all the time and have a really great marriage. You need some time when you are together relaxing—having fun, talking as friends, making love, and so forth—when conflict and problems are off-limits. This is such an important point that we devote three chapters of this book to sensuality, friendship, and fun.

For now, we emphasize two points embodied in this ground rule. First, make time for these great things. Second, if you're spending time together in one of these positive ways, don't bring up issues that you have to work on. And if an issue does come up, table it until later—for example, until your couple meeting.

The example we presented earlier in this chapter with Victoria and Warren makes this point well. They were out to have a relaxing and romantic weekend, and this wasn't the time to focus on one of their key issues, Victoria's mom. Using Time Out and the Speaker-Listener Technique helped them get refocused on the real reason they had gotten away. It's better still if you agree to keep difficult issues off-limits during such positive times in the first place.

*

One essential benefit for your relationship is embedded in all these ground rules. When you use them properly, *you are agreeing to control the difficult issues in your marriage rather than allowing them to control you.* Instead of having arguments whenever events come up, you are agreeing to deal with the issues when you are both able to do it well—and when you are both under control.

One of the most destructive things that can happen to an empty nest marriage is to have the growing sense that you are walking in a minefield. With the children gone, you are more vulnerable. You know the feeling: you begin to wonder where the next explosion will come from, and you don't feel in control of where you're going. You no longer feel free to just "be" with your partner. You don't know when you are about to "step in it," but you know right away when you did. It just doesn't have to be this way or ever get to be this way in the first place. These ground rules will go a long way toward getting you back on safe ground. They work. You can do it.

EXERCISE

Your exercise for this chapter is very straightforward: discuss the ground rules and begin to try them out. You may want to modify one or more of them in some specific manner to make them work better for you. That's fine. The key is to review these rules and give them a chance to work in your relationship. We have listed them again here.

Suggested Ground Rules for Handling Issues

1. When conflict is escalating, we will call a Time Out or a Stop Action and either (1) try talking again, using the Speaker-Listener Technique, or (2) agree to talk about the issue later, at a specified time, using the Speaker-Listener Technique.

2. When we are having trouble communicating, we will use the Speaker-Listener Technique.

3. When using the Speaker-Listener Technique, we will completely separate problem discussion from problem solution.

4. We can bring up issues at any time, but the Listener can say, "This is not a good time." If the Listener does not want to talk at that time, he or she takes responsibility for setting up a time to talk in the near future. (You need to decide how "the near future" is defined.)

5. We will have weekly couple meetings. (Schedule the time now for your weekly couple meeting. There is no time like the present.)

6. We will make time for the great things: fun, friendship, and sensuality. We will agree to protect these times from conflict and the need to deal with issues.

STEPS YOU CAN TAKE TO ACHIEVE FORGIVENESS AND RESTORATION

Now that you've had the opportunity to learn some new skills for handling issues and problems in your relationship, we want to revisit the subject of forgiveness. In Chapter Two, you had the opportunity to deal with some of the little irritations that were spoiling your marital soup. We encouraged you to forgive your spouse, move past those little idiosyncratic behaviors, and accept your partner as a package deal. We encouraged you to table the larger issues and promised that later in the book we would help you deal with them. The time is now. Equipped with your new skills, we invite you to follow seven steps that will help you walk through forgiving your spouse and restoring a close relationship. We want to give you a more specific and structured approach for making forgiveness happen. In suggesting specific steps, we don't mean to imply that forgiveness is easy. But we do want you to be able to move forward with some specific steps to get you through the toughest times.

First, spend some time alone in reflection about areas in which you may still harbor resentment, bitterness, and lack of forgiveness in your relationship. Write these things down. How old are these feelings? Are there patterns of behavior that continue to offend you? Do you hold things against your partner? Do you bring up past events in arguments? Are you willing to push yourself to forgive? Are you willing to give up your right to get even or to get back at your partner?

Second, spend some time reflecting on times you may have really hurt your partner. Have you taken responsibility? Did you apologize? Have you taken steps to change any recurrent patterns that give offense? Just as you may be holding onto some grudges, you may be standing in the way of reconciliation on some issues if you have never taken responsibility for your end.

If you have identified more significant hurts that the two of you have not fully dealt with, take the time to sit down together and tackle these meatier issues using our seven steps. Doing so is risky, but if you do it well, the resulting growth in your relationship and capacity for intimacy will be well worth it. The choice is yours.

The steps outlined here are much like the problem-solving process we described in Chapter Seven. These steps can work very well to guide you in approaching forgiveness when you have a specific event or recurring issue to deal with. Consider these seven steps as a road map for forgiving your partner.

Step 1: Schedule a Couple Meeting to Discuss the Specific Issue Related to Forgiveness

If an issue is important enough to focus on in this way, do it right. Set aside a time when you will be without distractions. Prepare yourselves to deal with the issue openly, honestly, and with respect. As we have discussed in this chapter, setting aside specific times for dealing with issues makes it more likely that you'll actually follow through and do it well. For instance, Beth and Jack Dillard in Chapter Two set a time to talk about Beth's role as a stepmother and her commitment to supporting Jack and his son. Even after an initial rush of anger, you can agree to set aside time to work through the issue.

Step 2: Set the Agenda to Work on the Issue in Question

Identify the problem or harmful event you plan to work on now. You must both agree that you are ready to discuss it in this format at this time. If not, wait for a better time.

Beth and Jack set the agenda to include a discussion of Beth's relationship with her stepson and the importance of her giving priority to that relationship in her life. They agreed.

Step 3: Fully Explore the Pain and Concerns Related to This Issue for Both of You

The goal in this step is to have an open, validating talk about what has happened that harmed one or both of you. You shouldn't try this unless you as an individual are motivated to hear and show respect for your partner's viewpoint. The foundation for forgiveness is best laid through such a talk or series of talks.

Validating discussions go a long way toward dealing with the painful issues in ways that bring you closer together. This would be a great time to use the Speaker-Listener Technique. If there's ever a time to have a safe and clear talk, this is it.

Using the Speaker-Listener Technique, Beth and Jack talked it out for about thirty minutes. He really listened to her sadness about missing the awards luncheon. He had calmed down and could see that being angry at her didn't make a lot of sense. By using the Speaker-Listener Technique, they soon felt closer than they had in quite awhile.

Step 4: The Offender Asks for Forgiveness

If you have offended your partner in some way, an outward appeal for forgiveness is not only appropriate but very healing. An apology would be a powerful addition to a request for forgiveness. A sincere apology validates your partner's pain. To say, "I'm sorry. I was wrong. Please forgive me," is one of the most healing things that one person can say to another.

Apologizing and asking for forgiveness are a big part of taking responsibility for having hurt your partner. (This doesn't mean that you sit around and beat yourself up for what you did. You have to forgive yourself, too!) Beth was clearly contrite when she asked for forgiveness from Jack, and this made it even easier for him to forgive her.

What if you don't think you have done anything wrong? You can still ask your partner to forgive you. Remember, forgiveness is a separate issue from why the infraction or mistake occurred. So even if you don't agree you did anything wrong, your partner can choose to forgive. It's harder to forgive under these circumstances, but it's doable.

Listen carefully to your partner's pain and concern. Even if you feel you have done no wrong, you may find something in what your partner says that can lead to a change on your part for the better of the relationship.

Step 5: The Offended Agrees to Forgive

Ideally, the one needing to forgive gives a clear, open acknowledgment of the desire to forgive. This may be unnecessary for minor infractions, but for anything of significance, this step is important. It makes forgiveness more real, more memorable, and increases accountability between the two of you to find the healing you are seeking.

There are several specific implications of this step. In forgiving, you are attempting to commit the event to the past. You are agreeing that you will not bring it up in the middle of future arguments or conflicts.

You both recognize that this commitment to forgive does not mean that the offended person will feel no pain or effects from what happened. But you're moving on. You're working to restore the relationship and repair the damage. Jack clearly gave Beth the message that he would forgive her for letting him and his stepson down and that he could move forward in their relationship.

Step 6: If Applicable, the Offender Makes a Positive Commitment to Change Recurrent Patterns or Attitudes That Give Offense

This step depends on your agreement that there is a specific problem with how one of you behaved. It also assumes that what happened is part of a pattern, not just a one-time event. Jack agreed that Beth typically did not forget important events and that she did not have an ongoing pattern of hurtful behavior.

If you have hurt your partner, it also helps to make amends. This is not the same as committing to make important changes. When you make amends, you make a peace offering of a sort—not because you "owe" your partner but because you want to demonstrate your desire to get back on track. It is a gesture of goodwill. One way to make amends is to do unexpected positive acts. This shows your investment and ongoing desire to keep building your relationship.

Step 7: Expect Change to Take Time

These steps are potent for getting you on track as a couple. They begin a process, but they don't sum it up. These steps can move that process along, but you may each be working on your side of the equation for some time to come. You can heal your relationship when painful events come between you. Forgiveness is your choice.

*

In Part Two, we have covered many deep and often misunderstood concepts, but we also have given you specific skills for dealing with them. Acting on what we have presented will take a lot of reflection and skill, but if you do the work, we believe it will be worth it. In Part Three, we look at key empty nest issues: unmet expectations, commitment, spirituality, and relating to aging parents and adult children.

Part III

Dealing with Empty Nest Issues

9

When What We Want
Isn't What We Get

In Chapter Six, we explained how hidden issues can fuel conflict and create distance between partners. Now we are ready to build on those concepts by focusing on expectations. We'll help you explore your expectations for your empty nest marriage—what they are, where they come from, and whether they are reasonable.

You might be thinking that you already understand everything there is about what you each expect in your marriage, or you might already have been surprised at what new expectations have been uncovered. However, this is a time of significant transition in your life together. Not only is it a time with great potential for growing closer together, but we think it's also a time when you will find that some of your expectations about life and marriage that worked with a full nest are not so right for your empty nest. At the end of this chapter, there's a very important exercise with which you'll explore and share your expectations for your relationship in this new stage of marriage. In fact, this chapter is primarily designed to prepare you for the exercise.

Exploring your expectations will also help you understand how issues—hidden or not—get triggered in your relationship. Exploring your expectations for the empty nest years, along with using all the skills you have learned so far, will give you the best shot at preventing the kinds of frustrating conflicts we've discussed so far in this book and will help you stabilize your relationship in the empty nest years.

HOW EXPECTATIONS AFFECT RELATIONSHIPS IN THE EMPTY NEST

We all have expectations for every aspect of our relationships. In Chapter Five, we discussed how expectations can become powerful filters distorting your understanding of what happens in your relationship. The reason, we explained, is that people tend to see what they expect to see. In that chapter, the focus was on how your perception can be distorted because of filters.

In this chapter, we focus on your expectations of the way you think things are supposed to be in your relationship now that the kids are grown—even if one or more still live with you. For example, you still have specific expectations regarding such minor things as who will refill the orange juice container or who will balance the checkbook—the stuff of everyday events. You have expectations about common issues, such as money, housework, in-laws, and sex. You also have expectations about the deeper, often hidden, issues: how power will be shared (or not shared), how caring will be demonstrated, or about what the commitment is in your relationship. These hidden issues become more critical when transitioning into a marriage without day-to-day parenting responsibilities.

For instance, roles that worked in the active parenting years may no longer function. If one spouse remained home to focus on parenting and to be the primary caregiver and home manager, she now may decide to go back to work, seeing the empty nest passage as her chance to pursue delayed vocational dreams. She may decide to get a graduate degree or start interviewing for jobs. She is ready to branch out and perhaps even begin a career. At this point, her expectations concerning household responsibilities may change—especially if she has handled most of the house stuff while the kids were growing up. Her spouse may or may not pick up the slack. He may be ready to pull back, take life a little easier, play more golf, spend more time at home, or travel and see the world. He might never even think about realigning household responsibilities.

Expectations affect everything! And couples entering the empty nest today have higher expectations. They want more from their marriage relationship than did past empty nesters. Why? As we discussed in Chapter One, one reason is that people are living longer. Years ago, the life cycle was simple. You grew up, you got married, you raised your family, you retired—and then you died. Today's empty nester may be married for another thirty-five or even forty years! A dysfunctional couple may look at each other and say, "I don't want another thirty years of this!"

Newly married couples in later life may feel a confusing mixture of expectations, some appropriate to newlyweds, others reflecting their greater life experience. A divorced woman married to a widower wrote of the impact of expectations in her everyday life: "I'm adjusting to living in the same house as his previous wife, attending the same church, and working in the school where she taught. I'm surrounded by my husband's past life with his previous wife." Here the expectations are unspoken, but they pressure this new wife (married just fifteen months) in every aspect of her life and marriage.

The fact is, if you are reading this book, you are wanting to build, keep, or return to a great relationship. Your chances of having that great relationship are much better when you are able to define together what it will look like in your future.

Another reason expectations are higher is that today's couples value relationships and want to have a close one with their spouse. Empty nest marriages are held together from within—this goes to the very heart of the relationship—and when that relationship is not working, expectations are not met.

To a large degree, we are disappointed or satisfied in life depending on how well what is happening matches what we expected— what we think *should* happen. Therefore, expectations play a crucial role in determining our level of satisfaction in marriage. If we don't expect a lot, what actually happens may easily exceed our expectations. If we expect too much, it's likely that what happens will fall short of what we desire.

Consider Linda and Max. This marriage is the second one for both of them; they have been married just a year, and things have gone pretty well. Both sets of children are grown, and both Linda and Max are well established in their careers. However, Max is upset about Linda's nights out with the girls. Like many remarried couples, both partners bring plenty of baggage from their previous marriages and have a lot of expectations and issues to resolve about what's OK and what's not.

Linda goes out for dinner once a week with her longtime girlfriends. These friends were her major support group after her divorce from Fred and during her "parenting alone" years. Frankly, this drives Maxwell nuts. Sometimes the event of her going out with her friends triggers huge arguments between them, like this one.

MAX: *(feeling agitated)* I don't see why you have to go out again tonight. You've been out a lot lately.

LINDA: *(obviously irritated, and rolling her eyes)* How many times do we have to argue about this? I go out once a week and that's it. I don't see any problem with that.

MAX: Well, I do. All of your girlfriends are divorced, and I know they keep their eyes open for guys.

LINDA: So?

MAX: So they are looking for guys, and you're married.

LINDA: *(angered, feeling attacked and accused of being loose)* We don't go out hunting for guys. I don't like it that you don't trust me.

MAX: I just don't think a married woman needs to be out so often with her single friends. Guys notice a group of women, and you can't tell me your friends aren't interested.

LINDA: *(turning away and walking toward the door)* You sound jealous. I have to leave now; I'll be back by ten.

Linda and Max are arguing about an expectation. He didn't expect that she would still go out with her girlfriends so often after they got married. He associates their "going out" with being divorced and single, not being married. Linda expected to cut back time with friends, but not to stop seeing them altogether. These nights out mean a lot to her. She sees nothing wrong, except that Max isn't handling it very well.

In this example, you couldn't really argue that either expectation is outrageous. What is much more important is that their expectations don't match, and this is fueling some conflict. You can easily imagine that hidden issues of caring and control are also at work. Max could be wondering if Linda really cares to be with him, because she still wants to go out regularly with her friends. She could be feeling he's trying to control her, a feeling she does not respond to warmly.

Studies show that when expectations are quite unreasonable, it is more likely that the relationship will be distressed. Do you think Max's or Linda's expectations are unreasonable? Like any other couple, they will be far better off if they can bring this issue into a more open discussion of what each expects and desires and of what the two of them are going to do to handle these dynamics well.

EXPECTATIONS AND HIDDEN ISSUES

When hidden issues get triggered by events, it's really because some expectation was not met. Underlying *power* issues are expectations about how decisions and control will or will not be shared. Underlying *caring* issues are expectations about how one is to be loved. Underlying *recognition* issues are expectations about how your partner should respond to who you are and what you do. Underlying *commitment* issues are expectations about how long the relationship should continue and, most important, about safety from abandonment. Underlying *integrity* issues are expectations about being trusted and respected. And underneath all these expectations, there are core expectations about being *accepted* by your partner.

A hidden issue can't get triggered in the first place unless an expectation is violated. Consider Sean and Nancy. In the middle of a thunderstorm, Nancy told Sean to get off the phone—he could get struck by lightning. Sean reacted by telling her it was ridiculous to worry about being struck by lightning. In doing so, he violated Nancy's expectation of being listened to and taken seriously.

Conversely, when Nancy told Sean not to use the phone, she stepped on his expectation not to be told what to do. The clash of expectations about these most basic issues ignited conflict. It takes a lot of skill to keep such clashes from happening.

WHERE EXPECTATIONS COME FROM

Expectations build up over a lifetime of experiences. These expectations are based in the past but operate in the present. There are three primary sources for our expectations: our family of origin, our previous relationships, and the culture we live in.

Family of Origin

We learn many expectations from our families as we grow up. Our family experiences lay down many patterns—good or bad—that become models for how we as adults think things are supposed to work. Expectations were transmitted both directly by what our parents said and indirectly by what we observed. Regardless of where the expectations came from, we learned them in many areas of life. No one comes to marriage a blank slate.

For example, if you observed your parents avoiding all manner of conflict, you may have developed the expectation that couples should seek peace at any price. If there's disagreement and conflict in your marriage, it may seem to you as though the world is going to end. If you observed your parents being very affectionate, you may have come to expect this in your marriage. If your parents divorced, you may have some expectation in the back of your mind that marriages don't really last.

Pattie and Hayden are a couple who had terrible conflicts about how they should relate to their young adult children. Pattie came from a home where her mother and stepfather were very controlling and very involved in her life, even after she left home. She had attended a nearby college and came home every weekend. She was in daily phone contact with her mother.

Hayden came from a very loose-knit family in which the kids could pretty much do whatever they wanted, and the parents were basically uninvolved. When he left for college, he came home only on major holidays and for a brief visit in the summer.

With her background, Pattie expected to be very involved in the lives of their adult children. Her expectations were based on past patterns from her family of origin. If she didn't hear from their adult children at least once a week, she became concerned and would call them. Hayden saw Pattie's behavior as being overinvolved and meddling. He thought she was trying to be too involved in their lives—that she should back off and give them some room.

The couple's expectations became powerful filters, distorting their perception of what was really going on with the relationships with their adult children. Actually, Hayden, like his parents, cared about his kids—he just didn't want to be overinvolved or try to manipulate them. Pattie also cared about her kids; she didn't want to lose contact, and she thought Hayden didn't love them as much as she did.

As a consequence of their expectations, Hayden and Pattie had difficulty agreeing on how much contact to have with their adult kids. And looking to the future, what kind of expectations do you think their children will have when they are married and have adult children—that mothers meddle and fathers are distant? In this example, you can see how expectations get handed down from generation to generation.

If we had the space, we could give literally thousands more examples. Suffice it to say that we all have many expectations based on our families of origin. Understanding this basic fact is the first step to dealing more effectively with those expectations and preventing increased conflict.

Previous Relationships

You also have developed expectations from all the other relationships in your life—most important, from previous relationships or marriages. Think back to when you first married. You had expectations about how to kiss, what is romantic, how to communicate about problems, how recreational time should be spent, who should take the first move to make up after a fight, and so on.

Suppose, for example, that you found in previous relationships that when you began to open up about painful childhood events, you got dumped. Logically, you might have developed the expectation that such a topic is off-limits with certain people. On a deeper level, you may expect that people can't be trusted with knowing the deepest parts of who you are. If so, you'll pull back and withhold a level of intimacy in your present relationship.

Studies show that people who have come to expect that others can't be trusted have more difficulties in relationships. If you look at these people's entire lives, it will usually make sense why they have such an expectation. Yet it can lead to trouble if the mistrust is so intense that they can't even allow someone they really love—such as their partner—to get close. Such mistrust based on previous relationships makes it critical for you to learn how to make it safer for verbal intimacy in your empty nest relationship. We believe this is a time in life when you can develop an even closer, more personal marriage relationship.

One couple, Marcy and Jonathan, told us how expectations had become very difficult as they entered the empty nest stage of life. It was a second marriage for both. Not only did they have conflicts about the monetary needs of each other's children, who were in college, but they had a lot of difficulty handling expectations about which parent of which child was supposed to pay for which part of college expenses.

In contrast to Marcy and Jonathan's issue, many expectations are about such minor things that it's hard to imagine they could become so important—but they can. Whether they do depends on what meanings and issues are attached to the expectations.

For example, Ross, who just remarried in his fifties, told us that his first wife had drilled it into him that she didn't want him opening doors for her. He thought, "OK, no big deal." Now, with his present wife Suzanna, he was finding quite the opposite. She liked men to hold doors, and she'd get upset with him if he forgot. He had to work hard to unlearn the expectation he had finally learned so well.

Events of the door-opening variety happen pretty often in life. For Ross and Suzanna, they triggered conflict because she would interpret his trouble remembering as a sign that he didn't care about what was important to her. This is another example of negative interpretations causing more damage than the actual events. With his devotion challenged, Ross would get angry at her, which in turn just confirmed what she already believed: "I knew he didn't care."

Are you aware of how many expectations you have for your partner that are really based in experiences with others? It's worth thinking about; after all, your partner isn't the same person as those whom you have known, dated, or been married to in the past. It may not be realistic or fair to hold the same expectations for your partner that you had with someone else in the past.

Cultural Influences

There are a variety of cultural factors that influence our expectations. Television, movies, religious teachings, and what we read can all have powerful effects on our expectations.

What expectations would you have about marriage, for example, based on watching thousands of hours of TV in America? For most of us, this is not a hypothetical question. Shows like *Home Improvement, The Simpsons, The Cosby Show, Roseanne, Seinfeld, Everyone Loves Raymond,* and *Seventh Heaven*—not to mention the daytime soaps and talk shows—all send (or, in their day, sent) very powerful messages about what is expected and acceptable and what is not. Whether we agree with those messages or not, such TV shows offer powerful and influential opinions to society that may shape our expectations about marriage.

WHAT TO DO ABOUT EXPECTATIONS

Expectations that you hold for your empty nest marriage can lead either to massive disappointment and frustration or to deeper connection between the two of you. There are three keys to handling expectations well:

1. Being *aware* of what you expect
2. Being *reasonable* in what you expect
3. Being *clear* about what you expect

Being Aware of What You Expect

Whether you are aware of them or not, unmet expectations can lead to great disappointment and frustration in your relationship. You don't have to be fully aware of the expectation to have it affect your relationship.

Clifford Sager, a pioneer in this field, noticed how people bring to marriage a host of expectations that are never made clear. These expectations form a contract for the marriage. The problem is, people are not clearly informed of what's in the contract when they get married. Sager went further to suggest that many expectations are virtually unconscious, making it very hard to be aware of them. We don't mean to say that all expectations are deeply unconscious. But many do become such a part of us that they function automatically. Like driving a car, much of what we do is so automatic that we don't even have to think about it.

At the end of this chapter, you'll have the opportunity to increase your awareness of your own expectations for your marriage. One great clue to your own empty nest expectations is disappointment. When you're disappointed in your relationship, some expectation hasn't been met. It's a good habit to stop a minute when you are disappointed and ask yourself what you expected. Doing this can help you become aware of important expectations that otherwise may be unconsciously affecting your relationship.

Jarred and Dorian entered the empty nest when their eighteen-year-old son joined the marines. Over the years, Jarred enjoyed boating, and now that their son was gone, he assumed he and Dorian could enjoy boating together. But when Jarred asked his wife to go boating with him, she'd say, "That's OK, go ahead without me and have a great time." She preferred to stay home and garden. Jarred worked very hard during the week as a repairman, and boating was the greatest relaxation for him. Dorian didn't care for boating but really wanted Jarred to feel OK about having a nice time without her.

Jarred's sadness was a clue that there was some important expectation at work. In thinking about it, he realized that he had expected that once their son left home they would share this very important interest of his. If Dorian didn't, what did that mean? If nothing else, he felt torn between spending time with her and time on his boat.

Although Dorian loved Jarred dearly, the expectation or hope that she would suddenly become interested in his hobby once their son left stirred sadness for Jarred about deeper issues of wanting to feel cared for. Once he was aware of his expectation and the reasons for his sadness, he was able to express what boating with her meant to him. Dorian had had no idea. Although she didn't love boating, she was glad to come along once in a while now that she knew it meant so much to him.

A vast number of the couples responding to the Arps' survey mentioned a desire to travel together. This is clearly an expectation that cuts across many different types of empty next couples. Others are identifying new goals for this stage in their lives:

"Some quiet spontaneous times—be able to make love wherever, whenever, in the house without worrying about the kids—look forward to being playful again."

"Time to focus on each other, travel more, spend money on us, develop shared hobbies (if that is possible), minister together."

"Being together as much as we want, doing mutual things together, travel, volunteerism."

"A growing relationship/friendship."

"Better sex life, more companionship, shift in career focus."

Still others are acknowledging that as they grow aware of their expectations, they also become aware of a mismatch with their partners. One women wrote of her thirty-year marriage filled with conflict and ambivalence: "The only thing is simply enduring. In my lucid deep moments, I want to be heading into the kind of marriage God intends." Another, not yet as hopeless, wrote, "I would like to work together in some ministry, but this is not an interest to my husband. I'm going that way alone right now." Becoming aware of unmet expectations can be painful, but is a necessary first step in allowing any change to occur. After becoming aware of an expectation, you next need to consider whether your expectation is really reasonable.

Being Reasonable in What You Expect

As we noted earlier, many key expectations people have for the empty nest just aren't reasonable or realistic. Some unreasonable expectations are very specific. For example, is it reasonable to expect that now that the kids are gone, your partner will never seriously disagree with you? Of course not. Yet you would be surprised just how many people expect this.

Another example of an unreasonable expectation would be to expect that once you're in the empty nest, your partner will forsake all contact with old friends and focus on you. Some people actually expect things like this, but of course, the expectation is not very reasonable.

Acting on unreasonable expectations is likely to lead to conflict. A specific example of this is Norma and Bud, who have been empty nesters for two years. Both had high-pressure jobs in accounting, so it was very critical that they learn how to handle conflict and "free time" well.

In counseling, they made tremendous progress with all the techniques we presented in Part Two of this book. They were handling what had been significant conflicts far better than they ever had before. Unfortunately, their progress was held back by Bud's expectation that because they knew these techniques, they wouldn't have any more negative events. That's just not a reasonable expectation.

Meanwhile, Norma felt really unappreciated for all the efforts she had made to change the relationship. Bud's unreasonable expectation colored everything so that minor conflicts were seen as evidence that they hadn't made any progress at all. Not only did he expect they would no longer have conflict, but this expectation created a perceptual filter that caused him to miss all the great changes that were actually occurring.

We hope couples who consistently apply our principles will have fewer, less intense negative events. But events will always happen, and sometimes these events trigger issues. There's a difference between not having any issues and handling issues well. Bud's expectation led him to discount virtually all the striking changes that were occurring in his marriage. His expectation of no conflict was unreasonable and actually generated a lot of conflict until we pushed him to take a hard look at it. To overcome it, he had to become aware of the unrealistic expectation and challenge it within himself. It wasn't so much an expectation they needed to meet as one for Bud to change—and he did.

Being Clear About What You Expect

A specific expectation may be perfectly reasonable but never clearly expressed between mates. It is not enough just to be aware of your expectations or to evaluate their reasonableness: you must be able to express them. We all *tend* to assume that our model of the ideal empty nest marriage (made up of the sum total of our expectations) is the same as our partner's. Why should we have to tell him or her what we expect? In effect, we assume that our spouse knows what we expect.

This assumption is actually itself a kind of unreasonable expectation. You are assuming that your partner should know what you want, so you don't bother to make it clear enough. For example, how many people assume that their partner should know just what is most pleasing sexually? We see this over and over again. One or both partners are angry that the other is failing to meet a desire or expectation. But more often than not, they have never expressed their expectations. They are expecting their partner to be good at mind reading.

Worse, when one partner fails to read the other's key expectations, it is too easy for hidden issues to be triggered. Some couples feel stymied by the need to express themselves. One husband wrote in the survey, "We have differences in how we want to spend our time. No 'kid' buffer, and old resentments never worked through are resurfacing. We don't know what to talk about—lots of quiet." This couple understands the need to be clear with each other yet feels scared of actually trying to clarify expectations because of a fear of renewed conflict from the past. These hidden issues are filters and are causing further distortion in this relationship, long after the events occurred.

Many empty nest couples bring up the issue of retirement planning when they talk about expectations. Significant conflicts arise around financial planning, age differences that will lead to different retirement dates and stress caused when one partner is retired and the other working, and differences in expectations about retirement plans—travel, saving money, or spending on children and grand-children, for example.

Caring for an aging or ailing parent or parents was cited by many survey respondents as a major cause of stress in their relationships. Few mentioned any plan for dealing with the impact of this care-taking role.

For example, Martha and Ray had regular eruptions of conflict whenever they went to visit his mother, who lived in a retirement community with long-term health care. Since his dad's death, his mother had been more difficult to relate to. She was showing symptoms of early Alzheimer's disease, and Martha had the expectation that Ray would stay close by during visits. She didn't like being left alone in conversations with his mother. Ray often sensed that Martha was distant after visiting, but didn't understand why.

Martha's expectation for Ray to stay nearer when visiting his mother was perfectly reasonable. Yet until she told him that was what she wanted, he was left to his own assumptions. Once she expressed her real expectation, he could act on it to help her have a better time. Unless you both make your expectations clear, you'll have trouble working as a team. You can't work from any kind of shared perspective if you don't share your perspective!

People whose expectations are not perceived and met by their partner can easily come to believe that this means their partner does not care. This can cause particular problems in the physical relationship—something we will revisit in Chapter Thirteen.

*

You need to be aware of your expectations, willing to evaluate them, and willing to discuss them. Otherwise, expectations have the power to trigger all the biggest issues in your relationship. Without dealing with them openly, you also miss an opportunity to define a mutual vision of how you want your marriage to be.

The exercises we are about to present are among the most important in this book. It takes time to do them well. They also take considerable follow-up. We hope you can find the time and motivation to do the work. If you do, you will improve your understanding of mutual expectations. Combining that knowledge with the skills you are learning can have a major impact on the strength of your relationship—both now and into the future.

From the standpoint of giving you a lot to think about, we expect that this is one of the hardest chapters in this book. In addition to going carefully through the exercises, you might want to read the chapter over a time or two more. Really think through what your key expectations are for the empty nest and how they affect your relationship.

In Chapter Ten, we move on to the concept of commitment. This is a topic of great importance for relationships—one in which people have quite a few expectations.

EXERCISES

Use the exercises here to explore your expectations of your relationship in the empty nest years. Spend some time thinking carefully about each area and then write your thoughts down so that you can share them with your partner. Each of you should use a separate pad of paper. Each point here is meant to stimulate your *own* thinking. There may be numerous other areas about which you have expectations. Please consider everything you can think of that seems significant to you. You won't get much out of this exercise unless you are able and willing to really put some time into it. Many couples have found this type of exercise extremely beneficial for their relationship.

Getting to Know Your Expectations

The goal is to consider your expectations concerning how you want the relationship to be in the empty nest or how you think it should be, not how it is and not how you guess it will be. Write down what you expect, whether or not you think the expectation is realistic. The expectation matters and will affect your relationship whether it is realistic or not. Consider each question in light of what you expect and want for the future.

It is essential that you write down what you really think, not what sounds like the "correct" or least embarrassing answer. It also can be valuable to consider what you observed and learned in each of these areas in your family when you were growing up. This is probably the source of many of your beliefs about what you want or don't want.

Explore your expectations regarding the following areas:

1. The longevity of this relationship. Is it "Till death do us part"?
2. Sexual fidelity.
3. Love. Do you expect to love each other always? Do you expect your love to change over time?
4. Your sexual relationship. Do you hold any expectations about frequency? Practices? Taboos?
5. Romance. What is romantic for you?
6. Health issues.
7. Adult children.
8. Grandchildren.
9. Children from previous marriages. If you or your partner has children from a previous marriage, how do you expect your spouse to relate to them?
10. Work, careers, and provision of income. Will both of you continue to work in the future? Will one start back to work? Whose job or career is more important?
11. Retirement.
12. Travel.

13. The degree of emotional dependency on the other. Do you want to taken care of? How? How much do you expect to rely on each other to get through the tough times?

14. Basic approach to the empty nest and the second half of marriage. Will you work as a team? As two independent individuals?

15. How do you feel about the importance of keeping promises? How does that affect your feelings about your partner and your relationship?

16. Loyalty. What does that mean to you?

17. Communication about problems in the relationship. Do you want to talk these out, and if so, how?

18. Power and control. Who do you expect will have more power, and in what kinds of decisions? For example, who will control the money? What happens when you disagree in a key area? Who has the power now, and how do you feel about that?

19. Household tasks. Who do you expect will do what? How much household work will each of you do in the future? How does the current breakdown of tasks match up with what you ideally expect?

20. Religious beliefs and observances. How, what, when, where?

21. Time together. How much time do you want to spend together? Alone? With friends, at work, with extended family, and so on?

22. Sharing feelings. How much of what you are each feeling do you expect should be shared?

23. Friendship with your partner. What is a friend? What would it mean to maintain or have a friendship with your partner?

24. The little things in life. Where do you squeeze the toothpaste? Is the toilet seat left up or down? Who controls the remote? Who sends greeting cards? Really think about the little things

that could irritate or have irritated you (or have been going really well). What do you want or expect in each area?

25. Forgiveness. How important is forgiveness in your relationship? How should forgiveness affect your relationship?

Now, with your mind primed from all the work you have just done, consider again the hidden issues we described in Chapter Six. Do you see any other ways now that they influence or are influenced by your expectations? What do you expect in the areas of power, caring, recognition, commitment, integrity, and acceptance?

List any other expectations that you feel are important about how you want things to be in the empty nest and that did not appear in the foregoing list.

Determining Whether Your Expectations Are Reasonable

Now go back to each area listed in the previous exercise and rate each expectation on a scale of 1 to 10 for how reasonable you think it really is. On this scale, 10 means "Completely reasonable—I really think it is OK to expect this in this type of relationship"; 1 means "Completely unreasonable—I can honestly say that even though I expect or want this, it is not a reasonable expectation in this type of relationship." For example, suppose you grew up in a family where problems were not discussed, and you are aware that you honestly expect or prefer to avoid such discussions. You might now rate such an expectation as really not very reasonable.

Next, place a big check mark by each expectation that you feel you have never clearly discussed with your partner.

Sharing Your Expectations

After you and your partner have finished the exercises so far, begin to plan time and spend time together discussing these expectations. *Please don't attempt to do this all at once.* You should plan on a number of discussions, each covering only one or two expectations. We strongly recommend you use the Speaker-Listener Technique to facilitate these discussions.

1. Discuss the degree to which you each felt that the expectation being discussed had been shared clearly in the past.

2. Talk about the degree to which you both feel the expectations are reasonable or unreasonable, and discuss what you can agree to do about them.

3. Talk about what your overall, long-term vision is for the relationship. What expectations do you share about your future together?

10

Applying the Glue of Commitment

Most married couples consider commitment the glue that holds their relationship together. The kind and depth of your commitment has a lot to do with your chances of staying together and being happy in the second half of marriage. What better time to think about your commitment than when you are facing the empty nest? After all, your relationship is what sets the foundation of security for your future, and commitment is at the foundation of your relationship.

THE COMPLEXITY OF COMMITMENT

In this chapter, we explore the meaning of commitment, and focus on how to apply the major concepts of commitment to maintaining a healthy and long-lasting marriage. To begin, we discuss two empty nest couples in some detail. Both marriages reflect commitment, but the type of commitment is very different. As you read, notice the similarities and differences between the two marriages.

Charlie and Carolyn Falk: Ball and Chain

Charlie and Carolyn have been married twenty-nine years and have a twenty-four-year-old son, Michael, and a twenty-two-year-old daughter, Melissa. Melissa just graduated from college and accepted a job in another state. Michael is a computer programmer and is engaged to be married. Although both Charlie and Carolyn were eager to experience the empty nest, reality had not lived up to their expectations. Things got tough for them after Melissa left for college, and they have not gotten any better.

Initially, Charlie and Carolyn felt awkward without their daughter being around. The stresses of parenting adolescents left them feeling tired and distant, and in the empty nest their relationship became even more strained. Their communication became almost nonexistent. They had spent the last quarter of a century relating in thirty-second sound bites as they handed off car keys and scrambled to keep up with their children's hectic schedules. During those years, they neglected their own relationship. Now, spending an entire evening together without interruption seemed like a challenge rather than a treat. They have little in common, and they don't know how to redefine their relationship.

Soon after they entered the empty nest, Carolyn went back to work full-time and threw herself into her job as a nutritionist at a local assisted living health care center. At the same time, Charlie was talking about cutting back on his work hours and suggested they take some time off and travel. Carolyn wasn't interested.

Carolyn actually had considered divorce on more than a few occasions and increasingly finds herself thinking about leaving. Charlie also feels unhappy in the marriage but hasn't considered divorce as much. He hopes for more in the relationship and doesn't understand why Carolyn wants to spend so much time at her job. Although Charlie has become anxious that Carolyn might leave him now that the kids are gone, he has come to believe that any energy invested in the marriage is wasted effort. Tension between them continues to escalate.

Carolyn and Charlie work around others they find attractive. Brad is a single, good-looking man whose wife died of cancer a couple of years ago. He has made it clear he's interested in Carolyn. She's been seriously contemplating leaving Charlie for another man. She finds herself thinking more and more about it.

Carolyn feels that over the years she put more into the marriage than Charlie, and with little in return for her time and effort. She resents that he doesn't seem to appreciate all she's done for him in providing support, making a home, and taking care of the kids. Now that she is finally getting a chance to concentrate on her career, why can't Charlie be more supportive?

As Carolyn thinks about divorce, she grapples with difficult questions. First, she wonders how their adult children would respond to divorce. Would it hurt them? Would it be hard to get a divorce? Would Charlie try to stop her? How could she find a lawyer? Who would get the house? Could either of them afford to keep the house separate from the other?

As Carolyn considers these questions, she decides that the costs of getting a divorce may be greater than she wants to bear, at least for now. She's not happy in the marriage, but she balances this against the pain and stress divorce could bring. A dark cloud of despair hangs over her, and she feels trapped—wearing a ball and chain. Although staying isn't great, she decides at least for now that it's better than leaving.

Bruce and Amy Johnson: Full Commitment

Amy and Bruce were married twenty-seven years ago, and now their first grandchild is on the way. Although they have had their stressful times, they have few regrets about marrying one another. Having children turned out to be much more difficult than either imagined. They had great difficulty getting through the adolescent years. Their son went through a rebellious time, dabbling in drugs; for a while their relationship with him was quite rocky. Then their daughter got pregnant, and her boyfriend skipped town. Now she was having her baby and as a single mom would be looking to them for support. Despite the challenges, Amy and Bruce feel each other's support as they face life together.

They not only approach life as a team but also regularly do things that affirm their mutual dedication. They talk about what they want to do in the future, even looking toward retirement. They change their schedules to accommodate each other's needs. Each has resisted the temptation to dwell on "what ifs" when they were more frustrated in the marriage or with their children. Most important, they keep a clear emphasis on "we" as they go through life.

Everyone has regrets at times in marriage, but for Amy and Bruce, these times are few. They genuinely respect and like each other, do things for each other, and talk openly about what they want in marriage and life. Because of religious convictions, each resists thinking about divorce, even in the rough times. Each is willing to support the other in attaining what they desire in life. Simply put, they feel like a team.

*

The Falks and Johnsons have very different marriages. The Falks are pretty miserable, and the Johnsons are enjoying life. Both marriages are likely to continue for the time being—reflecting some kind of commitment. But it's not just the level of happiness that differentiates these two marriages. The Johnsons have a much different, fuller kind of commitment. To understand the difference, we need to better understand what commitment is all about.

WHAT IS COMMITMENT?

What do you think of when you think about commitment? There are two common ways to think about commitment. The commitment characterized by what we call *personal dedication* refers to the desire (and associated behaviors) not only to continue in the relationship but also to improve it, sacrifice for it, invest in it, link personal goals to it, and seek the partner's welfare, not just one's own.

In contrast, *constraint commitment* refers to forces that keep individuals in relationships whether or not they're dedicated. Constraint commitment may arise from either external or internal pressures. Constraints help keep couples together by making ending the relationship more economically, socially, personally, or psychologically costly. If dedication is low, constraints can keep people in relationships they might otherwise want to leave.

Carolyn and Charlie Falk have a commitment characterized by constraint. Carolyn in particular is feeling a great deal of constraint and little dedication. She feels compelled to stay in a dissatisfying marriage for a host of reasons: their adult kids, money, family pressure, and so on. Charlie also has high constraint commitment and little dedication, though he's less dissatisfied with their day-to-day life.

Like Carolyn and Charlie, Amy and Bruce Johnson have a good deal of constraint commitment, but they also have a strong sense of dedication to each other. Our research at the University of Denver shows that constraints are a normal part of marriage; they accumulate over time with the developmental changes marriages go through. For example, when couples go from being engaged to being married, the constraints increase. Likewise when they go from being married without children to being married with children. The point is that any marriage will generate a significant amount of constraint over time. Happier, more dedicated couples are just as likely to have considerable constraints as are less satisfied, less dedicated couples at similar points in life. Happier couples just don't think a lot about constraints, and when they do, they often draw comfort from them.

Let's look more closely at the composition of the glue that holds relationships together. We could spend some time looking further at constraints, but we won't. The reason is that although constraints are very important in the underlying stability of a marriage, they are not nearly as important to the ongoing *quality* of your marriage as dedication. Dedication is all about daily choices you make—choices that will greatly influence the kind of marriage you are going to have in the future.

THE COMMITMENT
OF PERSONAL DEDICATION

In this section, we talk about the most common features of dedication in strong relationships.

Desiring the long term refers to wanting the relationship to continue into the future: wanting and expecting your relationship to last, wanting to grow old together. It's a core part of dedication. This long-term expectation for the relationship to continue plays a critical role in

the day-to-day quality of marriage. One survey respondent wrote
that she and her husband look forward to "growing older gracefully
if possible and being able to stay in the home where we've lived all
of our married life. In fact, my husband was born there." These are
partners who really are thinking of their relationship in terms of
lifetimes. A thirty-nine-year-old woman in a stressful relationship
also wrote of the long-term view in her relationship, saying, "We've
been together since I was fifteen years old. I just don't remember life
without him." This is a motivating factor for her to work on resolv-
ing issues and keeping the marriage alive.

The priority of the relationship refers to the importance you give
your relationship relative to everything else. When people are more
dedicated to their partners, they are more likely to make decisions
in favor of the relationship when it competes with other things for
time and attention. In contrast, when dedication is weaker, the relationship is more likely to take a back seat to work, hobbies, kids,
and the like. To some degree, making the relationship a lower priority can reflect as much a problem with overinvolvement elsewhere
as with a lack of dedication. Unfortunately, as partners get busier
and busier, too many of them end up doing what Scott Stanley, in
his book The Heart of Commitment, called "no"-ing each other rather
than knowing each other: "No, I don't have time to talk tonight."
"No, I'm too tired to even think about making love tonight." "No,
I can't take Friday off to make it to the doctor appointment; I have
that project that has to be done." "No, I promised Dad I'd come
over Saturday and help him put up that new fence." To protect your
relationship at this crucial time of transition, you have got to get
good at saying no to some of the other things in your life that seem
important but really don't matter nearly as much in the long run as
your happiness together.

Unfortunately, the Falks have allowed their marriage to become
a low priority, and they're suffering for this. Their marriage isn't so
much bad as it is neglected. It's possible to turn their relationship
around. Amy and Bruce Johnson are truly important to each other.

There are times when Bruce feels that Amy is overly focused on their pregnant daughter, but he doesn't seriously doubt that he matters to his wife. Likewise, Amy sometimes thinks Bruce is too involved with work, but she recognizes his dedication to her.

We-ness refers to the degree to which couples view their relationship as a team rather than as two separate individuals focusing mostly on what's best for themselves. This has been called we-ness because *we* transcends *I* in the way couples think about their relationship. It's crucial for you to have a sense of an identity together if your relationship is to grow and be satisfying. Without this sense of being a team, you and your partner are more likely to come into conflict as problems pit one of you against the other instead of the two of you against the problem. Our research clearly shows that couples who are thriving in their marriages have a strong sense of "us."

We aren't suggesting that you should merge your identities and lose your individual sense of self. Rather, we're suggesting that most couples do best with a clear sense of being two individuals coming together to form a team. Dedicated couples experience this sense of being a team. Instead of each selfishly grappling to get his or her own way, both partners feel that the team's goals are at least as important as their individual goals. This makes a big difference in how you view life together. One couple wrote in the survey that the best part of their marriage was their "shared memories and experiences and the comfortableness of having resolved differences and stresses and survived together."

In the empty nest phase of marital life, this dimension of dedication takes on special importance. Your day-to-day sense of family changes dramatically through this period. For many couples, the children were the essence of the glue of their marriage, and now that their children are leaving home, their identity as a couple shifts. This shift can take partners one of a number of ways.

Melissa and Will had a pretty stable and harmonious life up until the time their youngest left home to take a job in another state. As a couple, they had done a wonderful job raising their children. They had given them what they needed, not just materially but also in terms of the less tangible blessings. They had been emotionally supportive, sensitive, and affirming in their children's development, but they had never developed a very strong sense of an identity as a couple.

As the children left home, they took with them the glue that had bound Melissa and Will together. The couple drifted for some time. There was increasing distance and conflict between them, and they began developing lives that were largely independent from each other. After a painful year of growing distance and a few discussions in which even divorce had been mentioned as a possibility, they decided to take control of the direction of their relationship and began to draw together. They became more active in deciding what kinds of things they wanted to share together and what ways they wanted to be together, developing a growing sense of "us" that surpassed anything they had experienced earlier in their lives. We-ness had never really been there very strongly, but that did not mean they had to live the rest of their lives that way.

Other couples have nurtured and protected their couple identity since the start. Although their identity surely included being parents together, that was not the central feature of their marriage. If you are such a couple, you will likely have an easier time with the transition to the empty nest than other couples, because your identity is not being so disrupted. Nevertheless, your lives are changing, and you can look at this time of life as an opportunity to openly discuss and plan for how you want to express your "we" in the years ahead.

Satisfaction with sacrifice is the degree to which people feel a sense of satisfaction in doing things that are largely or solely for their partners' benefit. The point is not to find pleasure in being a martyr but to find joy in an honest choice to give of yourself for your partner. Research indicates that people who are doing the very best in their marriages are those who feel the best about giving to one another—and they are also those who report that they would give up the most for their marriage and their partner. In these marriages, partners get pleasure from giving to one another. Relationships are generally stronger when both partners are willing to make sacrifices. In the absence of this willingness to sacrifice, what do you have? You have a relationship in which at least one of you is in it mostly for what you can get, with little focus on what you can give. That's not a recipe for happiness or growth.

Carolyn and Charlie Falk have stopped giving to each other. Charlie doesn't think he'll get anything back if he gives more, and Carolyn already feels she's given more than her share. Neither feels like sacrificing anything at this point. They've lost the sense of "us" that promotes giving to one another without resentment.

Looking for new partners refers to how much you keep an eye out for potential alternative partners. The more you are attracted to or attuned to other potential partners, the less your personal dedication to your current partner. Do you find yourself frequently or seriously thinking about being with people other than your spouse? We must emphasize *seriously*, because almost everyone is attracted to other people from time to time.

Dedication is in jeopardy if this attraction to others has become strong, especially if you have a particular person in mind. There is some research evidence that highly dedicated people actually mentally devalue attractive potential partners so as to protect their commitment to their partner. This is an attitude and behavior about which you have a choice. Bruce has been tempted a couple of times by people at work, especially by a woman named Libby. Although he is aware of the attraction, Bruce considered it a threat to his marriage and made himself focus more on Libby's negative aspects rather than dwell on her positives. Though tempted to look, he focused on why the grass *wasn't* greener on the other side of the fence. If you're planning on keeping your marriage strong, keep your focus on tending to your own lawn rather than yearning for the grass on the other side of the fence.

HOW DOES COMMITMENT DEVELOP?
HOW DOES DEDICATION DIE?

Dedication is believed to develop mostly out of the initial attraction and satisfaction in relationships. Think back about your relationship. Because you liked being together, you became more dedicated to staying together.

As your dedication to one another became more apparent, you may have noticed you became more relaxed about the relationship. In most relationships, there's an awkward period during which the desire to be together is great but the commitment unclear. The lack of clarity produces anxiety about whether or not you'll stay together. As your mutual dedication became clearer, the relationship seemed safer to invest in.

Because of your dedication, you made decisions that increased constraint. For example, as dedication grows, a couple will decide to go from a dating relationship to an engaged relationship. As dedication grows further, they decide to become married, buy furniture, buy a home, have children, and so on. Each of these steps, taken as a reflection of dedication, also adds to the constraint. Essentially, today's dedication becomes tomorrow's constraint. It's normal for levels of constraint to grow in marriage.

Greater dedication will usually lead to greater satisfaction, and dedication grows out of satisfaction in the first place. When truly dedicated, people are more likely to behave in ways that protect their marriage and please their partner, so the effect on satisfaction is very positive. It's very comforting to see that your mate really cares about you and protects your relationship from all the other options available.

If most couples have high levels of dedication early on, such as when they are engaged or newly married, what happens over time to kill dedication for some couples? For one thing, if a couple doesn't handle conflict well, satisfaction with the marriage will steadily decline. And because satisfaction fuels dedication, dedication begins to erode along with satisfaction. With dedication in jeopardy, the partners' desire to give to one another erodes further, and satisfaction takes a big dive. There is a downward spiral, and it bottoms out when unhappy couples hit the empty nest.

For some couples, their constraints are primarily related to the presence of their children, and when their children leave home, so does most of the glue holding the couple together. Even if such a couple does not break up, the erosion of commitment can lead to insecurity about the future that makes it far harder to work to make the marriage all it can be. Dedication erodes further when people feel their efforts no longer make a difference. We believe that nearly any empty nest couple will find real benefits in making special efforts to increase and demonstrate their mutual dedication to one another.

The secret to satisfying commitment is to maintain not just constraint but high levels of dedication. Although constraint commitment can add a positive, stabilizing dimension to your marriage, it can't give you a great relationship. Dedication is the side of commitment that is associated with great relationships. Dedicated couples report not only more satisfaction with their relationships but also less conflict about the problems they have and greater levels of self-disclosure. As one husband put it, he is looking forward to "seeing the love we started with and knowing where our love is now and anticipating how much more our love will grow!" In contrast, another husband, married for twenty-nine years, wrote in the survey, "We are both committed to preserving [the marriage], but I'm curious to see my spouse want to improve and mature it." Are you just existing in your relationship, or are you making it what you hoped it would be?

✳

Now that you have a better understanding of commitment, let's focus on how to apply some of this information to maintaining healthy and long-lasting marriages by considering the special topics of selfishness and the importance of the long-term view.

SELFISHNESS

Our culture encourages devotion to self. Notions of sacrifice, teamwork, and placing a high priority on one's partner and the dedicated
relationship have not enjoyed much positive press lately. In fact,
our society seems to glorify self and vilify whatever gets in the way.
And we all pay for these attitudes.

In contrast, we suggest that dedication is fundamental to healthy
relationships and that selfishness is fundamentally destructive. Selfishness may sell in our culture, but it doesn't bring lifelong happy
marriages.

*Dedication is more about being team centered or other centered than
about being self-centered.* To be team centered is to be sensitive to
your partner, to take your partner's perspective, to seek to build your
partner up, and to protect your partner in healthy ways, because you
are a team. It means making your partner's health and happiness a
priority. It means doing what you know is good for your relationship—such as listening to your partner—even when you don't particularly want to. It means protecting your commitment from
alternative attractions.

These acts of giving to one another are particularly crucial when
you are in a major transition, as you are when entering the empty
nest. Your life is in upheaval of a sort now, and it's going to be for
some time, as you adjust to this new stage of marriage. If your last
child is leaving the nest, this change in who you are as a couple is
really profound. It's the best possible time to demonstrate your commitment to one another through solid teamwork and active giving
of yourself to the other.

Selfish attitudes and behavior can and will kill a relationship.
Such attitudes aren't compatible with dedication. Dedication
reflects we-ness and, at times, sacrifice. You just can't have a great
marriage when each partner is primarily focused on what's best for
self. In a culture that reinforces self, it's hard to ask, "What can I do

to make this better?" It's a lot easier to ask, "What can my partner do to make me happier?"

We are *not* advocating martyrdom. In the way the term is commonly used, a martyr does things for you not out of concern for what is best for you but because he or she wants to put you in debt. That is not dedication. It's usually insecurity and selfishness masquerading as "doing good."

The key is to think about not only what you do for your partner but also why you do it. Do you do things with an attitude that says, "You'd better appreciate what I'm doing?" Do you often feel your partner owes you? There's nothing wrong with doing positive things and wanting to be appreciated. There is something wrong with believing you are owed, as if your positive behavior were building up a debt for your partner. The kind of deeply intimate, caring, and lasting marriages most people seek are built and maintained on dedication to one another expressed in the kinds of constructive behavior we advocate throughout this book. Too many people are self-centered so much of the time that they'll never truly experience the kind of relationship they deeply desire.

THE IMPORTANCE OF A LONG-TERM VIEW

At the heart of it, when people are committed, they have a long-term outlook on the relationship. This is crucial for one simple reason: *no relationship is consistently satisfying*. What gets couples through tougher times is the long-term view that commitment brings. There's an expectation that the relationship will make it through thick and thin.

We're not saying everybody should devote herculean effort to save their marriage, no matter how abusive or destructive. However, for the great number of couples who genuinely love each other and want to make their marriages work, a long-term perspective is essential for encouraging each partner to take risks, disclose about self, and trust that the other will be there when it really counts. In the absence of a long-term view, people tend to focus on the immediate payoff. This is only natural. If the long term is uncertain, we concentrate on what we are getting in the present.

What in Chapter Six we called the hidden issue of commitment is easily triggered when the future of the relationship is uncertain. When commitment is unclear, there is a feeling of pressure to perform, rather than one of *acceptance*—a core issue for everyone. The message is, "You'd better produce, or I'll look for someone who can." Most of us resent feeling we could be abandoned by someone from whom we expect to find security and acceptance.

Any major transition in life can raise issues that you thought were long settled. So much can change at once. If potential conflicts are not dealt with, such change can affect the quality and balance of your marriage. A great marriage is just not possible if the commitment becomes unsettled. People generally do not invest in a relationship with an uncertain future and reward. The Falks are held together mostly by constraint. There isn't the sense of a future together that comes from both dedication and constraint, and they are suffering greatly for it.

In contrast, other couples don't have the perfect marriage (who does?), but they have a strong expectation of a future rooted in balanced commitment. They talk about their plans for life together. They have maintained their commitment, especially their dedication. They do things for one another, show respect, and protect their marriage in terms of priorities and alternatives. Some survey couples put it in these ways: "I believe [my marriage] is solid and will survive any obstacles"; "We love each other and are committed to each other for the duration"; "We have a better understanding of each other. We look forward to some more years together . . . we have been married for forty-five years"; "I look forward to spending the rest of my life with my best friend." These couples all have a deep commitment to their marriage that is reflected in the way they think and talk about their relationship.

For these couples, the long-term view allows each partner to "give the other some slack," leading to greater acceptance of weaknesses and failings over time. Whereas the Falks experience anxiety or resentment around the core issue of acceptance, the Johnsons feel the warmth of a secure commitment—each conveying a powerful message to the other: "I'll be here for you." That's the essence of commitment. It is believing not only that you will be there for one another in the future but also that you can count on one another through the ups and downs of life.

Trashing the Long-Term View

Sometimes commitment becomes a weapon in a fight. Although Carolyn and Charlie Falk aren't going to get a divorce anytime soon, the topic sometimes comes up in bad arguments. Consider the following conversation, and its effects on trust, the balance of power, and commitment:

CHARLIE: Why does this house always look like a pigsty?

CAROLYN: Because we have two big dogs, and I'm at work every day.

CHARLIE: I end up having to clean up all the time, and I'm tired of it.

CAROLYN: Oh, and didn't I clean up all those years the kids were at home? Even now, when you're here, you usually disappear into your shop. I'm the one cleaning up constantly—not you.

CHARLIE: Yeah, yeah, I disappear all the time. You just don't give a care about this marriage. I don't even know why we stay together.

CAROLYN: Me neither. Maybe you should move out.

CHARLIE: Not a bad idea. I'll think about it.

At the end of the fight each was trying to convince the other they weren't committed. You can't get much more short term than to suggest divorce. If you're trying to keep your marriage on track, don't bring up the topic of divorce—period. Likewise, don't threaten to have affairs. Such statements trash the long-term view. They erode trust and reinforce the perception that it's risky for your partner to invest.

TAKE THE OPPORTUNITY
YOU HAVE NOW

In recent years, it has become and more popular for couples to reaffirm their love and commitment at some later point in life. Often such ceremonies are performed in religious services, much like many wedding services that begin marriages. Sometimes, many couples participate in the event together, making it an event in celebration of marriage and of the marriages of the couples who are publicly proclaiming their commitment. For some couples, such an event means they are declaring before others the reality of a commitment that has not wavered. For others, it means reclaiming what has weakened through a decision to renew personal dedication.

You may or may not like this idea of a rededication ceremony as it is most commonly done. You may not be religious, or you may simply be a very private person who does not care to engage in such public events. However, if you are both willing, you can plan some way of reaffirming the love and commitment that you started with, whether you've been married thirty years or two. If you are entering the empty nest, things are changing and will continue to change. What better time to reaffirm the core of what you do not want to have change: the foundation of your relationship?

Dave and Claudia reaffirmed their commitment to their marriage by spending a week in New England the year they entered the empty nest. You could go away someplace special, perhaps to a place with personal historical meaning, such as where you took your honeymoon. You could plan some ongoing activity that has great symbolic value to the two of you in the affirmation of your union. Dancing lessons? Commitment to some public service as a team?

We don't know what would be most meaningful to you, but if the two of you like this idea, putting a little thought into it will lead you to a plan that has great meaning for you both.

∗

When you boil it all down, commitment is about knowing you will be there for each other in the future and that you can count on one another in the present. There's no better time of life than now to do all you can to affirm your commitment to one another.

In Chapter Eleven, we look at the importance of shared core beliefs and how shared beliefs relate to the second half of marriage.

EXERCISES

There are several exercises to help you get the most out of this chapter. They give you the opportunity to examine your constraint and dedication commitment, consider your priorities, and think about a rededication of your devotion to one another.

Assessing Constraint Commitment

Jot down your answer to each item using the following scale to indicate how true the statement seems to you: 1 = Strongly disagree, 4 = Neither agree nor disagree, and 7 = Strongly agree.

1. The steps I would need to take to end this relationship would require a great deal of time and effort.

1   2   3   4   5   6   7

2. A marriage is a sacred bond between two people that should not be broken.

1   2   3   4   5   6   7

3. I would have trouble finding a suitable partner if this relationship ended.

1   2   3   4   5   6   7

4. My friends or family really want this relationship to work.

1   2   3   4   5   6   7

5. I would lose valuable possessions if I left my partner.

1   2   3   4   5   6   7

6. I stay in this relationship partly because my partner would be emotionally devastated if I left.

1   2   3   4   5   6   7

7. I couldn't make it financially if we broke up or divorced.

1   2   3   4   5   6   7

8. My lifestyle would be worse in many ways if I left my partner.

1   2   3   4   5   6   7

9. I feel trapped in this relationship.

1   2   3   4   5   6   7

10. It is important to finish what you have started, no matter what.

1   2   3   4   5   6   7

Your answers to these few questions can tell you a lot. What constraints are you aware of? How powerful are these constraints? What kind of constraint seems most powerful?

Most important, do you feel trapped or stuck? It is normal to feel this way from time to time; just about everyone does. Having a good deal of constraint but not feeling trapped is normal in a healthy couple relationship. The best relationships are those in which both partners are dedicated to each other and feel comfortable with the stability implied by constraint.

Assessing Dedicated Commitment

These next items will help you gauge your level of dedication. Use the same rating scale you used to examine constraint commitment: 1 = Strongly disagree, 4 = Neither agree nor disagree, and 7 = Strongly agree. Jot down your responses on a separate piece of paper.

1. My relationship with my partner is more important to me than almost anything else in my life.

1   2   3   4   5   6   7

2. I want this relationship to stay strong no matter what rough times we may encounter.

1   2   3   4   5   6   7

3. It makes me feel good to sacrifice for my partner.

1   2   3   4   5   6   7

4. I like to think of myself and my partner more in terms of "us" and "we" than of "me" and "him [or her]."

1   2   3   4   5   6   7

5. I am not seriously attracted to anyone other than my partner.

1   2   3   4   5   6   7

6. My relationship with my partner is clearly part of my future life plans.

1   2   3   4   5   6   7

7. When push comes to shove, my relationship with my partner comes first.

1   2   3   4   5   6   7

8. I tend to think about how things affect us as a couple more than how things affect me as an individual.

1   2   3   4   5   6   7

9. I don't often find myself thinking about what it would be like to be in a relationship with someone else.

1   2   3   4   5   6   7

10. I want to grow old with my partner.

1   2   3   4   5   6   7

We can give you an idea of what your score means on these dedication items. To calculate your score, simply add up your ratings for each item. In our research—with a sample of people who were mostly happy and dedicated in their relationships (including couples who had been married for over thirty years)—the average person scored about 58 on the items in this scale. If you scored at or above 58, we'd bet you're pretty highly dedicated. Your dedication may be quite low if you scored below 45. Whatever your score, think about what it may mean for the future of your marriage.

Considering Priorities

An important way to look at dedication is to consider your priorities. How do you actually live your life? What does this say about your commitment?

Take a piece of paper you can divide into three columns. In the first column, list what you consider your top five priorities in life, with number one being the most important. Possible priority areas might include work and career, your partner, adult children, religion, house and home, sports, future goals, education, possessions, hobbies, pets, friends, relatives, coworkers, television, and car. Feel free to list whatever is important to you. Be as specific as you can. Now, in the second column, list what you think *your partner* would say are your top five priorities. For example, if you think your partner would say that work is your top priority, list that as number one. In the third column, list what you believe are *your partner's* top five priorities.

When both of you have completed your lists, compare them. Don't be defensive. Consider how the answers each of you have given affect your couple relationship. If you see a need to make your relationship a higher priority, talk together about specific steps you can take to make this happen. You might find it helpful to use the problem-solving process you learned in Chapter Seven. Part Four of this book, on enhancing your relationship, will provide additional suggestions of ways to make your relationship a higher priority.

Rededication of Your Devotion

The idea we raised near the end of the chapter may not be for everyone, but we want to encourage the two of you to consider whether or not you can work out something that would be right for you both. If you are open to the basic idea, don't try to come too quickly to a decision about how to enact it. Plan some time for brainstorming. Come up with all the ideas you can, and see what jumps out at you. You may find that several ideas have real meaning and appeal. You could plan to do a number of them!

11

Core Beliefs and Developing
Spiritual Intimacy

I n Chapters Nine and Ten, we focused on how understanding
expectations and deepening your commitment to each other can
enhance your relationship in the empty nest. Now we look at how
your core beliefs affect your relationship. Stop and consider what
you believe about life's core issues. Your core beliefs influence all
dimensions of your life and are played out daily in the values you
hold and the choices you make. What are your beliefs about life,
death, marriage, family, God or a higher being, prayer or medita-
tion, and so on? Consider your core relationship values. How much
value do you place on commitment, respect, intimacy, and forgiveness? Do the two of you share the same worldview?

Because the spiritual or religious realm reflects one's core belief
system, we will use core beliefs as the focus for much of what we
have to say. Although not everyone is religious or spiritually
inclined, everyone does have a core belief system. In addition, people tend to get more religious or spiritually inclined as they age—
perhaps because death gets closer. This tendency appears to be more
common for women than for men, which means that some partners
in marriage grow further apart spiritually later on than they were
when they started. For others, the challenges of life can change perspectives on religious or spiritual issues. So what looks unimportant
early in life can, for some couples, become more of an issue in the
empty nest.

If you aren't religious or spiritually inclined, you may be skeptical about the relevance of what we have to say. Or, if you're very committed to your faith, you may see this chapter as too broad or "watered down" in its approach. Whatever your persuasion, however, we invite you to explore your own core beliefs and consider the impact they may have on your marriage. We also hope this chapter will point the way for you and your partner to have some intimacy-enhancing discussions about your values and belief systems.

Because most of the relevant research has been conducted with a focus on religion, we'll look at the key implications of research findings that relate to all couples who want to build a better marriage. Then we ask you to consider these implications in light of your own beliefs. Let's start with some definitions.

Webster's New World Dictionary defines *spiritual* as "of the spirit or the soul"—*spirit* having several definitions, including "the life principle," "life, will, consciousness, thought, etc., regarded as separate from matter," and "essential or characteristic quality." Hence, the spiritual can be taken to pertain to the essence of the inner person, the core of the individual's life.

Religion is defined as "any specific system of belief, worship, conduct, etc., often involving a code of ethics and a philosophy." A recent participant in one of our training workshops for professionals put it this way: "Religion is typically a structure in which people express their spirituality." In religion, people find, among other things, codes and rituals—structures—that guide them in life. Hence, for many people, though not all, their religious faith embodies central, core beliefs about life, its meaning, and how one should live. Issues of the spirit are considered primarily in the religious domain for many people, whereas others hold views of spirituality quite apart from any particular religious tradition.

Most of the research we describe in this chapter is related to religious beliefs and practices rather than to spirituality. That's because you can't conduct research on things you can't measure—and although it isn't hard to measure religious activity or even core beliefs, it is extremely difficult to measure spirituality. We're not saying spirituality isn't important; it's just that most of the research is on religious behavior.

RESEARCH ON RELIGIOUS INVOLVEMENT

The impact of religion on marriage has been studied for years. Most of this research has been conducted with those involved in traditional religious systems, particularly within the Judeo-Christian spectrum. Even if you may not follow one of those traditions, the implications derived from these studies can benefit all couples. That's because many religions codify core beliefs, values, and practices that promote stability and health in relationships. Our goal here is to decode these findings and highlight key implications for all empty nest couples, religious or not. We do know that as people grow older they tend to become more introspective and ask more questions about life. Discussions of your core beliefs can enhance the level of intimacy between the two of you. You may have assumed for some time that you know what your partner thinks and believes about the big issues of life, but what better time of life than the empty nest years to explore what each of you thinks?

Numerous studies suggest that religion has a favorable impact on marriage. For example, couples who are more religious tend to be a bit more satisfied in their marriages. They're also less likely to divorce. In one of our studies, married subjects who rated themselves as more religious showed somewhat higher levels of satisfaction, lower levels of conflict about common issues, and higher levels of commitment. Other studies have shown an edge for religious couples in sexual and sensual satisfaction.

Our own research has shown that those who are more religious, especially those who are conservative in faith, were more likely to say that divorce is wrong. They also were more likely to believe that if they had problems, there would be significant social pressure for staying together and making the marriage work. They were more likely to report being satisfied in sacrificing for one another and having a stronger sense of couple identity. These findings make sense, considering the values that are emphasized in traditional religious groups.

For some couples, differences in core beliefs have caused conflicts for years. One study showed that although couples who attend religious services more often are less likely to divorce, couples are actually more likely to divorce if one partner attends a great deal and the other hardly at all. Many couples echo the following concern, written by a woman married thirty-one years, "Maybe we are both committed [because we] don't believe in divorce . . . [but we have] religious conflict—husband wants to worship at a different denomination than wife." Often, conflicts in this area are especially intense for couples while they are raising their children, the conflicts revolving around what the children should be taught. If that has been the case for you, it is possible that those differences between the two of you could become much less threatening. In fact, you might even find that you could enjoy talking about what you believe at this point in life as an aspect of your friendship together.

We want to be clear, though. It's not that more religious couples have substantially better marriages according to marital research. The effects in most of the studies we're talking about are consistent and statistically significant, but the differences are also often rather small. The exception to this is in cases of marriages in which both partners not only share similar core beliefs but also are involved together in the activities of their faith (prayer, attending services, attending retreats together, reading and talking together about spiritual things, and so on). These kinds of joint religious and faith activities tend to be strongly associated with marital quality.

Overall, it would be most accurate to say that something about the factors associated with religious involvement gives couples an edge in keeping their marriages strong. Considering the increasing empty nest divorce rate, there are concepts worth considering that you can learn from these studies, even if you are not religious.

To summarize, here's what the findings about the religious influence on marriage indicate. Couples who are more religiously inclined and from the same faith backgrounds appear to have an edge in maintaining satisfying marriages and avoiding divorce. We would now like to offer an analysis of why this might be so, in hopes of stimulating you to consider how to strengthen your own relationship.

Because this is a secular book, we'll focus our understanding on pretty down-to-earth explanations, though we recognize that some of you may also consider more spiritual explanations for such effects. So in our attempts to decode the research for all couples, we focus on two key factors: (1) the value of social support for your relationship and (2) the effect of having a shared worldview. Let's look at these in detail.

SOCIAL SUPPORT

Aside from whatever else they do, religious and spiritual beliefs bring groups of similarly minded people together. There's a clear benefit for most people in being part of a social group—religious or not—as long as the people have a clear sense that they belong or "fit" into the group. In fact, research by our colleague Ken Pargament has found that church and synagogue members who fit well into their religious community have higher levels of mental health than those who don't.

Studies have consistently shown that people who are more isolated are at greater risk for emotional problems such as depression and suicide, health problems, and poverty. Many studies in the field of stress management demonstrate how much more vulnerable you are if you have significant stressors but no social support system to help you. It's just not healthy for most humans to be isolated. To paraphrase John Donne, "No person is an island."

Religious involvement brings ready-made social structures. Religions specify codes of behavior and rituals, many of which create natural points of connection between those involved. For example, most religious and spiritual groups meet regularly for numerous kinds of activities. Spiritual activities include worship, prayer, reading, study, discussion groups, and so forth. Social activities can include coffee hour, ice cream socials, picnics, group outings, get-together dinners, softball leagues, and about anything else you can think of. Service activities are also common, including food drives, visiting shut-ins, ministries of service to disadvantaged groups, community outreach, volunteer work, support groups, and the like. Such social links to a community are important for most couples.

For example, William and Sandra are a couple in their fifties who met in an adult class at the church where they later got married. They had been involved in the same church for many years with their previous spouses, who are both deceased. So when they married, it was natural to invite the entire church as well as friends and family to their wedding. The turnout was large, and the outpouring of support very clear. They didn't get married just in front of friends but in front of a whole community that knew them, supported them, and would be regularly involved in their lives.

As you can imagine, such a couple has a tremendous support system. Their relationship is supported and encouraged in the social network and by teachings that place great value on marriage and commitment—especially dedication.

Of course there are other ways people get together in our culture: neighborhood get-togethers, political groups, interest groups, sports, support groups, clubs, and so on. Our point is that it is important for all couples to have a strong support system for their relationships. Are you socially connected to a group that supports and somehow helps your relationship? If not, do you want to be? These are important questions for you and your partner to address directly. (Please see Resources and Training at the back of this book for information about small-group curricula especially crafted for empty nest couples.)

SHARED WORLDVIEW

Now we turn to other key implications of the research we have described. When you consider the spiritual or religious realm, you are dealing with core beliefs about your worldview—in other words, how you make sense of all of life. Everyone has some explanation for the big questions, whether complex or simple, religious or not. Hence, everyone has some core belief system. When you, as a couple, share such a belief system, you have a shared worldview.

Many successful long-term marriages have partners who share a worldview. Fran Dickson, a communication expert at the University of Denver, has conducted studies that show that couples who have stayed together for fifty years have a shared relationship vision that includes personal dreams and goals for the future. When there's a shared belief system—including a mutual understanding about the meanings of life, death, and marriage—it's likely to be easier to develop a vision for your relationship. In turn, having a vision for your relationship helps nurture the long-term view of commitment.

In most religions, there is a common understanding of, and language system for thinking and talking about, core beliefs. So another explanation for the benefit of religious involvement is that these couples have a belief system that facilitates developing and maintaining the shared worldview. Spilka, Gorsuch, and Hood, experts in the study of religion, put it this way in their book, *The Psychology of Religion* (1985, Prentice Hall): "Since it is fairly likely that the religious feelings of spouses tend to be similar, among the more religious, who probably come from religious homes, there may be a *supportive complex of perceptions* leading to increased marital satisfaction" (p. 105, emphasis added). That is, a shared worldview.

It is important for both of you to consider the impact of your worldviews on your marriage. Before the empty nest, you had your kids in common. You could always talk about and focus on their activities and interests. Then comes the empty nest, and if your nest is healthy, your children are no longer the primary focus. Now it's time to focus on your own dreams and goals for the future. How are you handling your similarities and differences in views? Think about this question as we look at two specific areas in which your worldview affects your marriage: core relationship values and expectations.

Core Relationship Values

Let's focus on four key values that are emphasized in many belief systems—values with obvious positive implications for marriages and other significant relationships: commitment, respect, intimacy, and forgiveness. When you and your partner have similar core belief systems, it is likely you have a similar understanding about these values and how you can give life to them in your marriage.

Commitment in various aspects is greatly emphasized in many belief systems, in terms of both dedication and constraint. Although there are great differences among belief systems about the morality of divorce, there would be wide agreement across beliefs about the value of commitment in general. Long-term relationships need a sustained sense of commitment. One survey respondent, married twenty-eight years, wrote, "Our spiritual commitment and commitment to each other gets us through the hard times."

Respect is a core value emphasized in most religious and spiritual groups. Although various religions hold to specific beliefs that others may reject, most systems emphasize the value and worth of others. Respect is a core need of all people, and as a couple, you need to share a value system that strongly emphasizes respect for each other.

In Part Two we talked about how you can show respect for one another in how you communicate—validate each other—even if you have significant disagreements and differences. You show interest in and respect for your partner even when you see things quite differently. You can't have a good relationship without basic respect.

Intimacy is prized in most religious and spiritual systems. Although various systems may understand the idea differently, intimacy is usually emphasized and encouraged, especially in marriage.

All the traditional religious systems in Western cultures seem to place a high value on marriage and the relationship between the two partners.

Couples in the empty nest especially need to have clear ways to protect, preserve, and enhance intimacy. Many couples responding to the survey wrote of their belief that the answer to emotional distance was "growing together spiritually," as one husband, married twenty-eight years, put it. Another person wrote, "We pray together daily, and there is precious intimacy available in and through this area." "Reconciliation and restoration of intimacy" was the hope of one husband, married fifteen years.

Forgiveness is a core theme for relational health. Long-term, healthy relationships need an element of forgiveness. Otherwise, emotional debts can be allowed to build in ways that destroy the potential for intimacy and teamwork. That's why we began this book by looking at the restorative power of forgiveness. Forgiveness is the oil that lubricates a love relationship. Marriages—especially in the empty nest—need generous amounts of the oil of forgiveness to stay healthy and growing.

Expectations

Another way in which your worldview can significantly affect your marriage in the second half is in shaping your expectations regarding such areas as relationships with adult children, grandchildren, in-laws, and aging parents; personal health; intimacy; retirement issues; economic lifestyle; and redefining marital roles and career goals. This aspect of your worldview can have very significant implications for the day-to-day quality of your marriage.

The potential for differences in expectations to spark conflict is so great that we spent an entire chapter (Chapter Nine) encouraging you to make such expectations clear, regardless of where they came from. When two people share a perspective on key relationship expectations, they are going to have an easier time negotiating life. Shared expectations lead to shared rituals and routines that guide couples more smoothly through the transition to the empty nest and through the other transitions and trials of life.

In religious systems, such expectations tend to be very clear and codified in the beliefs and rituals, which encourage a shared world-view in terms of everyday events. This could explain, in part, the research findings showing that more religious couples and those with more similar belief backgrounds have a somewhat easier time in marriage. Sharing a structured belief system brings a clarity about many expectations—expectations that therefore don't have to be worked out or negotiated. Presumably, couples who aren't religiously involved could derive this same benefit if they share some philo-sophical view that makes it easier to maintain a shared view on expectations.

Three Types of Couples

Whatever your backgrounds and beliefs, you shouldn't take these things for granted in your relationship. You need to identify key similarities and differences in your viewpoints and talk about them in ways that help you work together as a team. Let's look at three different types of couples before we recommend some exercises for you to do.

Type 1: Shared View

For many empty nest couples, their similar core beliefs lead to a lower likelihood of conflict for the various reasons we have outlined. There is simply less to work out in all sorts of areas. However, all couples still must clarify key expectations regarding how they will handle various marital challenges of the empty nest. It's best when any differences in expectations are discussed early in a relationship so that you can make the decisions that form the "default settings" for your empty nest relationship. These defaults are basic agree-ments about how you will handle various things, so that you aren't constantly adjusting to differences in worldview in the context of events. Many couples wrote in the survey that sharing the "same belief and value system" was a strength of their marriage.

Type 2: Nonshared But Respected Views

For couples in this kind of relationship, there is a significant difference of opinion on core beliefs, but the partners handle the differences with respect. The differences don't produce alienation and may, in fact, be a source of intimacy if the spouses are able to enjoy the exchange of different perspectives. One woman, married twenty-three years, put it best: "We're at such different places in our spiritual journey, but I've learned that I can't coerce my husband to attend or do something that I know he will not enjoy. I finally realized that one of the privileges of marriage is we don't have to settle theological issues."

For a couple to accept each others' differing views, the partners would need at least two things: (1) the skills needed to maintain respect in light of the differences and (2) enough personal security about the core beliefs not to be overly threatened by the absence of agreement. For these couples, their views and expectations aren't shared in the sense of being similar but can be shared in the sense that there is open expression that doesn't trigger hidden issues of acceptance.

Type 3: Nonshared Views with Conflict

These partners don't share the same perspective, and this sparks conflict—especially in the empty nest—that is generally not handled well. Such couples aren't able to talk freely about differences in views and maintain mutual respect at the same time. Either they argue unpleasantly about the differences or avoid talking about them. It is easy to trigger hidden issues of basic acceptance. The differences in core beliefs become a barrier; the partners are unable to share openly about their perspectives on the deepest issues of life. A wife married thirty-two years wrote in the survey, "[The marriage] could be so much more than there is. I've felt for a long time God wants to use us together—won't happen if nothing changes." She continues, "I want a breakthrough in the emotional distance between us . . . being the couple God wants us to be."

Key life transitions—such as moving into the empty nest—have a habit of bringing us more in touch with our core beliefs. In fact, we'd suggest that having a shared worldview is most beneficial to your relationship when you are going through such major life transitions. At those times, a similarity in core beliefs guides you through with less stress and disruption. These transitions would also be the times when having social support is most critical. Without the shared view, the next best thing you can do is to be clear about your expectations and agree how you will proceed as a couple. Anticipate the key transitions of life so that you can talk together about how you will handle things.

*

In summary, you and your partner may come from different perspectives, even if you were raised similarly. When you think about religious and spiritual differences, a lot is at stake. Likewise for any core belief system, such as a philosophy of life. Everyone believes something, and it is unlikely that there is a couple in which both partners line up perfectly on these dimensions.

The point here is that you need to grapple with the effects on your relationship. The exercises for this chapter are designed to help you do just that—grapple. We want you to explore your beliefs on religious or spiritual dimensions and talk them over together.

Exploring and sharing clearly what you believe and expect about some of these key questions of life can be an enriching if not eye-opening experience in your relationship. Talking about these issues with respect can be a very intimate experience. Try it and see what we mean.

In Chapter Twelve, we discuss the challenges of balancing the generational seesaw with adult children and possible grandchildren on one end, aging parents on the other end, and your marriage in the middle!

EXERCISES

There are three exercises for this chapter. They parallel the key themes we used to explain the research findings regarding the impact of religion and spiritual values on relationships. First, you will consider what your core values are, where they come from, and how they affect your marriage. Second, you will take stock of your social support system. Third, you will explore your core belief systems and the expectations specifically related to them. You will each need a separate pad of paper to do these exercises.

Thinking About Core Values

We'd like you to consider what your core values are in life. What values are central for you? Where did these values come from? Spend some time alone thinking about these questions. Jot down some notes on your ideas. Then share with each other what you've been thinking about. As always, we encourage you to use the Speaker-Listener Technique to facilitate your discussion.

You may have some additional ideas after you work on the other exercises. In addition to other ideas that come up for you, specifically discuss together your views of the core relationship values mentioned in this chapter: commitment, respect, intimacy, and forgiveness. What is your view of these values?

Discussing Social Support

Talk together about your social support system. Do you have a strong system—people to rely on, to encourage you, to hold you accountable at times? Are you involved in a community that supports and nurtures your growth in your marriage? Do you want to be? What could you do as a couple to build up more support if you see the need to do that?

Exploring Core Beliefs

Now we want you to explore on your own and, later, share with your partner issues relevant to your core belief system. For many people, their religious faith or spiritual orientation reflects or determines their core philosophical, moral, and cultural beliefs and practices. If that's the case for you, it will make the most sense to answer these questions in that light. For others, these questions may seem related less to religion and more to philosophy.

Whether your core belief system is based in spiritual or religious beliefs or other philosophies of life, it can be very important for you and your partner to understand each other's core beliefs. This exercise will help you accomplish this goal. It is very much like what you did in the chapter on expectations, but this exercise is focused on the area of core belief systems.

The following questions are designed to get you thinking about a broad range of issues related to your beliefs. There may be other important questions that we have left out, so feel free to answer questions we haven't asked. Write down an answer to each question as it applies to you. Doing so will help you think more clearly about the issues and will also help you when it comes time to talk with your partner about them.

As you think about and answer each question, it can be especially valuable to note what you were taught as a child versus what you believe or expect now as an adult.

Questions for Reflection

1. What is your core belief system or worldview? What do you believe in?

2. How did you come to have this viewpoint?

3. In your core belief system, what is the meaning or purpose of life?

4. What was your belief growing up? How was this core belief practiced in your family of origin? Through religious practice? Or in some other way?

5. Do you make a distinction between the spiritual and the religious? What is your view on these matters?

6. In your belief system, what is the meaning of marriage?

7. What vows did you say? How do these tie into your belief system?

8. What is your belief about divorce? How does this fit in with your belief system?

9. How do you practice your beliefs as part of your relationship? (This could mean religious involvement, spiritual practices, or other activities, depending on your belief system.) How do you want to practice your beliefs in the future?

10. What do you think should be the day-to-day impact of your belief system on your relationship?

11. Are there specific views on sexuality in your belief system? What are they? How do they affect the two of you?

12. Do you give financial support to a religious institution or other effort related to your belief system? How much? How do you decide to what and whom to give? Do the two of you generally agree?

13. Do you see potential areas of conflict regarding your belief systems? What are they?

14. What do you believe about forgiveness in general? How does forgiveness apply in a relationship such as the one with your partner?

15. In your belief system, what is your view of your responsibility to parents as they age and develop health problems?

16. How do you observe religious holidays? What has changed since your kids left home? How might this change when your children marry and have children of their own?

17. In your belief system, what is the basis for respecting others?

18. Are there any other questions you can think of and answer?

After you and your partner have finished the entire exercise, begin to plan time and spend time together discussing these expectations. You should plan on a number of discussions. Discuss the degree to which you each feel the expectation had been shared clearly in the past. Use the Speaker-Listener Technique if you would like some additional structure to deal with these sometimes difficult issues.

Regarding any expectations that come up, talk out the degree to which you both feel they are reasonable or unreasonable, and discuss what you want to agree to do about these.

12

Relating to Adult Children and Aging Parents

Someone once said, "Life is an opportunity for every person to create a new story that can be passed along to the next generation." Sounds lovely, but it's not that simple to do! In our empty nest survey, when we asked what was putting the most stress on their marriage, participants often responded with a comment about their adult children.

One wife wrote how hard it was to "let go" of her adult daughter. Another mentioned the stress of dealing with her "fragile adult child." Still another survey participant wrote, "Our twenty-three-year-old son is unemployed and living with us." A husband responded, "My daughter is going through a divorce and needs our support." Another wife wrote, "I looked forward to the empty nest, but now I spend every weekday caring for my two-year-old grandson while my daughter works. Where is all that time my husband and I were supposed to have to travel together and to enjoy our empty nest?"

Many respondents also reported stress related to difficulties with their aging parents—sometimes combined with their children's problems. "The greatest stress in my marriage," one participant wrote, "is being caught between our twenty-year-old son who makes such foolish choices, and my elderly mom, who just had a hip replacement and needs extra care. After dealing with my son and trying to help Mom, I have no time and energy left to invest in my marriage. I thought the empty nest was supposed to be empty!"

"Whatever I do for my parents, I can never meet all of their expectations," responded a wife who had been married for thirty years. A husband wrote, "We're draining our savings, caring for my wife's mother and my ailing dad. I don't know what we will do in our old age unless our kids take care of us."

Other comments like these confirm that intergenerational stress is a major issue in the second half of life. How can you build your marriage in the middle of family pressure—adolescent or adult children and maybe even grandchildren on one end, aging parents on the other? You love them, but you also love your spouse. How can you find balance?

BALANCING THE GENERATIONS

If you are part of the sandwich generation, how can you cope? Maybe you keep waiting for your nest to empty, and it's not happening. Did you realize that of unmarried American men between the ages of twenty-five and thirty-four, more than one-third are still living at home? Even if your children have left the nest, your love and concern for them never empties out. Or sometimes the nest refills, when children return and perhaps bring spouses and grandchildren to live with you. Or just as your kids move out, an elderly parent moves in.

Today it's not unusual for couples to have teenage children and elderly parents all living under the same roof. One reason for this trend is that some couples are waiting later to have their families, so at the traditional "empty nest" time of life, they are still parenting their children. This becomes more complicated when, at the same time, their own parents are aging and may be experiencing health problems. One wife, married twenty-three years and the mother of two teenagers, is experiencing intergenerational stress that is affecting her marriage. She wrote:

I just don't have time to even think about my marriage. My thirteen-year-old son is driving me crazy. He's not doing well in school—just doesn't seem to care. And my mom just had gall bladder surgery and will be staying with us when she gets out of the hospital. I'm an only child, so there's no one else to care for her. Yesterday after a conference with my son's teacher and hearing about how terrible he was doing, I raced to the hospital to be with my mom during her surgery. I really don't know how I will manage with Mom with us. She gets really nervous when there's noise and confusion around, and with two teenagers, that's a given. Sometimes, I want to run away from home—but I can't, I'm supposed to be the responsible adult.

How can this wife find balance and fight for her marriage in the middle of all this stress? Are you in a similar situation? Are intergenerational stresses affecting your marriage? First, you must understand that each generation, from the adolescent to the elderly, needs the same things. Besides basic physiological needs, we all need love, affection, tenderness, respect, acceptance, trust, and hope. This wife and mom in the middle of her stressful complicated situation has the same needs and must take care of herself. As marital researchers, educators, and workshop leaders, we (all the authors) travel in our work. Each time we board a plane and are getting settled in our seat, the flight attendant makes the announcement to explain how the oxygen system works. "In case of emergency, the oxygen mask will drop down in front of you. If you are traveling with a small child, first put the mask on yourself, then put a mask on the child." The same principle applies here. You have to take care of yourself first. Although this may seem impossible, it is critical if you and your marriage are going to survive. If you are in a stressful situation right now, look for ways to meet your own basic needs; then you will be better equipped to help your loved one.

Second, realize that whatever your family situation, its effect on your marriage—positive or negative—depends more on *you* than on the circumstances. A negative situation can bring you closer together. The key is to make your marriage the anchor relationship and to give each other the needed understanding and support. One survey participant put it this way: "We are friends who survived many catastrophes (death of a child and cancer). Both of these can draw you apart or reinforce your marriage." If you are struggling with an immature young adult child, most likely he or she will eventually mature and grow up. If parents are demanding and are looking to you for help with their problems, do what you can to help them. But remember that you, and your marriage, are likely to outlive your parents, so now is the time to keep your relationship with your partner healthy and growing.

Third, lean on the skills you've learned in the earlier chapters of this book. You will need to watch for the four danger signs with your extended family just as you have learned to do with your partner. The pressure of past family patterns and remembered family history easily leads to negative interpretations; to withdraw as perhaps you used to do as a child; or to let it all out, allowing your negative comments to escalate and, before you know it, saying things you regret. You're angry and frustrated. Many adults are surprised by how quickly they return to childhood patterns of functioning, despite years of appropriate adult functioning, under the stimulus of their parents' assumptions and expectations. But this doesn't have to happen. Now you know how to stop the negative process!

Even if your parent or adult child isn't interested in learning the Speaker-Listener Technique, you can put yourself in the role of Listener. You may be surprised by what you will hear and how just listening will help your intergenerational relationships. You will also now be able to look beneath the events and better identify the real issues you need to deal with. And don't forget the ground rules. Perhaps you used Time Outs during the years your children were growing up. You may need to introduce the concept again, but this time you both take Time Outs. And just as we have encouraged you to have couple meetings, you can schedule time to discuss problems together with your parents or adult children. What you have learned about fighting for your marriage will also help you fight for better relationships with your parents and children.

We could write a whole book about intergenerational issues. Given the focus of this book on preserving and enhancing your marital relationship, we have chosen to focus on issues with both adult children and aging parents that directly affect the well-being of your marriage. First, let's consider your relationship with your adult children.

RELATING TO AND RELEASING ADULT CHILDREN

The transition into adult relationships with your children can be challenging and can greatly affect your marriage. And when your children marry, the family circle expands, and relationships become more complicated. Maybe your child has married and is now divorced. When grandchildren come along, they add a totally new dimension. Or perhaps your son or daughter isn't acting like an adult, and daily makes unwise decisions—is involved with drugs, can't hold down a job, or is an unmarried parent raising your grandchild alone. A wife, married twenty-three years, wrote in the survey, "Our twenty-year-old daughter, who became pregnant in high school, is still living at home with her now four-year-old son, while she attends college. Our younger daughter is a senior in high school. We are incredibly BUSY. Time is a big stressor, and we anticipate money becoming more of a problem with the younger daughter in college. Making time for the relationship is very hard right now." How can you find the balance between helping your adult children and still maintaining a partner-focused marriage, as we talked about in Chapter Three?

The View from the Other Side

We need to consider what our children are facing. It's not easy to separate from a parent and become an independent adult. Erica, a generation Xer, wrote the following letter, in which she described the tension she was feeling with her parents:

> I'm twenty-seven years old, and the complaint that I have is that my parents are smothering me! They have become so needy and insecure during their "empty nest" stage. For instance, their hugs and kisses are too aggressive and they cross a lot of relational boundaries. They call every day just to check on me. Why can't they give me a little space to build my own life? I know they want my love, but their behavior is driving me away. I want to be around parents who are confident and self-assured and respect my boundaries. All of that intense bear-hugging, cheek-pinching and telephoning is driving me away. My friends feel the same way. I just thought I would tell you this, because it's something many of us don't feel comfortable telling our parents. It has a bearing on their relationship with their adult children, which feeds their self-esteem in a way that affects a huge part of their lives.

Strategies for Releasing

From this young woman's comments, we can immediately identify several potential areas of stress in the relationships between parents and their adult children. Lack of trust, refusing to give adult status, and trying to manipulate or control your adult child will lead to strained relationships. Some parents are distant and don't give their children enough help. Relating to and releasing your children as they move into adulthood is one of the greatest challenges of the empty nest stage. What follows are some suggestions for helping that transition go more smoothly.

Give adult status. Your young adult can vote, defend our country in war, have children, have his or her own bank accounts and credit cards, and sign contracts that you are not responsible for. Most adult children rise to the occasion and live responsible lives. If they don't, however, they are still adults. Erica's issue of boundaries is closely related to her need for adult status.

Are you willing to let go—to release your child into adulthood? If you want to have healthy relationships with your adult children, it is critical that you respect their boundaries and relate to them as adults. Why is this so hard for parents to do? One reason might be that they are feeling insecure at this transitional time and may be basing their sense of identity on their children—or leaning too much on their children and not on their mate. This is an unfair burden for any child and especially for a young adult, who has enough struggles coping with the new responsibilities of adulthood. In some families, one partner is unable to progress through the releasing of the child, leaving the other partner feeling lonely and ignored. When survey participants indicated that the best aspect of their marriage was their children and their grandchildren, it usually followed that their marital satisfaction was at a very low level.

Practice letting go. You will build your marriage when you learn to let go of your adult children. This is especially critical when they marry. Letting go means being willing to take a lower priority in your son or daughter's life. This may be particularly difficult if you are very close to your child. In some cultures and economic situations, married couples still live with parents and grandparents. Although we don't recommend this kind of living arrangement, the key is to let go emotionally, which goes much deeper than physically distancing yourself.

Give advice sparingly. You can build a more adult relationship with your children if you avoid giving advice. And when you feel you must, give it sparingly and only when requested. Before giving advice, a good check is to ask yourself, Will what I'm about to say be welcomed or rejected by my child?

Even when asked for your opinion, you might want to end with a comment like, "I'm sure you'll make the best decision" or "I know you'll figure it all out." Follow this general principle: If in doubt, don't! One wife joked, "Better to have calluses on my tongue than damaged relationships."

Tolerate small irritations. Your child will make some choices you would not make. Give some grace. Accept your child as a package deal (as you did your spouse). No one is perfect—not even you—so try to concentrate on your child's positive traits.

Resist the urge to manipulate. It won't help build your relationship, and, frankly, it doesn't work. And be honest: it probably didn't work when your children were young, either. Realize that your job of parenting your adult son or daughter is over. Now you can enjoy relating to him or her on an adult level—if you resist the urge to manipulate. Unfortunately, Millie's mother didn't.

Millie, who has been married for thirty-two years and has three adult children, complained about her relationship with her eighty-three-year-old mother: "Mom is forever trying manipulate me. If I forget to call her, she'll play the martyr. Then the next time I talk to her she'll say something like, 'Honey, don't worry about me, I'll be just fine here alone by myself. You can't imagine how lonely it is to live by yourself, but don't you worry, I know you have things you need to do with your own family.'"

Does Millie enjoy being around her mother? What do you think? Aside from her lack of desire to be with her mom, Millie needs to watch that she doesn't repeat this manipulative, negative pattern with her own adult children.

It helps to realize that one isn't responsible for things one can't control. And parents cannot control their adult children. Neither are they responsible for their children's decisions. But how can you help them? How can you handle your own frustrations with your children's problems? What about the effect they have on your marriage?

Dealing with Serious Problems

We acknowledge that many parents face more serious relationship problems and heavier issues than we have addressed so far. How do you cope if your adult child has a drug problem, can't hold a job, is going through a divorce, or moves back home and brings grandchildren along? We have no simple answers. If you are presently facing a serious issue, we encourage you to get help. Finding a Counselor When You Need One at the back of this book may assist you in finding the kind of help and support you need at this time.

When Your Adult Bird Flies Home

How can you keep your perspective when you have to live under the same roof with your adult children? What can you do to make this time harmonious and peaceful? When adult children come home, it's easy for them to slip back into the child role. We suggest setting specific guidelines and having a definite plan. Perhaps one stipulation you might want to make before they actually move back in is to teach them the skills described in Part Two of this book—especially the Speaker-Listener Technique. The best advice we can give is to talk, talk, talk, and listen, listen, listen! Together work out the guidelines for financial arrangements and household chores, and rules for pets. If there are grandchildren, include baby-sitting arrangements and what you will and will not do. You may want to renegotiate each month and set a time for evaluation to ask each other, "How is this working?"

It may help to remind yourself why you are doing this in the first place. It may be a way of helping your offspring temporarily. If it's permanent, do what you can to give each other privacy and breathing space. Don't be a doormat or a dictator. You'll have to work to find balance. Here are some of the best tips we have received from couples whose nests have refilled:

- Keep your sense of humor and be flexible.

- Talk and listen to each other. Have planned times of communication. You may decide you will touch base each Monday evening and resolve any issues.

- Set reasonable house rules—for example: If you get it out, you put it back, or, You mess up the kitchen, you clean the kitchen.

- Write down guidelines and financial arrangements so that there are no misunderstandings about what was agreed on.

- Respect each other's privacy.

- Together talk about what each person needs most to make this work. ("I need a living room without clutter." "I need real coffee in the morning." "I need a time to relax and play the piano." "I need space.")

It can feel awkward to request written contracts and agreements with your adult children. It may help to emphasize the adult aspects of the situation over the child aspects; if you were renting out your spare room, you would certainly want everything down in writing to protect both sides. Often, though, children return home in the midst of an emotional crisis—a sudden request for divorce, financial chaos, the death of a spouse. Though you may not feel able to say no to your child's return home, it is still your home, and it is not unreasonable to expect him or her to accept your limits and requirements. Be reasonable—curfews and reporting to you about their whereabouts are not likely to be accepted, whereas financial arrangements and cleaning responsibilities are. As we discuss in Chapter Nine on expectations, though, be sure to discuss your expectations openly and fully to minimize unpleasant confrontations.

No one ever said it was easy to adjust to having adult kids move back in, but with your newly acquired skills, you will be well equipped to keep your relationships healthy and strong. Just remember, take care of your needs first. Your spouse will still be your spouse, if and when the kids leave again—especially if you keep fighting for your marriage.

RELATING TO AND CARING FOR AGING PARENTS

On the other end of the family seesaw are aging parents. Perhaps you have noticed that as people age, they tend to grow more saintly, loving, and caring, or they become more bitter, complaining, and self-centered. Although you can't choose how your parents will be in their old age, you can choose for yourself how you will relate to your children when you are older. History does not have to repeat itself. And whatever the situation, your relationship with your elderly parents affects your marriage. A wife, married twenty-eight years, wrote that she fears "that the needs of our three elderly parents will be overwhelming to us and cause problems between us (they already have)." Another wife, married thirty-two years, wrote, "My mother lives with us—this causes a lot of stress. My husband is unaffectionate and emotionally distant—seems full of resentment." Let's discuss how to improve relationships with both your parents and with your partner in this situation.

It's About Respect

Relational problems often occur when there is a lack of respect. If your parent demonstrates little trust and respect for you, it will be hard for you to have a close relationship. In such a situation, you may need to be more independent and to have a more distant relationship with your parent. Not all elderly parent–adult child relationships are close. But however close or distant your relationship with your parent is, you need to do what you can to nurture mutual respect.

Let's begin by looking at several respect issues. (You may note that many of these ideas are the flip side of what we previously discussed in relating to your children, except that now you are the adult child.)

Respect for Being an Adult

Remember Millie from the preceding section? She struggles with her mother's lack of respect for her adult status.

> Within ten minutes, Mom has reduced me to a ten-year-old. I get so frustrated. I'm over fifty with married children, but when I'm around Mom, I instantly become the child. Do you know how frustrating that is? She is always asking me if I remembered to turn off the oven, or if I set my alarm before I left my house. Or she will make some comment about my diet. Am I getting enough fruits and vegetables? Of course she then brings up all the vegetables I didn't like as a child. I feel just like a kid again. Why can't she respect the fact that I am a competent adult?

It may help to realize that when our parents treat us as children, it's probably not personal—it's how they see all their adult children. Consider this dialogue between Millie and her mom:

MOM: Millie, I just don't know what will ever happen to your brother.

MILLIE: Mom, he's fifty-eight years old. He's already happened!

One way Millie copes with her mother is by trying to keep a sense of humor. What else can Millie do to help her mother respect her as an adult? Probably not much, but she can treat her mother with respect, and who knows, maybe her mother will change the way she relates to Millie, but probably not. On the other side of the seesaw, Millie can concentrate on showing respect to her children. She was definitely thinking ahead when she said, "I don't want to someday be an eighty-three-year-old mother standing at the sink saying, 'I don't know what will ever happen to my sixty-year-old son!' That's just not how I want to spend my senior years—or for that matter—any year!"

Respect for Reality

If there is little mutual respect and honest communication with your parents, it will be harder to help them deal with reality. One survey participant told us how his dad would not discuss the future: "He lives daily in denial. It's been months since he was physically able to drive a car, but he still talks all the time about getting a new sports car. There is no way I can get him to consider moving into a retirement community. I'm an only child. What can I do?"

What can he do to help his dad have a healthy respect for reality? Perhaps this is just his dad's way of coping with aging. He knows he will never buy a sports car, but he likes to talk about it. It doesn't hurt to talk about it. His long-term care is something they do need to talk about. Perhaps his dad would be more willing to talk about that if he were allowed to talk about the car. Again there are no easy answers.

Respect for Boundaries

Parents who don't respect boundaries tend to be more manipulative. "My mom is like an emotional octopus," another survey participant wrote. "She attaches her emotional tentacles to me and sucks out my patience and energy."

Although we want to love and respect our parents, we need to affirm that our allegiance is first to our spouse. A marriage in which one mate refuses to realign his priority from his parents to his spouse—or in which one or both of the spouse's parents expect their adult child to put them before his mate—will have problems.

So how does the wife we just quoted not get caught by her mother's tentacles? She must establish her own boundaries, and in so doing, perhaps eventually her mother will learn to respect them. To her mother's unreasonable demands, she could respond, "Mom, I can't do . . . , but I can do. . . ." For example:

"I can't visit you every day, but I can visit you tomorrow."

"I can't drive you to the grocery store this afternoon, but I can pick up a few things for you at the store on my way home from the dentist."

This daughter can do what she can do, and realizing that is what she can do, she will be able to respect herself for establishing needful boundaries. Whatever stresses you are experiencing with your parents, you need to continue to invest in your marriage while loving, respecting, and caring for your aging parents. Now let's consider what you can do to enhance your relationship with aging parents.

Building Positive Bridges

Remember our ground rules in Chapter Eight? Part of ground rule 6 can help you build a better relationship with your parent: making time for fun and friendship, and protecting those times from conflict and the need to deal with issues.

Maybe you are blessed with parents who are positive, are in excellent health, and each day look for the best. Or you may be in a more distressing situation. You may have to look harder to find positive bridges to a better relationship, but we challenge you to look until you find some. One husband in our survey, married for thirty years, wrote, "The empty nest is stressful, but inherently it is not as stressful as parenting teenagers."

To help you focus on the positive, make a list of things that are positive about your mom or dad. We often forget to express the tender feelings and thoughts we have about our loved ones. Write out several positive sentences and then use them the next time you talk to your parent. Here are some other ways to build positive bridges:

Collect family history. You can sidetrack the "body recital" of aches and pains when you are with your parents by asking them about when they were younger. Taking notes is one way to preserve family history and show interest, especially when the story being told is a repeat. Did you know that we usually talk at around one hundred words a minute (older people tend to talk much slower), whereas we think at around four hundred words per minute? That's why it's harder to listen than to talk, especially if we have already heard about the hip replacement operation numerous times.

Recently Bill, in a phone conversation, got his dad talking about his experience in Europe during World War Two. Bill took notes on his computer and then e-mailed them to the rest of the family. A treasured bit of Arp history is the story Dave's grandmother told of her first car, a Model T—it was the first car in her county—and she actually forded streams to get to the next town. We even have the blanket she used to cover up and stay warm in that car. Now that's family history!

Collect family wisdom. When your parents come out with one of their unique sayings, write it down. Dave's dad used to say, "I was just born too soon," and two favorites from Claudia's mom were "You're as cute as an Indian rubber bouncing ball" and "Bless your little angel heart!" Our having kept a journal helps us appreciate the unique characters that our parents were.

Do something out of character. Dave's dad seldom ate a meal out, so when Dave suggested taking him out for a steak dinner to celebrate his eighty-fourth birthday, we were both surprised when he wanted to do it. We took him to a restaurant he had never been to before, even though he had lived in Albuquerque for over thirty years. We had a great evening doing something that was out of character.

Give gifts of love. Do something your parent would like to do. Claudia's mother, who lived in northern Georgia and died at ninety, loved to go to Atlanta for the day to shop. Whatever you do, plan ahead. Although surprises can be nice, at least half the fun is the anticipation. Knowing you are going to call or come to visit may be as important and enjoyable as the actual call or visit.

Provide lots of pictures. Put together a photo album or video and send it to your parents. You'll be the hero, and you will help your parents keep up with their grandchildren. Beside each picture in the scrapbook, identify who is in the picture and be sure to include the middle name, especially if it happens to be the name of one of your parents. They may have forgotten that someone was named after them!

Tips for Keeping Your Balance

Whatever your situation with your aging parents, don't let it consume all of your emotional and physical energy. You need to balance your parent's needs with those of your marriage. Consider the following four balancing tips:

1. *Deal with false guilt.* Help your parents as much as you can, but having done so, you can't dictate their responses. Do what you can do and then accept that that is what you can do! The year before my dad died, I (Dave) made several trips out west to see Dad, who had a rare form of Parkinson's disease. My greatest frustration was not being able to solve his problems and make him well again. Once I even had to leave for the airport when he was agitated with me. I felt so guilty, although I had not said or done anything to upset him. Fortunately I was able to identify that I was dealing with false guilt and did not let it consume me. I also shared my concerns with Claudia and allowed her to give me emotional support. This strengthened our relationship and gave me more strength to deal with my dad's terminal illness and death.

2. *Don't feel responsible for what you can't control.* Remember, anxiety tends to appear when we feel responsible for things we can't control. So remember the prayer used in Alcoholics Anonymous: "God grant me the serenity to accept the things I cannot change, the courage to change the things I can, and the wisdom to know the difference." It may be helpful to write a list of those things you can control and those things you cannot control. This can be a good reality check.

3. *Get advice from others.* Friends who are just a little bit older than you can be a great source of information. Develop couple

friends who have good relationships with their parents and learn their secrets for relating to their elderly parents. Research old age. Read books. Check out the Internet and find helpful websites. Do whatever you can to gather helpful information. Research this together with your spouse. It will help you stay connected as you face the future together.

4. *Get a life*. Whatever your situation with your parents and with your own children, you need to get a life of your own. Pursue a hobby or interest just for you. Take a nap or soak in the tub. Go for a short walk. Remember that in these stressful years your marriage needs maintenance. Plan a date with your spouse, and on your date resist discussing other family members—on both sides of the generational seesaw.

Identifying Potential Problems and Being Proactive

Sam, a seminar participant, told us,

> My seventy-five-year-old dad is driving me crazy. We had to put him in an extended care center because after his stroke he couldn't be left alone. Both my wife and I work, so it wouldn't work to have him move in with us. Plus we would not be about to give the level of care he needs. His mind is failing, and he doesn't always know where he is. Right now the greatest irritation is that he calls me early each morning before our alarm even goes off. I'm working the late shift at work and just not getting enough sleep to function properly. I know Dad is lonely—especially since Mom died a year ago—but I can't meet his need for a constant companion. I visit him several times each week, but I feel flooded with his phone calls and other demands. I love him, but I don't know what to do.

In regard to our aging parents, it is tempting to put our head in the sand and not face the present and future with objectivity. Is your mom or dad forgetting more? Acting hostile at times? Weird? Do you know where to turn for help? Decisions about long-term health care, home safety when parents' health begins to fail, maintaining a healthy diet, and financial responsibilities are just a few of the topics you need to broach with your parents—before situations become chronic or serious. Although Sam is still in a frustrating situation, he did make the decision for his dad to be cared for in an extended-care center close to him.

You also may want to check out local agencies in the town or city where your parents live, such as the Office on the Aging, AARP, and so on. Take the initiative today. Don't put your head in the sand.

✳

We've looked briefly at relationships with adult children and aging parents. Either can challenge your marriage. Balancing both at the same time is not an easy assignment when there are conflicting needs on both sides just waiting to be met. And what about those family situations that are much more complicated and serious? With the high divorce rate and so many blended families, family relationships can get really complicated. Unfortunately, there are no easy answers. But we do know this: your marriage is greatly influenced by other family relationships. Our best advice is to keep your marriage as the anchor relationship. It is most important not to forget to include your partner in how you are feeling. He or she can be your sounding board, your source of support, and, at your request, a source of good ideas and advice. Problem Discussion focusing on having your partner understand and validate your feelings about your aging parent or your adult child is the key here. Problem Solution may be helpful to clarify your choices. If you have adult children or aged parents living in your home, use your regular couple meetings to vent frustration and develop better attitudes, as well as to come up with solutions where necessary.

We have to face the fact that some families are just closer than others. Some of us grew up in happy, healthy families, and others grew up in unhealthy families. Some of us started our marriages with liabilities but, over the course of our own marriage, have turned them into assets to pass on to the next generation. So be thankful for the healthy relationships that you have. Accept your own family situation. Wherever you are in life, you can leave a legacy of a healthy marriage! You can create a new story to pass along to the next generation.

Having discussed many of the heavier empty nest issues, let's turn the page. In Part Four, we consider how to energize your marriage with romance, friendship, and fun. Then we will help you design your own strategy for keeping your relationship strong.

EXERCISES

The following exercises are intended to help you look clearly at your relationships with your adult children and with your aging parents—to face your concerns, but also to find new ways of connecting and rebuilding strained relationships. Because all these relationships influence your marriage, you may want to share your list with your spouse. You could also do the exercises together and focus on how your children and parents affect your marriage relationship.

Adult Child Relationship Checkup

In thinking about your relationship with your adult children, answer the following questions for each adult child.

1. What are the best aspects of your relationship with your child?

2. What are the areas that cause the greatest stress in your relationship with your child?

3. What do you fear the most in the future concerning your child?

4. What are you looking forward to in the future concerning your child?

Letter of Encouragement to Your Adult Child

Write a short note to your child telling her the things you admire and appreciate about her. You might include character qualities, personality traits, moral strengths, and virtues that you admire.

List of Fun Things to Do with Your Adult Child

Just as your relationship between you and your partner can benefit immensely from positive times you spend together, so can your relationship between you and your adult children. Having a list of ideas ready when you have the opportunity makes it more likely that you will actually do something different and positive next time you are together.

Parent Relationship Checkup

In thinking about your relationship with each of your parents, answer the following questions.

1. What are the best aspects of your relationship with your parent?

2. What are the areas that cause the greatest stress in your relationship with your parent?

3. What do you fear the most in the future concerning your parent?

4. What are you looking forward to in the future concerning your parent?

Letter of Encouragement to Your Parent

Write a short note to your parent and tell him the things you admire and appreciate about him. You might include character qualities, personality traits, moral strengths, and virtues that you admire.

List of Fun Things to Do with Your Parent

The point here is the same as that regarding your adult children. Positive times together are like money in the bank. Sure, there will be withdrawals from the account now and then, but maintaining a positive balance goes a long way toward easing the more difficult times.

Part IV

Feathering Your Own Empty Nest

13

Becoming Empty Nest Lovers

Y ou can tell you are in the second half of life when people start
telling you Viagra jokes, such as this one we heard recently. A
husband complained to the pharmacist that $10 a pill was just too
expensive. His wife disagreed: "Why, honey, that's only forty dollars a year!"

This joke obviously plays into the fallacy that sex is reserved for
the young. Wrong! Our research shows that sexual satisfaction is
often quite high for couples in the empty nest. Actually, your love
life can be much better when the kids are no longer around. Just
think, the whole house is yours again!

Al and Stacy know what we're talking about. They have been
married for twenty-seven years and are the parents of two children:
Sam, twenty, a college sophomore, and Carl, twenty-four, a website
designer. Al and Stacy celebrated reaching the empty nest by building a new house that they designed around their own desires and
needs. For instance, the master bedroom was set off from the rest of
the house, so when their sons returned for visits or summer vacations, the couple would have privacy. But when it was just the two
of them, the whole house would be their love nest! During construction, they joked about the fun they would have christening
each room.

Fast-forward to the first few days in their new home. One
evening, exhausted from all the unpacking, Al and Stacy decided

to take a break and enjoy their new living room. Sitting side by side on the couch with romantic music in the background, they begin to hug and kiss. "I think I can really get used to the empty nest!" Stacy said.

"Me too!" Al responded. "Let's see how our gas logs work." Al walked over to the fireplace and turned them on. Then with the background music and the soft glow of the logs, the spark of their love ignited, and they "christened" their new living room. However, Al and Stacy were not the only things that were heating up. Al had assumed the fireplace damper was open. It wasn't. Their new house came very close to catching on fire. Fortunately, they realized the room was getting really hot and checked the fireplace. To this day they laugh about how their "hot love" christened their new home. Since that time, they have continued to claim the whole house as their love nest, but when they're using the living room, they first check the fireplace damper!

Al and Stacy have a great love life in the empty nest because they understand that it is OK not only to be sexual but also to be sensual. What's the difference?

SENSUALITY AND SEXUALITY

What comes to mind when you think about sexuality? For many, the first thought is of sexual intercourse and all the pleasurable acts that may come before and after. Anything else? Perhaps thoughts of what is arousing to you or your partner, or feelings you have when you want to make love with your partner.

Now think about sensuality. What comes to mind? Usually, some pleasant experience that involves touching, seeing, smelling, tasting, or feeling—such as walking on the beach or being massaged with sweet-smelling oil. How about the roughness of a beard or the silkiness of hair? The smell of your partner after a shower? Chocolate? You get the idea. These are sensual experiences not necessarily goal oriented or connected with sexuality.

Sensuality includes physical touch or other senses but is not always associated with making love. We would include hugging, affectionate cuddling, and nonsexual massages—all acts that provide physical pleasure in nonsexual ways.

This distinction between sensuality and sexuality is important. In the early stages of relationships, touching, holding hands, hugging, and caressing are common. Unfortunately, over time many couples tend to bypass the sensual and move more exclusively to goal-oriented sexual behavior. Less time is spent on the kinds of touching and sensing that had been so delightful before. This shift leads to problems, because such touching is a basic, pleasurable part of your overall intimacy. And by the time they reach the empty nest, many couples have forgotten how to be sensual and are not happy with sex, either. Thus a major avenue of connection and bonding can become lost.

Leanne and Jerry had been married for thirty years. Like most couples, in the early days of their marriage they used to spend a lot of time just cuddling and caressing each other. As time went by, they got busier with kids, work, and home—as most of us do. Over the years, they had settled into a pattern of having sex about twice a week. Given time pressures and other cares of life, less and less time was devoted to sensuality. At night, in bed, one or the other would initiate sex, and they would quickly have intercourse, usually finishing in about ten minutes.

Then the adolescent years hit, and the frequency of sex dropped to once a week or once every other week—and those times were boring. After all, they didn't want their teenagers to hear them! When they hit the empty nest, Leanne and Jerry were in a deep rut.

What had happened here? Over the years of their marriage Leanne and Jerry had become quite efficient about making love— or rather, having intercourse. They didn't have or make a lot of extra time, so they made do. In fact, they were making do rather than making love. Their focus on sexual intercourse rather than sensuality led to dissatisfaction for both. They began to assume they were too old to be sensual. They never talked about their sex life, and both assumed that lack of a great sex life must just be part of growing older. Many couples don't realize that an unsatisfying sex life is just part of a deteriorating marriage. Most couples in the survey who complained about their physical relationship did so in the context of loss of closeness in many areas, as in this example of stressors in the marriage: "Lack of intimacy. Lack of sexual interest by partner. Parallel marriage, different interest and social groups. Poor communication."

Assumptions about the effects of age and time are just wrong, in our opinion. But if you want to have a great sex life in the empty nest, sensual touching—both in and outside the context of making love—must be part of your relationship. The distinction between sensuality and sexuality is similar to the distinction between problem discussion and problem solution. Just as the pressures of life lead many couples to problem-solve prematurely, too many couples shortchange the sensual and prematurely focus on just sex. Just focusing on sexuality without the overall context of touching can be very problematic in the second half of marriage—and can lead to a boring or nonexistent sex life!

In the empty nest, touch becomes even more important for both partners. If the husband is slow in getting an erection, touching can be a very important stimulant. Also, the wife may need more lubrication than her body provides at this stage of life—again an opportunity to touch and to make the application of lubricant sensual. So it is critical to make sensual experiences a regular part of your relationship, apart from sexuality. Furthermore, sensual experiences set the stage for better sexual experiences. The whole climate for physical intimacy is better when you have preserved the sensual. Those couples who haven't may be the ones who struggle with sexual dysfunction. Marriage education pioneers Drs. David and Vera Mace write in their book *Letters to a Retired Couple* (1985, p. 70), "Clearly, some older couples continue to enjoy their sex life as the years pass, while others reduce its frequency or have to give it up altogether as their general health and vigor deteriorate. What really matters is that good sex is the expression of a warm and close love relationship. If that relationship exists, its continuity is not seriously disturbed when the sexual aspect can no longer continue."

What about those couples who don't have a loving and warm sexual or sensual relationship? They may feel they are in a rut and don't know how to get out of it—like George and Nancy in the movie *The Out of Towners*. New empty nesters, George and Nancy visit New York City. They have been robbed and mugged, and when chased by a dog, they escape into a church, where quite unintentionally they join a sex therapy group. After a while the leader asked them what their problem with sex was. George says, "We're from Ohio. We don't discuss sex in public." His wife Nancy says, "That's part of the problem. We don't talk about it. Actually, we don't even do it much anymore."

The leader prods, "So when you do have sex, is it programmed and lacking spontaneity?"

"Exactly!" Nancy says. "It's like we're two dead people." We would certainly diagnose this couple as missing out on sensuality and emotional intimacy.

SUGGESTIONS FOR SENSUAL CONNECTION

There are many simple things you can do that will keep your sensual connection thriving. It is not hard to do any of these, and the positive effects for you can be enormous. Here are some ideas that work.

Practice Love Talk

To preserve or revive sensuality in your love life, you need to talk. Tell your partner what is sensual for you. Talking will help you understand each other and get your love life back on the front burner. It is critical for you to communicate about your physical relationship in ways that protect and enhance this important way of being intimate.

Couples who have the best sexual relationships have ways of communicating both verbally and nonverbally about what they like. In their book *Love Life for Parents* (1998), Dave and Claudia actually describe a lovemaking menu called "Love a la Carte." Why not write your own menu and include things you would like to do or things you think your partner would like? You may not have the same sexual appetite, but with a menu, you can pick and choose what is appetizing to you. Every day will not be one of long, relaxing gourmet sex, but having a sexual menu can help you develop a satisfying and well-balanced love diet. Consider the following treats from Dave and Claudia's suggested menu:

Appetizers. An appetizer is a come-on. It creates interest, increases the appetite, and precedes a main course. An appetizer could be a ten-second kiss, a back rub, a handwritten love note, or one long-stemmed red rose. Appetizers help keep sex from being too goal oriented.

Snacks and fast foods. Snacks are similar to appetizers but may lead to intercourse. A snack might be only one partner pleasuring the other, ten minutes of nondemand touching (sensuality that doesn't lead to sexual intercourse), or a quickie. (A quickie might be when one spouse is just too exhausted or has no huge appetite for sex and gives a gift of love by having quick sex.) But remember, you can't build a healthy love life by having only fast foods!

Main courses. Main courses give energy and strength to a relationship and satisfy deep hunger. Also, main courses often require planning. A main course might include an evening of uninterrupted lovemaking, a twenty-four-hour getaway, or an afternoon at a hotel. Or for a creative main course, plan to rendezvous at a restaurant, flirt with each other over appetizers, then drive in separate cars to a hotel, where you meet for the main course adventure.

Desserts. Desserts bring little pleasures and complement the main course. They can be light, rich, or gourmet. In lovemaking, desserts can create intimacy, which is so important. Also, sometimes desserts are simply desserts and don't include sex. A dessert could be something as simple as snuggling and holding each other before going to sleep, or ten minutes of afterplay, or lying together on a blanket and gazing at the stars.

Use your imagination and come up with your own love menu. Plan your empty nest love feast and don't forget to set the "table" with things like candlelight, romantic music, perfume, flowers, silk pajamas, and so on.

Besides talking about their love life, couples with great sex lives unselfishly desire to please one another. There's a strong sense of teamwork involved, even in lovemaking, through which each gives to and receives from the intimacy they share. The giving combined with the direct communication leads to great lovemaking.

We recommend that you communicate clearly about what feels pleasurable to you while you are touching or making love. Your partner doesn't know what you want unless you say something. We're not suggesting that you have a Speaker-Listener discussion in the middle of lovemaking. (Though if it really excites you to do so, let us know how it goes!)

We're suggesting that you keep conflict out of the bedroom. If you are keeping conflict out of the bedroom, handling conflict well in the rest of your relationship, and taking the time and energy to preserve sensuality, this kind of communication will be much easier to do.

One caution: you need to initiate this intimate conversation in an atmosphere of trust, unconditional love, and acceptance. If one partner is reluctant to talk, the other needs to be patient, gentle, and accepting. The following questions may help you get started:

1. What do you think of when you think of intimacy and closeness?
2. What is romance to you? Do you need romance to set the mood?
3. What are the positive aspects of your love life?
4. What brings you the most sensual fulfillment?
5. How much hugging and cuddling do you need? (You can put this in terms of minutes per day if necessary.)

Take Marriage Vitamins

Think of sensuality as marital vitamins. Once you understand each other's desires, romance your mate by giving each other at least one vitamin a day. Make the time for sensual experiences that don't necessarily lead to sex. Consider the following marital vitamins:

- Hug for twenty seconds each day.

- Flirt with each other—especially when there isn't time for sex. If you communicate your desire, it keeps the passion alive.

- Kiss for ten seconds every morning when you say good-bye and every evening when you say hello. (Time it—it's longer than you think!)

- Think about sex. While doing the laundry, dishes, and the like, daydream about making love.

- Give your spouse a one-minute shoulder rub.

- Rent a romantic movie and watch it together.

It's also important to keep sensuality as a regular part of your lovemaking. When you keep a focus on a variety of touching, you preserve and elevate the importance of the whole sensual experience. Most couples prefer this broader sensual focus to a narrow focus on sex. It provides for a fuller expression of intimacy in your physical relationship.

Risk Trying New Things

If your empty love nest is a little blah, try some new ideas to break out of ruts. Read a book on how to give a massage and then practice on each other. Or read a book on sex. That might help you talk about these issues. Agree to surprise each other one night. Try something new, even if just once. Exploring both the sensual and sexual sides of your relationship may relieve many concerns about performance and help you find even more pleasure.

✳

We aren't saying every empty nest couple can have a wonderful physical relationship. You both have to want it, protect it, and nurture it. If things are going well in your physical relationship, keep it that way. If some problems have developed, the things we are emphasizing here can help you get back on track.

PROTECTING PHYSICAL INTIMACY FROM ANXIETY

Arousal is the natural process by which we are stimulated to sexual pleasure. It is a state of pleasurable excitement. Although just about everyone is capable of being aroused, this pleasurable feeling can be short-circuited by anxiety—especially in the empty nest. Numerous studies suggest that anxiety is the key inhibiting factor to arousal.

There are two primary kinds of anxiety in this context that we would like to discuss: performance anxiety and the tension created by conflict in your marriage.

The Barrier of Performance Anxiety

Performance anxiety is anxiety about how you are "performing" when you make love. Asking yourself such questions as "How am I doing?" or "Is my partner enjoying this?" on a regular basis reflects performance anxiety.

In the second half of life, couples are at greater risk for performance anxiety than in the earlier years. One reason is that as you get older, your body undergoes normal physical, psychological, and hormonal changes. The good news is that these hormonal changes can actually bring couples into closer balance. Women may even become more assertive and more interested in sex when they reach menopause. Menopause is a well-known and accepted change in life for women, but less is known about hormonal changes that men go through. These changes can affect desire for and interest in sex. Because of reduced blood flow, a middle-aged man's erection may not be as firm as it was when the man was younger. This may cause some anxiety, and the solution may be as simple as understanding that a softer erection does not prevent the man from reaching orgasm or prevent his partner from enjoying intercourse.

Actually, age-related changes can enhance your sexual relationship if you understand them. We believe that your sexual relationship can be more satisfying in your fifties than in your twenties! For instance, as a man's response time slows down, he has time to increase his wife's pleasure. In the empty nest, just think of your sexual experience as a delightful stroll—not a sprint. Enjoy the experience!

Other issues can also cause performance anxiety. For example, when you are keeping an eye on your performance, you put distance between you and your partner. You're focused on how you are doing rather than on being there with your partner. Many people report feeling distant when making love, as though they were just watching what's going on instead of participating. This kind of detachment is believed to lead to a variety of sexual problems. The focus is no longer on the pleasure you're sharing. Instead, your self-esteem feels at stake. It's as if the event of making love has triggered issues of acceptance and the fear of rejection.

The focus on performance interferes with arousal because you are distracted from your own sensations of pleasure. This distraction leads to many of the most common sexual problems people experience: premature ejaculation, problems keeping erections for men, and difficulty lubricating or having orgasms for women. You can't be both anxious and pleasantly aroused at the same time. And you can't be relaxed and enjoy being with your partner if you are concentrating on not making mistakes.

Consider Jerry and Leanne again. Leanne became aware over time that Jerry was less interested in lovemaking. Without the kids around, she was more interested, so she would try to let Jerry know in indirect ways. But without a focus on sensuality and touching throughout their relationship, Jerry just wasn't picking up on her hints. At the same time, he was becoming more concerned about his own performance. What if he failed to get an erection or keep it? This feeling intensified because several times recently he had almost not made it. As unsatisfying as their lovemaking was for both of them, it seemed to Leanne that Jerry was avoiding her. She wondered if he was seeing someone else. Her concern grew.

Jerry sensed her concern but assumed she was concerned about his ability to perform. Instead of talking about his concerns, he decided he'd just try to do a better job of making love to Leanne. This wasn't all bad, as ideas go. However, he became more and more focused on performing, and his anxiety grew. Thoughts about performance became his constant companions during their lovemaking: "Am I going to keep an erection? How's Leanne doing? Can I still excite her? Does she like this? I wonder if she's worried I might not make it?"

Pretty soon he was growing tenser and tenser about what he was doing when they made love. Neither Leanne nor Jerry was feeling connected or satisfied in their lovemaking. Leanne had this growing sense that Jerry was somewhere else when they made love. They certainly weren't sharing a sensual experience.

The key for Leanne and Jerry was to rediscover the sensual side of their relationship. They also had to learn about how their bodies worked at this stage of life, and they had to talk out loud about what was going on. Leanne and Jerry had a lot of love and respect for each other, so once they started dealing with their concerns, the situation quickly improved. Leanne was relieved that Jerry was not having an affair, and Jerry could relax about feeling criticized for his performance.

The Barrier of Relationship Conflict and Anxiety

Mishandled conflicts can destroy your physical relationship by adding tension both in and out of the bedroom. Let's face it: when you've been arguing and angry at each other, you don't often feel like being sensual or making love. Although for some couples the sexual relationship is temporarily enhanced by conflict followed by "making up," for most couples poorly handled conflict adds a layer of tension that affects everything else in the relationship.

Tension isn't compatible with enjoyable, intimate lovemaking for most people. In fact, there may be no area of intimate connection that's more vulnerable to the effects of conflict and resentment than your physical relationship. If you are experiencing conflict in other areas of your relationship, it can be difficult to feel positive about sharing an intimate physical experience. Worse, these conflicts too often erupt in the context of lovemaking.

Whereas touching sensually or making love is a powerful way to connect, destructive conflict builds barriers. If you can protect your times for physical intimacy from conflict, you can do a great deal to keep your physical relationship alive and well. To do this, you must work to handle conflict well—for example, by using the ground rules and other techniques we've been stressing. *It is critical to agree to keep problems and disagreements off-limits when you have the time to be together to touch or make love.* Some couples agree that they simply will not discuss difficult issues in the bedroom. Other couples agree that when they are in the sensual mode, the ground rule is that no issues can be discussed. (We highly recommend you do this.) The time is therefore protected, and you are far more likely to be able to relax and connect.

WHEN EXPECTATIONS
GET IN THE WAY

Far too many couples experience so much less than they could together because the partners assume they know what their spouse likes. Sure, it's likely you've known each other a long time, but that doesn't mean you have really shared what feels good to you, and why, and how it affects you emotionally. It's a mistake to assume that your partner will like whatever you like or that you can read each other's minds. Those assumptions are filters that distort any communication you may have about your sexual relationship. Would you go out to a restaurant and order for your partner without talking about what he or she wanted to eat? Of course not.

It's also too easy for some people to assume that their partner won't like the things they like. In this case again, they are making assumptions. And because many empty nest couples have trouble communicating about their physical relationship, it's really easy for these assumptions to take control. You don't know what your partner's expectations are until you ask, and the same is true for your partner.

Of course, because of your previous experiences together, you can often assume correctly, and things can work out fine based on those assumptions. Assumptions about positive things, such as trying to please your partner, are more likely to succeed or at least not to spark conflict. Assumptions that are associated with negative emotions, such as anger, frustration, and distrust, are much more likely to harm the relationship. In any case, keep in mind that people change, so checking in with each other about desires and expectations is valuable for having a good sexual relationship. We can't tell you how many older couples we've talked with in which one partner expects the other to know what he or she likes most when making love. It's as though people believe that "it just isn't romantic or exciting if I have to tell you what I want. You should know!" That's an unreasonable expectation. If you hold this fantasy, you should probably challenge it for the health of your relationship. Try a Speaker-Listener discussion, so that you both can feel safe talking about this sensitive area.

WHAT IF THERE ARE PHYSICAL PROBLEMS?

A relationship between general health and sexual activity does exist. And as we age, we tend to experience more health problems. If you have health issues that are affecting your sex life, we encourage you to consult your doctor. Many situations can be improved. New products come on the market almost daily. Viagra is just one of them. And when something like Viagra works, it's no laughing matter—it's a gift to your marriage!

The Maces say that when couples cannot engage in sexual intercourse, they can compensate with "emotional intimacy," sitting and lying close to each other, touching, and holding hands. One wife, age sixty-one and married one-and-a-half years, wrote of the stress caused by problems with sexuality. "My husband had been celibate for ten years and was unaware he would be impotent. It really rocked our boat. We are now adapting." Sensuality plays a critical role here, as couples explore what a physical relationship can mean without intercourse. Thus we see the importance of the sensual side of a sexual relationship for the rest of your lives together.

*

In this chapter, we have looked at several keys to keeping your physical relationship growing and vibrant in the empty nest years. Now it's up to you.

We don't intend this chapter to be a substitute for sex therapy if you have a history of significant sexual difficulties. If you do, we encourage you to work together to overcome the problems. When there are significant problems, working with an experienced sex therapist can usually accomplish a great deal. Our focus here has been more to help couples who have a satisfying physical relationship keep things that way—and make it even better. As is true of so many areas we've discussed, working on this aspect of your marriage in some wise ways can produce great benefits. Physical intimacy isn't all that marriage is about, but it's an important part that affects the rest of your relationship. You really can develop a lasting, satisfying ability to connect. Part of that connection is connecting as friends. In Chapter Fourteen, we move on to look at the benefits of building your friendship.

EXERCISES

These exercises can help you enhance your abilities to connect physically; many couples have used them successfully. If you're ready for sensual and sexual enhancement, read on.

Sensate-Focus Exercise

Years ago, Masters and Johnson began studying the various ways in which problems develop in sexual relationships. They created an exercise that can benefit you whether or not you have faced difficulties in your physical relationship. This exercise is called the Sensate-Focus. Its purpose is twofold: (1) to keep you focused on sensuality and touching in your physical relationship and (2) to help you learn to communicate more openly and naturally about what you like and don't like in your lovemaking.

This isn't the time for sexual intercourse. That would defeat the purpose, because the focus is on sensuality. Don't be goal oriented, except toward the goal of relaxing and doing this exercise in a way that you each enjoy. If you want to make love following the exercise, that's up to you. But if you've been having a lot of concerns about feeling pressured into having sexual intercourse, we would recommend that you completely separate these practice times from times when you have sex. In fact, you shouldn't have sex unless both of you fully and openly agree to do so. No mind reading or assumptions!

The general idea is that you each take turns giving and receiving pleasure. The first few times, you are either the Giver or the Receiver until you switch roles halfway through the exercise. When in the Receiver role, your job is to enjoy the touching and give feedback on what feels good and what doesn't. Your partner does not know this unless you tell him or her. You can give either verbal or hand-guided feedback.

Verbal feedback means telling your partner what actions feel good, how hard to rub, or what areas you like to have touched.

Hand-guided feedback consists of gently moving your partner's hand around the part of the body being massaged to provide feedback about what really feels good.

As the Giver, your role is to provide pleasure by touching your partner and being responsive to feedback. Ask for feedback as often as necessary. Be aware of changes in how your partner is reacting; what feels good one minute may hurt the next. You are to focus on what your partner is wanting, not on what you think would feel good.

Choose roles and give a massage of hands or feet for about ten to twenty minutes, asking for and giving feedback. We recommend massages of areas like the hands, back, legs, and feet the first few times so as to get the hang of the technique. This also helps you relax if there are some issues about sexuality between you. Then switch roles. Repeat as often as you like, but also remember to practice these roles in other aspects of your sensual and sexual relationship.

We recommend that you try the Sensate-Focus exercise over the course of several weeks, several times a week. As you work on the exercise, there are some variations of the technique to work in over time. Assuming all is going well in your exercises, begin to move to other areas for touching. Wherever you want to be touched, including the sexual areas, is great.

Over time, you can drop the rigid emphasis on the Giver and Receiver roles, and work on both of you giving and receiving at the same time, while still keeping an emphasis on sensuality and communication of desires. Or you can vary the degree to which you want to stay in these roles. If you practice this exercise over time, it will become easier for you to communicate openly about touch. It will also be easier for you to work together as you try to keep physical intimacy vibrant and alive.

Exploring the Sensual

In addition to the Sensate-Focus exercise, set aside a specific time for sensual activities together. This works for all couples, regardless of whether or not they are engaging in sexual activity. Be sure you will not be interrupted. (This is the time for the answering machine!)

At the start of this exercise, talk about what is sensual for each of you and what you would like to try doing to keep sensual experiences in your relationship. Here are some ideas:

- Give a massage to your partner, using the Sensate-Focus technique.

- Share a fantasy you have had about your partner.

- Cuddle and hug as you talk to your partner about the positive things you love about him or her.

- Plan a sensual or sexual activity for your next encounter.

- Plan a wonderful meal together. Prepare it together and sit close together. Share the meal.

- Wash your partner's hair.

- Spend some time just kissing.

- Design your own Love a la Carte menu.

14

Building Your Friendship

Saturday morning. Time to catch our breath. The previous week, heavy with writing deadlines, was history. The night before, Dave had raced time and traffic to FedEx and won. Now was our time to kick back, be lazy, and enjoy the beautiful late spring day. But what started out as a lazy spring friendship-building Saturday turned into a friendship strainer. Here's our story.

We were sitting on our screened porch with our second cup of coffee, reading the paper and talking as friends about things other than work deadlines. Then it happened. Claudia saw a bargain in the paper that promised to make us slim, sleek, and sexy. She immediately recognized it as a great opportunity to build our friendship and have some fun together.

We must confess. We are among the myriad of empty nesters who would like to firm up and drop a few pounds, and this exercise ski machine, advertised for only $39.99, would be our answer to cellulite. After all, we like to ski. Now we could have fun firming up and watching our love handles disappear.

Dave, though reluctant and skeptical, was willing to indulge Claudia's enthusiasm for this unbelievable bargain and said, "Sure, why don't you check it out?"

Fast-forward a couple of hours, when most sane empty nesters are pouring another cup of coffee. Claudia arrived home. The bargain was bulging out of the trunk of our car—unassembled—and

Dave suddenly realized that someone had to put that baby together. The sixteen-page instruction booklet for assembling the ski exerciser was a clue that it was not going to be a fun, friendship-building morning.

Soon our living room resembled a bicycle repair shop. Hundreds of nuts, bolts, and parts carpeted the floor. By step eighteen, we knew we were in trouble. The needed screw was missing. Our frustration and irritation levels were rising. Claudia was disappointed in Dave's lack of ingenuity, and Dave silently wished Claudia had just skipped reading the Saturday paper. What had started out as a friendship builder was becoming just the opposite. Our story is a great example of how a friendship moment can be destroyed by irritability and conflict.

Can you think of times when you were trying to build your friendship, and it backfired? In working with couples in the second half of life, we find that most friendship blockers are not the big disappointments in life. Instead, it's the chronic ongoing daily things that keep fun and friendship at bay, such as not investing enough time in each other, not protecting your friendship from conflicts, or simply failing to intentionally plan fun times together. In this chapter we look at how you can overcome these barriers. We want to help you preserve and enhance the really great things in your relationship.

And just how did we preserve our friendship that frustrating Saturday when we had the unassembled ski machine spread out on our living room floor? Dave wanted to junk it and chalk up the $39.99 to experience. Claudia wasn't ready to give up that easily, but neither of us wanted to spend the rest of our Saturday looking for screws. "Claudia," Dave said. "Let's just cut our losses, return it, and get on with life."

Whereas most of Claudia's bargains are great, this one was the pits. Together we agreed we'd had enough exercise for one day. We boxed up our bargain, loaded it in our trunk, and took it back to the discount store. On the way home, we stopped for another cup of coffee and decided that talking while walking will remain our favorite friendship-builder exercise.

HOW'S YOUR FRIENDSHIP FACTOR?

What are you doing to build your friendship in the empty nest? Is your partner your best friend? According to our research, friendship is what people want the most from their mate. And from our survey we confirmed that the greatest indicator of a successful second half marriage is the level of the couple's friendship.

If so many couples want their mate to be their best friend, why is this desire for lifelong intimacy more of a hope than a reality? It's not that it is an unreasonable expectation to have your mate be your best friend. It's just that friendships need to be nurtured in ways that many couples fail to recognize until their friendship is gone. You may not even realize it's not there until you hit the empty nest. Or maybe you breezed into the empty nest as best friends. If you are among this fortunate group, we want to help you preserve and deepen your friendship; if your friendship factor is registering low, we want to help you enhance and upgrade it.

WHAT IS A FRIEND?

How would you answer that question? When we've asked people, they have said that a friend is someone who supports you, is there for you to talk with, and is a companion in life. In short, friends are people we relax with, open up to, and count on. We talk and do fun things with friends. In friendship, your support and care for one another help buffer you both from the trials and tribulations of life. There is a great deal of research that backs up this point. People who have more friends (especially at least one really good one) do better in almost every conceivable way in life, especially in terms of physical and mental health. One wife, married twenty-three years, wrote that the best aspects of her relationship revolve around "our friendship, humor, easygoing, things are good, and feel secure we will manage through the experiences." Friendship is clearly the solid base on which this marriage is built.

One of the aspects of friendship that is most powerful is that of deeper intimacy. Intimacy can take many forms. In part, it means being able to share what's in your heart—your hopes, fears, dreams, and burdens. It's also important to learn to hear your partner's heart in the ways he or she can readily share it. Sharing at this level will mean different things to different people. In fact, we're all different, so this is one of those areas in which there can be a really unique blending of who each of you is. Whether you are quiet or quite outspoken, a key to great friendship in your marriage will be in learning to share, and listen carefully for, what is in each other's hearts.

Friendship goes to the heart of many people's greatest desires in marriage. One survey respondent wrote that he was looking forward to "the same thing I have now—excellent companionship, a warm bed, someone to take walks with, someone with whom I might enjoy a good conversation, etc."—certainly a good definition of a friend. Another wrote that the best aspect of her marriage was "our friendship with each other and the fact that we enjoy spending time with each other, even to working together." One husband, himself a couples counselor and married eleven years, wrote of his own marriage that the best area of his relationship has been "friendship—closest to my wife as compared to anyone else. Similar tastes in life's things and experiences. Similar values in regard to family time and spiritual life." But why aren't more married couples good friends? Let's look at some common barriers.

BARRIERS TO FRIENDSHIP

Over the years of a marriage, many couples don't preserve and protect their friendship. What follows are some of the complaints we hear.

There's No Time

Couples tell us, "We just don't have time to build our friendship." We all lead busy lives, but that's no excuse. But we (the Arps) are guilty too. As we've already told you, when we hit the empty nest the pace of living just increased instead of decreased. Between work, the needs of our adult children and aging parents, the upkeep of our home and yard, writing deadlines, and traveling across the country leading seminars, our friendship at times was frayed. And unfortunately our experience is not that unusual. Friendship, the very core of your relationship, often takes a back seat to all the many competing interests.

For example, Eunice and Howard are a dual-career couple who had been together about ten years and actually got married as empty nesters. Eunice's fifteen-year-old granddaughter Linda lived with them at the time we met them. Even though they were happy with their marriage and life together, they were feeling like something was slipping away.

HOWARD: We used to sit around for hours just talking about things. You know, like politics or the meaning of life. But we just don't seem to have the time for that anymore.

EUNICE: You're right. It used to be so much fun just being together, listening to how we each thought about things.

HOWARD: Those talks really brought us together. Why don't we still have them?

EUNICE: We don't take that kind of time like we used to. Now that we've got Linda living with us we're back to dealing with adolescent concerns, and the yard work has to be done—not to mention that we each bring too much work home.

HOWARD: It seems like we're letting something slip away.

All too often, couples fail to take the time just to talk as friends. The other needs and cares of life crowd out this time to relax and talk. Often this is a matter of priorities. When couples date before marriage, they will usually find a lot of time for being together. Life is often less busy then, but it's also a higher priority to find the time to be together. But that's not the only reason friendship weakens over time.

We've Lost That Friendship Feeling

Many people have told us that they were friends with their spouses to begin with, but not any more—they're "just married." A husband, married twenty-eight years, wrote that he fears "letting it get stale, drifting, taking each other for granted." It's as if once you're married, you can't be friends anymore; you can be one or the other, but not both. That's a mistaken belief.

The strongest marriages we've seen have maintained a solid friendship over the years. Take Geena and Pierre, who have been happily married for more than forty years. While at one of our workshops, we asked them what their secret was. They said commitment and friendship. They started out with a great friendship, and they never let it go. They have maintained a deep respect for one another as friends who freely share thoughts and feelings about all sorts of things, in an atmosphere of deep acceptance. That's kept their bond strong and alive.

Don't buy into an expectation that says that because you're married—or have teenagers still at home—you can't stay friends. You can!

We Don't Talk Like Friends Anymore

If you have been married for some time, think for a moment about a friendship you enjoy with someone other than your mate. How often do you have to talk with that person about problems between the two of you? Not often, we'd bet. Friends aren't people with whom we argue a lot. If you argue a lot with a friend, you won't long think of that person as a friend. In fact, one of the nicest things about friendships is that you don't usually have to work out a lot of issues. Instead, you are able to focus on mutual interests in a way that's fun or meaningful for both of you.

Friends talk about sports, spiritual matters, politics, philosophy of life, fun things they've done or will do, dreams about the future, and thoughts about what each is going through at this point in life. In contrast, what do couples talk about most after they've been together for years? Let's list some of the common subjects: problems with the kids and grandkids, problems with money and budgets, problems with getting the car fixed, concerns about who has time to complete some project around the home, concerns about the health of parents, problems with the neighbor's dog, concerns about each other's health . . . the list goes on and on.

If couples aren't careful, most of their talks end up being about problems and concerns—not points of view and points of interest. Problems and concerns are part of married life, and they must be dealt with, but too many couples let these issues crowd out the other, more relaxed talks they once shared and enjoyed. And because problems and concerns can easily become events that trigger issues, there's much more potential for conflict in talking with a spouse than with a friend. That brings us to the next barrier.

We Have Conflicts That Erode Our Friendship

One of the key reasons couples have trouble staying friends in the empty nest is that friendship-building activities and discussions get disrupted when issues arise in the relationship. For example, when you're angry with your partner about something that has happened, you're not going to feel much like being friends right then. Or worse, when you do have the time to be friends, conflicts come up that take you right out of that relaxed mode of being together. We believe that this is the chief reason that some couples talk less and less like friends over the years—they aren't keeping their issues from damaging their friendship.

One couple, Samantha and Ken, were having real trouble preserving friendship in their relationship. They had been married twenty-six years, had three kids—one still at home—and were rarely able to get away just to be together. They bred dogs together but hadn't been away to a dog show together for several years. The parenting years had taken their toll on their "friendship time alone."

They were sitting in the hot tub of the hotel, really enjoying talking together about the show and the dogs they breed, when a conflict came up that ended their enjoyable time together.

SAMANTHA: *(very relaxed)* This is such a nice setting for the dog show.

KEN: *(equally relaxed, holding Samantha's hand)* Yeah. This is great. I can't believe the size of that shepherd.

SAMANTHA: Me neither. I don't think I've ever seen a German shepherd that big. This reminds me. If we're going to breed Sasha again this year, we'd better fix that pen.

KEN: *(tensing up a bit)* But I told you how big a job that was. We'd have to tear out that fence along the property line, build up the side of the hill, and pour concrete for the perimeter of the fence.

SAMANTHA: *(sensing his tension and now her own)* Would we really have to do all that? I know we have to get the pen fixed, but I don't think we'd have to make that big of a deal out of getting it done.

KEN: *(growing angry)* There you go, coming up with things for me to do. I hate having all these projects lined up. That's a really big job if we're going to do it right.

SAMANTHA: *(getting ticked off too)* You always make such a big production out of these projects. We don't have to do the job that well to make the pen usable again. We could do it on a Saturday.

KEN: *(turning away)* Maybe you could. But I don't want to do it unless we do it right, and we can't afford to fix that fence the right way right now.

SAMANTHA: *(looking right at Ken, with growing contempt)* Heck, if you watched how you spent money for a couple of months, we could pay someone else to do the whole thing right, if that's so important to you.

KEN: *(angry and getting out of the tub)* You spend just as much as I do on stuff. I'm going up to the room.

Notice what happened here. There they were, relaxed, spending some time together, being friends. But their talk turned into a conflict about issues. As Samantha raised the issue of breeding their dog Sasha, they got into an argument in which many issues were triggered: projects around the home, their different styles of getting things done, and money. Perhaps some hidden issues were triggered as well. What had been a great talk as friends turned into a nasty argument.

When couples aren't doing a good job of keeping issues from erupting into their more relaxed time together, it becomes hard to keep such positive times going in the relationship. The worst thing that can happen is that time to talk and be together as friends becomes something to avoid. As we said earlier in the book, spouses can come to perceive that talking leads to fighting—including talking as friends. So the baby gets thrown out with the bath water. This is one of the chief reasons why some couples lose touch with friendship over time—and it's the key reason that many empty nest marriages become just empty marriages. But as you will see, you *can* prevent this from happening.

We Use Reckless Words

One of the major barriers to friendship in marriage occurs when things shared at tender and intimate moments are used later as weapons in fights. When spouses do this, it is incredibly destructive to their friendship.

Bennett and Lillian had been married for twenty-eight years, and Lillian has just gone back to work as an editor for a woman's magazine. She had been feeling overwhelmed by the demands of her career, so she had begun talking with a counselor at church. After one particularly emotional but productive session, she shared with Bennett that she was feeling vulnerable and not very confident about her ability as an editor. Later that week, they got into a fight over how much time she was spending on the computer, editing for the magazine. After all, Bennett figured that this was a time of life when they would be spending more, not less, time together. The fight had begun when she got up from watching television with him to go work. He responded harshly, "Why is this work so important to you anyway? You yourself said you were not all that good at it. Why don't you just quit that and do something that takes less time?"

This devastated Lillian. That night, she slept in the guest bedroom and cried herself to sleep. She vowed never to tell him anything personal again. Unfortunately, events like this take place all too often in relationships. Through positive, intimate experiences as friends, we learn things that can be used as powerful weapons later when we feel more like enemies. But who is going to keep sharing personal and vulnerable information if it might be used later in a fight? This kind of pattern is devastating to friendship.

PROTECTING FRIENDSHIP IN YOUR MARRIAGE

We have found some core principles that help us protect and enhance friendship. If you have a good friendship going, these principles will help prevent your friendship from weakening over time. If while the kids were growing up you lost something in terms of being friends, these ideas will help you regain what you've been missing.

Make the Time

Although it's great to be friends no matter what you're doing, you can still benefit from setting time apart specifically for talking as friends—and that means you must *make* the time. Otherwise, all the busy stuff of life will keep you occupied with problems and concerns. The couples who are doing wonderfully well as life moves on are those who express their commitment to each other and to their marriage by carving out time for the best parts of being together.

In our research at the University of Denver, we find that there really aren't many clear differences in marital happiness between those who have children in the home and those who do not. Many people assume that children have some large negative effect on marriages, but some marital researchers are beginning to question that belief. Where we see the clearest difference between those who have children in the home and those who do not is in the degree to which the spouses report regularly talking as friends. People with children in the home are not doing this as often as they could. But this is a book about the empty nest. Here's your chance. When you had children at home, you may have let time for being together as friends slide, but there is now every reason in the world to reestablish friendship as a cornerstone of your marriage.

We mentioned how Geena and Pierre had preserved and deepened their friendship over the forty years they had been married. One of the things they did to keep friendship alive is plan time to be alone together. They would take long walks together and talk as they walked. They would go out to dinner. They would take weekend vacations from time to time, without the kids. They made the time for each other, and it's been paying off for over forty years.

If you are really serious about friendship, you need to plan time to be together as friends. That means putting a priority on this aspect of your intimacy. This is one of the key investments you can make in your relationship. The problem we all face is that there is much less *quality* time when there is little *quantity* time. A great many of the most magical times in married life come about precisely because something spontaneous and wonderful develops out of a block of quantity time. You will need to put some boundaries around all the other things you do in life so as to carve out time for friendship. But that's not all you need to do.

Protect Your Friendship from Conflict and Issues

You might be surprised how simple yet powerful it can be for the two of you to agree that some times are "friend time" and therefore off-limits for conflicts and issues. For example, you could decide that whenever you take a walk in your neighborhood, it's automatically friend time. Or you could go out to dinner and specifically agree, "This is friend time, tonight, OK?" That way, you are working together to define the times you are "off duty" in your marriage. Even better, you can agree that unless you have both agreed to deal with an issue at a particular time, the understanding is that you are more in friend mode. Think about how you can act out this principle in your relationship. The key is to realize together that you are not at the mercy of your issues. You can keep issues in their place and thereby give place to the promise of deepening friendship in your marriage.

Talk Like Friends

Now let's discuss how you can talk like good friends. We want to highlight some points about how friends talk that can help you protect and enhance your relationship.

Listen Like a Friend

Good friends listen with little defensiveness. With a friend, you don't have to worry so much about feelings getting hurt or whether he or she will be offended. That's because a friend cares about what you think and feel, and relationship issues are rarely at stake. Our friend and colleague Bill Coffin once noted, "A friend is someone who's glad to see you and doesn't have any immediate plans for your improvement." When you're talking as friends, you aren't trying to change one another. You can both relax and just enjoy the conversation. Even when we let our hair down and talk about something really serious, we don't want a friend to tell us what to do—we just want him or her to listen. It feels good to know someone cares. Friends often provide that kind of support, and you can do this for each other in your marriage.

Don't Focus on Getting Something "Done"

Most of the time, when with a friend, you don't have to accomplish something. There may be a limited amount of time, but there's no pressure to get something done. That lack of pressure allows your conversations to go to interesting places—to places of personal interest that you may not talk about much with other people who do not have the time to go there with you.

Talk About the Things Friends Talk About

This may be most important. What do friends talk about? What do you talk about most often with friends other than your mate? When it comes to talking as friends, the list of possibilities is endless: hobbies, investments, philosophy, great books (crummy books), sports, current events, politics, movies, fears, dreams, hopes for the future— you get the idea. When you are talking as friends with someone, you are most often talking about something that interests one or both of you, and there is a certain joy in just talking that way. If you've gotten away from doing this over the years, it's time to get back to it in a big way.

*

Like so many other things you've learned in this book, friendship is a skill. To keep your friendship strong, you may have to work on it a bit. We can't think of anything of greater importance for the long-term health of your empty nest marriage than to stay friends.

In this chapter, we've tried to outline some of the things that really make friendships work—especially in how you communicate. As we move to Chapter Fifteen, we change the focus to fun. This is another key area of intimacy and friendship in marriage that's often taken for granted.

EXERCISES

Plan some time for these exercises. Have fun, relax, and enjoy your friendship.

Talking as Friends

Plan a quiet, uninterrupted time. Take turns picking topics of interest for each of you. Ban relationship conflict issues and problem solutions. Then consider some of the following topics.

- Some aspect of your family of origin that you've been thinking about.

- Personal goals, dreams, or aspirations.

- A recent book or movie. Pretend you're professional critics, if you like.

- Current events: sports, politics, and so on.

Interviewing

Take turns pretending to be your favorite TV interviewers. Interview your partner about his or her life story. This can be a lot of fun, and it really is in the spirit of listening as friends. The best interviewers on TV are very good at listening and drawing their guests out of themselves. Try to draw one another out in your sharing together as friends.

Planning for Friendship

Talk together about how you can build time for friendship into your weekly routine. If you both believe friendship should be a priority, how do you want to implement that?

15

Having Fun When the Nest Empties

And what did you do on your last date?" the radio host asked. Dave and Claudia stared at each other. They were on a national radio program promoting their latest book on dating, and neither could answer the question! At that point, they knew they had some work to do. If the Arps, who are known as "the fun dating couple," still have to work at dating and having fun together, then probably you do too! Fun plays a vital role in the health of empty nest marriages.

RESEARCH ON FUN

In 1996, when we (Scott and Howard) conducted a nationwide random phone survey, we found that fun was an indicator of how couples were doing across the board. The survey included over fifty questions on all aspects of their relationships—satisfaction, commitment, communication, sex, and just about anything else you can think of. We were very surprised to find that among all the variables, the amount of fun these partners had together emerged as a key factor in understanding their overall marital happiness. That's not to say that there weren't other things going on in these relationships, but good relationships stay great when you are preserving both the quantity and the quality of your fun times together.

We have already mentioned that in Dave and Claudia's national survey, the friendship factor was the key indicator of successful empty nest marriages. And as we saw in Chapter Fourteen, fun and friendship go together. So if you aren't friends, you probably aren't having fun together, and if you aren't having fun together, you probably aren't friends!

BARRIERS TO FUN

Most couples have tons of fun early in their relationship. But for too many, fun fizzles out as time goes on. The children start arriving, limiting couples' fun times together. Then the adolescent years hit. For years, we have observed how fun-loving couples become serious and sober when they begin parenting adolescents. No wonder the fun level is so low when they get to the empty nest. Here are some of the reasons we hear from other couples.

We're Too Busy

Busy couples often stop making the time for fun. Early in relationships, people tend to put a high priority on going out to the movies, window shopping, walking hand in hand, going bowling, and so forth. In the phone survey mentioned earlier, we asked people how long it had been, in weeks, since they had dated their partner. What would you say? Overall, those who said they had been out most recently were those couples who were later in life, and likely did not have children at home anymore. If that's you, keep it up. It's great for your marriage, your health, and your spirit. But we also found that many other couples were neglecting to "date" one another: males reported that it had been, on average, about six weeks; women said it had been, on average, about eleven weeks. We'll discuss the discrepancy in those numbers later, but you can start thinking about it now. Particularly striking was that so many couples, especially in the years of heaviest family responsibility and child rearing, had not been out for fifteen weeks or more. That's a long time without intentionally going out on a date together. We interpret that data to mean that a huge number of couples in those years are neglecting this important aspect of their connection due to the time pressures of life.

That's the way it was for Mickey and Nicole, an empty nest couple. In their twenties, they would spend many Saturdays together at the beach swimming and talking and lying in the sun. They would also take long walks in the sand and talk about their future together. When they got married, they continued to go to the beach, but less frequently. A few years later, they had their first child and began to spend much less time having fun. Sure, their daughter, Amanda, was a delight for them, but it became rare for Mickey and Nicole to actually go out and have fun like they used to. Then when Amanda became a teenager, they did even less together.

Mickey and Nicole noticed over time that life wasn't as much fun as it used to be. They were happy together, and their marriage was solid, but now that Amanda was in college, they realized they had let something slip away. It was decision time for them.

It's really pretty simple: life is more fun when you *do* fun, and the rest of life will crowd fun out if you don't make time for fun to happen. One wife, married twenty-three years, wrote in the survey that friendship was the best aspect of her marriage, but the greatest stress was caused "by being too easygoing—we find we haven't planned for a recreational weekend." We want to encourage you to find the time to keep up the fun and playfulness that can make your relationship more delightful.

Karen and Frank are a good example of a couple who have preserved time for fun in their marriage. They've been married for twenty-five years and haven't let fun slip away. Every Friday night, for most of those years, they've gone out on a date to have fun together. That's just one way they have preserved fun in their relationship. When the kids were younger, they made use of baby-sitters, and over the years they haven't let things come between them and this time together. It's a priority in their marriage.

They also vary what they do for fun: dinner and a movie one week, swimming together another, dance lessons at times, walking in the park and watching the sun set, and so forth. They've tried lots of things, and they've made the time. Their marriage has benefited. Their fun experiences have built a storehouse of pleasant times and memories together. You can't overestimate the value of that.

Play Is for Kids

Many preschool experts say that playing is the work that children need to do. Through play, children gain developmentally relevant social, emotional, and cognitive abilities. We believe that the developmental importance of play doesn't stop after childhood but continues throughout life. Fun and play allow a release of oneself from all the pressures and hassles of being an adult.

The relaxed togetherness of playful times is important in the initial development of the bond between two people. That's because when people are engaged in fun through play, they are often relaxed and more themselves. It's under these conditions that people fall in love—when one sees in the other the relaxed self in the context of fun times together. It's not too often that you hear someone say, "I really fell in love with him when I saw how much he loved to work."

We mentioned how Mickey and Nicole used to go to the ocean more often earlier in their relationship. During their time there, they would splash in the water, make sand castles together, rub suntan lotion on one another, and bury each other—they'd play together like kids! During these times, they would frequently look at one another and smile in the delight of the moment. You can't put a price on time like that, which builds such basic bonds between you.

Mickey and Nicole occasionally still experience that kind of bond, but they could use a lot more of this kind of time together in their empty nest. As we said earlier, the couples in really super marriages create this time to play together, which keeps refreshing the bond. So be a kid from time to time.

We're Too Serious

During the stressful and draining adolescent years, many parents lose their sense of humor and become much too serious. Then they enter the empty nest sad, sober, and serious. Let us encourage you to loosen up, look for humor, and renew laughter and fun. We (Dave and Claudia) like to say, "Fun in marriage is serious business." And this is especially true in the empty nest.

If you're humor-challenged, get together with some funny friends. Read a humorous book. Look for humor—you can find it. Wear a fake nose to dinner. Stuff your partner's closet with balloons. Whatever you do to add humor will make your empty nest more fun.

Recently at a dinner party we met a fun-loving couple. Clark and April are part of a group of empty nesters that gets together every other Friday night. The group had studied our book *The Second Half of Marriage*. When they realized we were leading a conference in their city, Clark and April invited us to join the group for an evening dinner party they were hosting. From the moment we entered their home, we knew that an empty nest couple who liked to play lived there. A spiral staircase led to the lower level, where a hot tub was just waiting to be enjoyed. Their bedroom suite was a lovers' delight, complete with a heart-shaped Jacuzzi.

When we commented on how much we liked their home, they responded, "It's our empty nest playhouse!" It was obvious that they were the "players." But it had not always been that way. Like many couples, when Clark and April transitioned into the empty nest, they hit some rough places in their marriage. Both were teachers, and teaching was the focus of their lives. One day, after another heated argument, they both admitted their empty nest marriage was boring and that they needed to do something about it. About that time they received an invitation to join a group of empty nesters for a book study group. That's where they got the idea that the empty nest could be fun. And they took it very seriously. Clark and April actually sold their family home and bought this house nearer their friends. The spark between them was delightful to observe. Hard to believe that at one time they were bored with each other! Clark and April proved to us that play and fun in marriage is serious business— especially in the empty nest.

Conflict Spoils Our Fun Times

As we discussed in the chapter on friendship, mishandled conflict is a real killer of fun times together. We made the same point in the chapter on sensuality, too. Poorly handled conflict can ruin the most enjoyable aspects of any relationship.

Noreen and David were a middle-aged couple we talked with who were making the time for fun. That wasn't the problem. Instead, all too often they would be out to have a fun time, and some event would trigger an issue that would kill the playfulness of the moment.

One night, for example, they went out to take a class in couples' massage. They thought, "This will push us a bit to have some fun in a new way." Great idea! The instructor was making a point to the class about paying attention to the reactions of the partner. David whispered to Noreen, "That's a great point." Noreen whispered back, "I've been trying to tell you that for years." David was instantly offended. Feeling attacked, he pulled away from Noreen, folding his hands across his chest in disgust.

This event triggered some hot issues for David and Noreen. For years, Noreen had felt that David didn't listen well to what she was saying—triggering a hidden issue of caring. She was hurt that he hadn't cared enough to remember her making the same point the instructor was making. David had been feeling that Noreen was critical about nearly everything and now was attacking him when he was really getting into this massage workshop with her. He felt rejected and dejected. "Can't she even lay off when we're out to have fun?" On this evening, they didn't recover well. David suggested they leave the class early and go home. They did—in silence.

There will be times for all couples when conflict erupts during fun times. But if it begins to happen a lot, fun times won't be so much fun anymore. The whole idea of fun is that you are doing something together that is relaxing and that brings out positive emotions you can share together. Poorly handled conflict will disrupt these times. The sense that conflict could erupt at any moment isn't compatible with relaxed playfulness. Couples set themselves to fail at fun when they carry over grievances or anger into their special fun times.

A PRIMER FOR HAVING FUN

Now that we've spent some time discussing what prevents fun from being a regular part of some relationships over time, we want to present some ideas for keeping fun a significant part of your relationship. You may be thinking that you know how to have fun and don't need strategies and skills. That's great. But we have some pointers we think are useful for any couple, and they can help keep you on track.

Making the Time

It's hard to have fun together without setting aside time for it to happen. Sure, you could have a moment of fun just about anywhere, anytime, if the mood strikes you both. Even a quick joke together or seeing something funny on TV can be fun. But to get the full benefit, we suggest you make fun times a priority so that you can get into the flow of fun together. That means you need to be serious about setting time for not being so serious.

Most people are so busy and harried by life that it takes some time just to switch gears into the fun mode. That's why for many couples the first day or two of a vacation can be more stressful than fun. They are making a transition. The same holds true for shorter periods of fun time. It often takes time just to wind down and get relaxed. But once you are relaxed and playing together in some way, the opportunity to draw closer together in the bond of the positive emotion really takes hold.

To make the time for fun, you might actually have to pull out a schedule and arrange the time together. This may not sound all that spontaneous, but for most couples, there's so much else going on that it takes deliberate acts to make the time happen.

Designating a special fun time serves another purpose. Remember, we mentioned earlier in this chapter that Scott and Howard's national survey revealed a significant discrepancy in the length of time men and women reported had elapsed since their last date. Our research indicates that men and women define fun time together differently, leading to this difference in perception. For example, a man might think of watching TV together as a date, whereas his partner gives that title only to activities they do outside their home. When you have scheduled "fun time" together, both partners can feel satisfied with their commitment to this crucial piece of their relationship.

Try to arrange for time without the possibility of distraction. For example, if your job requires you to wear a beeper, do you have to wear it when you've carved out time to play with your spouse? It's not very relaxing to know you could get beeped at any moment. Make the time and shut out the distractions of the rest of your life. It's worth it. It might even give you something to look forward to.

Protecting Fun from Conflict

As we said with regard to friendship, the material on handling conflict presented in Part Two is critical if you are going to preserve fun in your relationship. Together as a couple, you need to control the times and conditions under which you deal with the difficult and conflictual issues in your relationship. When you have blocked out time to have fun, don't "do" conflict. Block out a separate time to handle the tricky issues.

Many couples eventually buy into the wisdom of "date night" or some such idea as a way to get away to enjoy each other. In our experience, however, many couples try to do too much with the time they have set aside. They try to have fun together *and* resolve difficult issues "while we have this time together."

For example, one night Frank and Karen went out to an ice skating show. As they were seated and waiting for the show to start, Frank said, "We haven't had time to talk out that budget problem. Let's see what we can get done right now." Big mistake. Their budget was a serious conflict area between them, and it deserved far more focused time to deal with than they were going to have waiting for an ice show to start. As you can imagine, they didn't get anywhere in the time they had, and only succeeded in getting on edge with each other when they were out to have fun.

Although it's unavoidable that conflict will sometimes occur while a couple is trying to enjoy a fun time together, we don't understand why some couples deliberately use their limited and precious fun time to deal with issues. Dealing with issues just isn't compatible with the greatest benefit of having fun time together—being relaxed and upbeat with one another. Deal with the important relationship issues during meetings arranged for that purpose—not during times for fun. When issues get triggered during times you set aside for fun, table them. Call a Time Out. Come back to them later. It's not hard to do once you try it a few times. In our experience, there's no more powerful change couples can quickly make in their relationship than to agree to keep conflict out of time set aside to have fun.

So What Can We Do for Fun?

OK, you've set aside the time for fun, and you've agreed to put conflicts aside to protect the time. Now what? For many couples, this is a difficult question. For others, like those couples in the super marriages we have described, there are plenty of ideas. Some of you have gotten rusty at coming up with fun things to do together. One wife wrote in the survey that her husband "is not athletic, so we don't recreate." What? Only athletic activities count as recreation? That's news to us.

In many ways, coming up with fun things to do is a skill like all the other skills we emphasize in this book. You have to practice such skills if they are going to work for you. If you're rusty at fun or want to keep your fun skills sharp, here are some of our ideas that might help.

Brainstorming Fun Activities

What do you do for fun? Not much? Then sit down together and think about the most enjoyable, interesting, and fun things you've ever done together, or things you would like to do. You might even want to think about things you used to do before you were married or before your nest first filled up with kids. Make a list to which you both contribute, putting down all ideas no matter how foolish or outrageous they may seem. Part of the fun is brainstorming about fun—throwing out the wackiest ideas you can. Avoid getting into ruts.

Ideas We've Heard from Couples

To help you get started, we'd like to mention some of the great ideas we've heard from other empty nest couples. Maybe one of these ideas will cause a cascade of ideas in your own mind. Try the ones that appeal to you and watch your friendship soar!

> "We like to cook together. Lately, we've been learning to cook northern Italian."
>
> "We pick apples together."
>
> "We take our boat out Sunday after church, and find a quiet cove and read the Sunday paper together."
>
> "We keep our grandchildren—one child at a time."
>
> "We signed up at the local health club and work out together each week."
>
> "We like to rock in our double rocker on our screened porch."
>
> "We recently learned how to surf the Net and use e-mail. We now stay in better touch with our children and grandchildren."

"We took a massage class and practice on each other."

"On our thirtieth wedding anniversary, we made a list of thirty things we wanted to do. We are working our way through our list."

Fun doesn't have to be something that's elaborate or costly. The ideas here involve activities couples can do almost anywhere if they enjoy them. In contrast, skiing is a wonderfully fun activity, but it can be very expensive.

Many couples enjoy going to the movies. That's not a very original idea, and you've probably already thought of it, but how long has it been? You can bake cookies together and make a big mess. You can climb a mountain or collect seashells. You can go swimming or play tag. How about renting a classic movie and cuddling together on the sofa with a bowl of popcorn? How long has it been since you had a soda with two straws? Have you ever tried preparing a meal together, then feeding it to each other?

Even things that seem like work can be fun if you have the right attitude. According to one husband, "My wife and I found out that it was really fun to do yard work together. It's fun to be together sprucing up our home, and at the end of the day, it's rewarding to see what we accomplished. And in the summertime, seeing the flowers we planted together bloom is something that gives us great pleasure and pride. These things are fun for us because it's us doing them together." One wife wrote, "We both like to do things together such as walking, yard work, etc. I like dancing better, but he will do it."

Over the years, we have noticed that when we ask couples to brainstorm about fun things to do, sex usually isn't mentioned until other things come up. Couples tend to forget that sexual intimacy is one of the most fun things they can do together. Several variations, to suit personal preferences of course, should be on your list. How about setting aside an evening with no other agenda but to make love?

Fun time you have together should be something you eagerly anticipate! Be creative.

Make a Fun Deck of Cards

Some couples find it handy to make a personal fun deck. To do this, take a stack of index cards and write down on each card one of the items from your brainstorming or any other ideas you've come up with. We suggest maybe twenty-five to thirty ideas to start with; they can cover a whole range of topics. Once you've made the deck, set aside particular times to choose activities and do them. Don't let anything stop you.

Because you'll have more fun if you are both up for the activities you choose, here's one way to use the fun deck to make sure that happens. Each of you picks three cards from the deck describing things you would find fun to do that day. Trade cards. Then you each choose one card from the three your partner picked, and each of you take responsibility for making that one activity happen. That way, you are each picking something you know your partner will like, and because you get to choose among the three, you are likely to like it too. Don't worry about which one your partner wants you to pick. If you don't get to it today, you'll have another chance tomorrow!

✳

Now it's your turn for fun. If you follow the key points in this chapter, you'll be qualified for a degree in relationship fun. You can do it. It's not hard if you make the time, protect this time, and make fun happen.

Whatever you do to put more fun in your relationship will help you keep your relationship strong in the empty nest. In the concluding chapter, we look at how to put into action the concepts we have shared in this and previous chapters. To build a successful marriage at this time of life, it's not just of matter of knowing what to do—it's a matter of doing what you know!

EXERCISES

Brainstorm together and make a list you can call "Fun Things We Will Do in the Empty Nest." Be creative. Anything goes, so have fun coming up with ideas. There are several things you can do with your list:

1. Make your own fun deck by writing your ideas down on index cards. Your fun deck will come in handy when you don't have much time to decide what to do but are ready for some fun. Pick out three things from the deck that you would enjoy doing. Hand these three to your partner. Each of you should take responsibility for making one of your partner's three things happen in the time you have set aside.

2. Make a list of dates you want to have. Choose a date night each week and begin working through your list.

3. You can surprise your mate—choose something from the list that you know your partner would really like to do, such as attending a sporting event. Buy the tickets ahead of time and kidnap your spouse for the evening.

16

Keeping Your Relationship Strong

Since joining the empty nest set, we've sold our Arp family home and moved into a condo community. We still have a yard, but we don't have to keep it up. And we just love it when every Tuesday the crew comes through and grooms our yard! But planting extra trees and shrubs is our responsibility, so when we wanted to add a few trees, our friend Radio agreed to help. Because we were leaving for a conference, Radio suggested we place our new trees where we wanted them planted.

It was early fall, so we left our indoor ficus tree outside on the deck. It is a temperamental plant that lives inside in the winter and almost dies. Then come spring, we put it outside for the summer, and it gets healthy again. So we wanted one last week in the sun for Mr. Ficus Tree.

After we left, a huge storm raced through Knoxville. When Radio came to plant the new trees, they were more or less in the area we wanted them planted, even though the storm had rearranged them. That part worked out fine, but our ficus tree had blown off the deck, and Radio planted it too!

The prognosis for a tropical plant surviving a Tennessee winter is not good. So after our ficus tree enjoyed several more weeks of glorying in the fall sunshine—and, we might add, thriving—we replanted it in a larger pot. After allowing it a few days of acclimating, we moved our tree inside for the winter. The results? It has never been so healthy! Being uprooted and replanted was like a shot of vitamins for our little tree. Years later, it's still growing!

Why are we telling you this story here? Because it illustrates what can happen to an empty nest marriage for those willing to do some replanting. We know from our own experience that the second half of marriage is a time of change and challenges—but whereas change is inevitable, growth is optional. This can be a time of uprooting negative habits and replacing them with healthier ones. It can be a time of replanting a root-bound marriage in healthy soil that will cause it to grow with vigor and zest. But it won't happen without effort. It's up to you.

We have covered many topics in this book, including communication and conflict management, commitment, forgiveness, sensuality, the impact of core belief systems and social support on your relationship, and, in the last two chapters, the importance of friendship and fun. We are confident that these ideas and techniques can go a long way toward helping you keep your marriage strong.

You could think of this book as a guide to helping you revitalize your marriage. You now have the skills for cultivating a better relationship for the empty next years. The key for you now is to put these to use. With a strong commitment, you make a great marriage happen. Based on our experience with couples through our research, surveys, seminars, and workshops, the recommendations we have made in this book will help you keep your relationship strong and vital for years to come. Now we have some final important points to make.

YOU ARE NOT ALONE

When people have relationship problems, the mistakes they make are fairly similar to those of other couples—escalation, withdrawal, invalidation, and negative interpretations. In contrast, there are many, many ways to have a good relationship. Happy, healthier couples can look very different from other couples who are doing well, yet they all have great marriages with intimacy and teamwork. In other words, couples who are struggling look more alike than couples who are doing well.

During a workshop we conducted recently, the husband's eyes lit up when he heard that other couples were making the same mistakes he and his wife were making. He was happy to hear that they weren't alone. In fact, this is a common reaction when we work with couples. There's frustration about whatever negative patterns they have going, but also relief: "Even though our marriage is pretty good, we blow it from time to time like everyone else."

You're in good company if you exhibit some of the negative patterns and attitudes discussed throughout this book. We all do. They're common. But divorce is common, too, so it's important to be concerned about the negative patterns. It's even better to do something with your concern.

Fortunately, the news is good. There's hope for couples who are invested in stopping negative patterns and preserving all the great things in their marriage. Our research shows that you can prevent such problems from building up and harming your relationship—but you have to work at it. This brings us to the issue of motivation.

MOTIVATION

Our principles, knowledge base, research, and techniques aren't going to work for you unless you are motivated to do what it takes to have a good relationship. Sometimes it's hardest to motivate the couples who can do the most to prevent serious problems from developing in the first place—engaged and newlywed couples. There is just too much else going on. When they are still early in the relationship, it's hard for these couples to imagine having serious trouble later on. If that's your situation, please keep in mind that working to implement the kinds of strategies recommended here can do a lot to keep your relationship vibrant.

If you have been together for some time, you probably fall into one of three categories:

1. Those who are doing great and want to keep it that way
2. Those who are having some struggles and are in need of a tune-up
3. Those who have been having significant problems and need major changes to get back on track

Whichever category you are in, you can't get the most out of this approach with a halfhearted effort. Even though we emphasize relatively straightforward techniques and ideas, it still takes effort to make any kind of meaningful change in life.

But My Partner Won't Try These Things

What if your partner isn't motivated to learn some of things we have presented? That can be a very frustrating problem if you really like the ideas. You could try several approaches.

Work on Yourself First

It's wisest to begin working on what *you* can change about how *you* handle yourself in the relationship—regardless of what your partner is willing to do. It's too easy for all of us to get focused on what our partners can do. Instead, focus your attention on the person over whom you have the most control: yourself!

Do you have a tendency to make negative interpretations? Do you tend to withdraw from talking about issues? Do you bring up gripes when you are out to have a fun evening with your partner? You can make substantial changes in such patterns no matter what your partner is doing. There are many ways in which you can work on maintaining and demonstrating your dedication without your partner ever reading this book.

You could also demonstrate some of the ground rules without necessarily working on them together. For example, if you are out together and begin to get in some conflict, you can say, "You know, we're out to have fun tonight; let's deal with that tomorrow when we have more time so that we can focus on relaxing together this evening." Most partners would get the idea even if they've never heard of ground rules. Making some of these changes is really pretty basic—but powerful nevertheless.

Although all the things we've suggested work best when you are working together, you can accomplish a lot on your own if you are willing to try and your partner isn't actively working to damage the relationship.

Try Lighter Topics

You could try to get your partner interested in some of the lighter topics we've discussed, such as fun or friendship. You might want to try some of our fun dating suggestions and begin the tradition of a weekly date night. (Remember, this is for fun, not problem solving.) As a start, you could suggest some of the ideas in Chapters Fourteen and Fifteen to your partner. That could get some potent and positive changes going that could open up interest in other features of this program. As you may have noticed, many of the key ideas about fun and friendship wouldn't depend on knowledge of other key concepts in this book. For more suggestions for fun times together, see the Marriage Alive International listings in the Resource section.

Marriage Lite Ideas

If the ideas above fail to spark your partner's interest, then you have a choice to make. Give some thought to the significance of your partner's reluctance. It could simply mean that your partner is less interested than you are in a particular approach to strengthening your marriage. If that's the case, it would be a serious and inaccurate negative interpretation to assume that your partner isn't as interested as you are in keeping your marriage strong.

In fact, we often talk to couples in which one partner—more often the woman—thinks the other isn't doing enough for their marriage and the other—more often the man—brings up all sorts of things that he feels he's doing because he does care for the relationship.

One couple we saw in counseling had a big problem with this kind of thinking. She loved to read self-help books and he didn't. She interpreted his lack of interest as a lack of motivation in the marriage. Yet he was doing all sorts of other things that showed his investment—being actively involved in counseling, wanting to go out and be together, and being a reliable provider for the family.

So be careful how you interpret things. Perhaps you can talk together about the ways you each think you can make progress as a couple. Your partner may have very different ideas about what's best for the marriage and how to get there. Listen up!

But My Partner *Really* Isn't Interested

If you're pretty convinced that your partner is substantially less motivated to work on the relationship in any way, you have a tougher situation. What you choose to do is up to you, but to give your relationship the best chance, we still recommend that you do the best you can to strengthen your marriage according to the principles we are advocating here.

As we said, one person can cause substantial changes in a marriage; it's just a lot easier and more fun when you are working together. If you value your marriage, your own positive investment gives you the best chance of achieving changes you desire. Just keep in mind that sometimes the most positive investment you can make is to confront head-on any problems you see. You might need to sit your partner down and say something like this: "I've been concerned for some time about where we're headed. I'm really committed to making this a great marriage, not just one where we get by. I'm willing to do what it takes to make that happen. I'm hoping we can work together, and I want you to know that I'll be trying hard. Let me know if you want to try some of the same things."

WHEN YOU WANT MORE HELP

Although we think almost all couples can benefit from the educational approach we have outlined, there are times when couples can benefit from professional help—times when motivation alone isn't enough to get you on a better path. We'd wish that everyone could work on *preventing* serious problems from developing so that there wouldn't be such a demand for marital counselors. But as marital therapists as well as researchers, we recognize there are times when couples can really benefit from a professional's skill.

We are not intending this book to be a substitute for therapy when that is what you really need. There are many reasons why a couple or individual might wisely seek professional guidance—for example, in cases of physical abuse, substance abuse, depression, and ongoing conflict that never gets resolved. These danger signs indicate that the educational approach may not be enough.

The most common reason couples seek professional help is that they feel stuck—wanting or hoping for some significant changes to occur but not being able to bring them about. For example, you might both read this book, love the approach, and try some of the techniques, but find that you are having trouble changing ingrained patterns.

If this is your situation, a good counselor can help you in numerous ways—in a sense serving the role of a gardener who can recommend proper nourishment and soil preparation for growing your marriage and who can also help you pull a weed or two. Counselors can give you different perspectives on a problem. They can provide a structured, safe place to talk about difficult issues—much like the structure provided by some of the techniques we recommend. They can hold you more accountable for making certain changes happen. They can coach you in learning skills you may be having trouble with on your own. They can also help you explore the effect of your family backgrounds and expectations in general on your relationship.

If you decide that getting professional help is something for you to consider, seek help sooner rather than later. Studies show that people suffer through as many as seven years of stress before they start seeking help. That's a very long time to wait. It is far easier to change patterns earlier than it is to do so later, especially if you wait so long that one of you has given up.

If you are at the point that you think professional help would be useful, Finding a Counselor When You Need One in the back of this book includes some tips for finding a competent couples counselor.

WHAT TO DO NOW

Bill Coffin, a colleague and prevention specialist who works for the U.S. Navy, suggests that couples think about relationship fitness as they might think about physical fitness. Physical fitness experts recommend that you work out three or four times a week for twenty to thirty minutes each time; couples should devote at least that much time to working on their relationships. This means not only having couple meetings but also planning fun times together, having friendship talks, making love, giving each other back rubs, just hanging out together reading a book in the same room, listening to music, or playing with the grandchildren. Make the time for your relationship to be regularly renewed in these ways.

If you're serious about putting some of these key ideas into practice, here are some important points to keep in mind.

Review

To get the most out of what we have presented in this book, be sure to review the material. We all learn better when we go over key concepts again and again. Perhaps you have highlighted key sections as you've read them. Go back and read those sections again. For example, it would be a great time to go back to Chapter Eight and review the ground rules. Are you using them? Have you kept at it?

It would be especially valuable to review the rules for the Speaker-Listener Technique (Chapter Five), the problem-solving process (Chapter Seven), and principles of forgiveness (Chapters Two and Eight). None of these rules or ideas are all that complicated, but you need to master them to yield the greatest benefit for your marriage. Better yet, read through the whole book again, together.

Practice

Our approach is a very specific, skills-oriented model for building solid relationships. The key is to practice the skills and ways of thinking we have recommended. It's not enough just to review the ideas—you need to make them a part of your life. Practice the techniques and strategies so that you can use them easily. We know they will feel artificial at first—they aren't like the behaviors you naturally do. But if you practice enough, the solid skills, techniques, and ways of thinking we have emphasized will become regular habits in your relationship.

Create Rituals and Routines

All couples can benefit from the kinds of patterns that work for happy couples and that help unhappy couples fix problems. For too many couples, relationship problems control them. We want couples to take control. Rituals are well-organized habits that guide people in life. A colleague of ours, Bob Weiss, at the University of Oregon, considers the benefit of rituals to be that they put people's lives under *rule control* rather than *stimulus control*. To be under stimulus control means that you are constantly reacting to the things happening around you—the stimuli of your life.

We've given you some pretty good rules, but it's up to you to make them habits. In effect, we're suggesting that you get out of patterns of reacting to events and instead build rituals into your lifestyle that give you—as a couple—control over important aspects of your life.

Many rituals take place during important life transitions. That is because transitions—such as birth, a wedding, leaving the nest, and death—are stressful. Rituals and routines can reduce stress by providing some structure during these times of change. For example, almost all cultures have ritualized ways of dealing with death and mourning. Rituals provide a map or structure to help participants handle these transitions. The daily conflicts that come up in life are stressful, too; rituals and routines to handle these situations can yield the same stress-reducing benefits.

You may already have many rituals in your relationship—simple routines for getting ready for bed or how you handle special meals on holidays. Clearly young children benefit from routines for family life. But kids aren't the only ones who benefit from structure. For example, if you're having a weekly couple meeting to deal with issues in your relationship, you've begun a ritual that we believe will have a very positive payoff over the long term. Meeting regularly helps prevent destructive conflict and enhances intimacy. It gives you a routine for anticipating issues that will occur.

We aren't suggesting you get weighed down by all sorts of rules. Sometimes people misunderstand this aspect of our model; they think we believe that all aspects of relationships benefit from structure. In fact, we do not think structure is all that useful (at least not in the sense we've talked about it in this book) when it comes to the most positive aspects of your relationship. We find that when couples are doing a good job of managing the differences and conflicts they have, the positive aspects of their marriage—sensuality, friendship, and fun—happen more naturally and spontaneously. We aren't saying people can't learn more about how to enhance those areas; in fact, we've made many suggestions to help you do just that. However, we are suggesting that some solid, commonsense skills can make all the difference in the world in how the tougher issues affect your relationship. When such skills and ways of thinking become routine, you'll get the greatest benefit.

Preserve spontaneity and creativity in the more wonderful aspects of your relationship. Structure conflict, let loose with fun.

Date Your Mate

One important ritual to develop that will feather your empty nest is having regular dates. Actually, we suggest that you develop what we call the dating mentality. Look for dating opportunities. Dating your mate means framing fun activities as dates. We have found that putting things into a dating context adds a really nice spin. Even activities that otherwise would be tasks, such as grocery shopping or running errands, can be turned into fun dates. So you can have dates that are set aside for having fun and being friends, and you can also have dates that are set aside for getting something important done.

Chapter Fifteen is jam-packed with creative ideas of things you can do for fun dates. Although you can have dates that are structured for improving your marriage (we recommend Dave and Claudia's *10 Great Dates* program for couples), here we want to focus just on increasing your enjoyment together. Setting aside times to build your relationship is a very healthy and preventive thing to do. Here's a simple example of prevention in action from the Arps:

Each October we actually have a standing date to get our flu shot. Let us explain. Each year on the third Saturday of October, the Academy of Medicine here in Knoxville, Tennessee, offers free flu shots. For us, attending this event has become a tradition. We see friends. We contribute to the Empty Stocking Fund to help needy families. And our friend, Dr. Bob, tells us that by not getting the flu we gain ten days in the coming flu season to invest in our marriage. Dave holds Claudia's hand while she gets her shot, and vice versa. Afterwards we stop for coffee at our favorite gourmet market and pick up the groceries we need. Each fall we joke about and almost look forward to getting our flu shot because now it's a date—something we plan and something we do together! This is an example of thinking preventively and getting the most out of the whole experience for our marriage. What are some tasks or chores you have to do anyway that you could do together and turn into a date?

When it comes to great fun dates, you should plan some dates where you really go for it. We're not talking about dates you make and keep to deal with problems. Remember we emphasized that you need to protect your fun times from conflict; that definitely applies to dates with your mate. Instead we are talking about big planned fun dates.

Over the years we (Claudia and Dave) have collected dating suggestions from seminar participants and catalogued them in a book, *52 Dates for You and Your Mate*. Here are five of our favorites:

- Formal Dinner in the Park Date. Put on your black tie or evening gown and grab the picnic basket for an evening under the stars.

- Breakfast on a Motorcycle Date. Surprise your partner by turning your bike (or card table) into a sidewalk café next to his or her office building.

- Photo Date. Go to your favorite haunt and snap away. Simply set the timer on your camera and run back and smile.

- Yellow Road Date. Choose a fifty-mile radius around your home and see what you can discover. Avoid four-lane roads and fast-food restaurants.

- Proposal Date. Go to a public place and ask your mate to marry you all over again. Then go to your favorite romantic restaurant and celebrate your engagement!

Engage the Skills

As you consolidate your skills through practice and the development of positive rituals such as dating, the most important thing is for you to be able to engage the skills when you need them. Knowing how to use the Speaker-Listener Technique or the problem-solving model is great, but the real benefit comes from using these skills when you need them most. Unfortunately, the times you need the most skill are the same times that it is hardest to use them, so being able to make the shift to engage more skills is critical. That's where practice and good habits really pay off.

It's hardest to engage the skills the first few times. For example, as you work on ground rule 1—the Time Out ground rule—it will be harder at the start than after you have used it a few times. It can seem like avoidance when you start using Time Outs, but the habit gets stronger as you see that they work. Your relationship benefits from the increased control over how and when you deal with difficult issues.

Reinforce, Reinforce, Reinforce

When we train other professionals and paraprofessionals to work with couples, we emphasize over and over the need to be active in reinforcing the positive steps couples make when learning the skills we teach. It's very important to reinforce new skills, as well as to reinforce the positive things that are already happening.

We make the same suggestion to you. As you are working on learning new patterns and ways of thinking, reinforce each other. Praise your partner for trying new skills out, for listening well, for working with you to handle issues well, for being committed, and so forth. Don't take each other for granted. Show your appreciation for positive effort. And don't dwell on the past. In other words, don't say "Why couldn't you have done this seven years ago?" Instead, *focus on reinforcing the positive changes that are occurring now!*

When was the last time you said, "Gee, honey, I sure like how you do that?" Or "I really felt great the other night when you dropped what you were doing and spent time just listening to me talk about my concerns at work." It's not hard to say "Thanks" or "Great job" or "I really appreciated the way you did that." The effects on your relationship can be dramatic. Too often we get too focused on the negative. Instead, try looking for how to reward the positive. That's the best way to encourage more positive behavior in the future.

In general, our entire culture greatly underestimates the power of verbal reinforcement. Maybe that's because we are so focused on material rewards here in America. Don't succumb to this cultural tendency. Positive verbal reinforcement is the most potent change agent ever devised. Use it. If you like some things you see going on, say so. Reinforce, reinforce, reinforce!

Do It Now!

Perhaps your partner is as excited about getting started working on your relationship as you are. We'd like to close with this exercise that you can do together to nurture your empty nest marriage. Why not take another empty nest marriage checkup and see what you need to weed or plant in your own marriage garden? Answer the following three questions:

1. What are the best parts of your relationship (such as friendship, sense of humor, flexibility, good communication, common faith, and so on)?

2. What are some negative habits you need to replace (such as taking on too many activities or watching too much television)? Do you need to throw away the remote?

3. What are some positive habits you would like to develop (such as getting more exercise, having more fun dates, or working on "active listening")?

Are you willing to accept the challenge to grow through the changes that come your way in the empty nest years? You can develop new habits to foster positive changes in your relationship. But it's up to you to define what you are going to do in the next weeks, months, and years to enrich your empty nest and make the rest of your marriage the best it can be.

A SENSE OF HOPE

Throughout this book, we have quoted real couples who have attended our seminars or responded to our written survey. We want to close with a sampling of what they said about their sense of the strengths of their marriage and their hopes for the future:

"After forty years of marriage, our love has grown and continues to grow. The special look we have for one another is still there."

"Commitment to persevere, no matter what occurs. I hope we will become closer than ever before and that our family will be whole again."

"Building a better relationship, injecting more fun and getting my best friend back."

"Being married to my best friend. I love him, but more important I like him. He is the man of my dreams."

"Being with my wife—her encouragement and partnership in life is the best part of my marriage."

"Friendship, concern for each other, tenderness, taking care of each other."

"I'm looking forward to getting to know each other in a more honest way and relaxing and enjoying our kids and grandkids as we let them enjoy us."

"The comfort and sense of stability in the relationship."

These couples have said it better than we could. Let them challenge you to choose to grow.

Choose to Grow

It is as you attempt growth that you make progress and have the potential for growing closer together. Along the way, you will have your "ficus trees" that you need to uproot and replant. But it's encouraging to know that even your mistakes can shake you out of complacency and jump-start growth. Our ficus tree is a living example. Each time we see our ficus, which now lives by a window in our living room, we are reminded of its days of glory in the sun. It reminds us to never give up adventure and, rather than remain root-bound, to take the risk to grow and keep on planting good things in our marriage.

Won't you join us in accepting this challenge? Trust us: your empty nest marriage can be the better half—if you are willing to take the risk and fight for it!

Research References and Further Reading

The following list is for those of you interested in further reading in the fields of study underlying this work. Some of the works, like this book, were written for the typical reader. Some were written for researchers and students interested in deeper study.

Arp, D., & Arp, C. (1993). *52 dates for you and your mate*. Nashville, TN: Nelson.

Arp, D., & Arp, C. (1996). *The second half of marriage: Facing the eight challenges of the empty nest years*. Grand Rapids, MI: Zondervan.

Arp, D., & Arp, C. (1997). *10 great dates to revitalize your marriage*. Grand Rapids, MI: Zondervan.

Arp, D., & Arp, C. (1998). *Love life for parents: How to have kids and a sex life too*. Grand Rapids, MI: Zondervan.

Baucom, D., & Epstein, N. (1990). *Cognitive-behavioral marital therapy*. New York: Guilford Press.

Clements, M., Stanley, S. M., & Markman, H. J. (1997). *Predicting divorce*. Unpublished manuscript, Penn State University.

Eidelson, R. J., & Epstein, N. (1981). Unrealistic beliefs of clinical couples: Their relationship to expectations, goals and satisfaction. *American Journal of Family Therapy, 9*(4), 13–22.

Floyd, F., Markman, H., Kelly, S., Blumberg, S., & Stanley, S. (1996). Prevention: Conceptual, research, and clinical issues. In N. Jacobson & A. Gurman (Eds.), *Handbook of marital therapy, second edition*.

Gottman, J. (1993). A theory of marital dissolution and stability. *Journal of Family Psychology, 7, 57–75*.

Gottman, J. (1994). *Why marriages succeed or fail*. New York: Simon & Schuster.

Gottman, J., Notarius, C., Gonso J., & Markman, H. J. (1976). *A couple's guide to communication*. Champaign, IL: Research Press.

Grych, J., & Fincham, F. (1990). Marital conflict and children's adjustment. *Psychological Bulletin, 108, 267–290*.

Guerney, B. G., Jr. (1977). *Relationship enhancement*. San Francisco: Jossey-Bass.

Hahlweg, K., Markman, H. J., Thurmaier, F., Engl, J., & Eckert, V. (1998). Prevention of marital distress: Results of a German prospective longitudinal study. *Journal of Family Psychology, 12, 543–556*.

Halford, K., Kelly, A., & Markman, H. J. (1997). The concept of a healthy marriage. In K. Halford & H. J. Markman (Eds.), *Clinical handbook of marriage and couples intervention* (pp. 3–12). London: Wiley.

Hartman, S., Whitton, S., Markman, H. J., & Stanley, S. (under review). Premarital intervention. In E. Craighead (Ed.), *Encyclopedia of psychology and neuropsychology*.

Johnson, D. J., & Rusbult, C. E. (1989). Resisting temptation: Devaluation of alternative partners as a means of maintaining commitment in close relationships. *Journal of Personality and Social Psychology, 57, 967–980*.

Johnson, M. P. (1982). The social and cognitive features of the dissolution of commitment to relationships. In S. Duck (Ed.), *Personal relationships: Dissolving personal relationships*. New York: Academic Press.

Jordan, P. L., Stanley, S. M., & Markman, H. J. (1999). *Becoming parents: How to strengthen your marriage as your family grows*. San Francisco: Jossey-Bass.

Karney, B. R., & Bradbury, T. N. (1995). The longitudinal course of marital quality and stability: A review of theory, method, and research. *Psychological Bulletin, 118*, 3–34.

Knox, D. (1971). *Marriage happiness*. Champaign, IL: Research Press.

Kurdek, L. A. (1993). Predicting marital dissolution: A five-year prospective longitudinal study of newlywed couples. *Journal of Personality and Social Psychology, 64*, 221–242.

Levenson, R. W., & Gottman, J. M. (1985). Physiological and affective predictors of change in relationship satisfaction. *Journal of Personality and Social Psychology, 49*(1), 85–94.

Levinger, G. (1965). Marital cohesiveness and dissolution: An integrative review. *Journal of Marriage and the Family, 27*, 19–28.

Mace, D., & Mace, V. (1985). *Letters to a retired couple*. Valley Forge, PA: Judson.

Mahoney, A., Pargament, K. I., Jewell, T., Swank, A. B., Scott, E., Emery, E., & Rye, M. (1999). Marriage and the spiritual realm: The role of proximal and distal religious constructs in marital functioning. *Journal of Family Psychology, 13*, 321–338.

Markman, H. J., Floyd, F. J., Stanley, S. M., & Storaasli, R. D. (1988). Prevention of marital distress: A longitudinal investigation. *Journal of Consulting and Clinical Psychology, 56*, 210–217.

Markman, H. J., & Hahlweg, K. (1993). The prediction and prevention of marital distress: An international perspective. *Clinical Psychology Review, 13*, 29–43.

Markman, H. J., Renick, M. J., Floyd, F., Stanley, S. M., & Clements, M. (1993). Preventing marital distress through communication and conflict management training: A four- and five-year follow-up. *Journal of Consulting and Clinical Psychology, 62*, 1–8.

Markman, H. J., Stanley, S. M., & Blumberg, S. L. (1994). *Fighting for your marriage: Positive steps for a loving and lasting relationship*. San Francisco: Jossey-Bass.

Matthews, L. S., Wickrama, K.A.S., & Conger, R. D. (1996). Predicting marital instability from spouse and observer reports of marital interaction. *Journal of Marriage and the Family, 58,* 641–655.

McManus, M. (1993). *Marriage savers.* Grand Rapids, MI: Zondervan.

Notarius, C., & Markman, H. J. (1993). *We can work it out: Making sense of marital conflict.* New York: Putnam.

Rusbult, C. E., & Buunk, B. P. (1993). Commitment processes in close relationships: An interdependence analysis. *Journal of Social and Personal Relationships, 10,* 175–204.

Sager, C. J. (1976). *Marriage contracts and couple therapy: Hidden forces in intimate relationships.* New York: Brunner/Mazel.

Sheehy, G. (1995). *New passages.* New York: Random House.

Silliman, B., Stanley, S. M., Coffin, W., Markman, H. J., & Jordan, P. L. (in press). Preventive interventions for couples. In H. Liddle, D. Santisteban, R. Levant, & J. Bray (Eds.), *Family psychology intervention science.* Washington, DC: American Psychological Association.

Smalley, G. (1996). *Making love last forever.* Dallas: Word Publishing.

Stanley, S. M. (1998). *The heart of commitment: Compelling research that reveals the secrets of a lifelong, intimate marriage.* Nashville, TN: Nelson.

Stanley, S. M., Blumberg, S. L., & Markman, H. J. (1999). Helping couples fight *for* their marriages: The PREP approach. In R. Berger & M. Hannah (Eds.), *Handbook of preventive approaches in couple therapy* (pp. 279–303). New York: Brunner/Mazel.

Stanley, S. M., Bradbury, T. N., & Markman, H. J. (in press). Structural flaws in the bridge from basic research on marriage to interventions for couples: Illustrations from Gottman, Coan, Carrere, and Swanson (1998). *Journal of Marriage and the Family, 62*(1), 256–264.

Stanley, S. M., Lobitz, W. C., & Dickson, F. (1999). Using what we know: Commitment and cognitions in marital therapy.

In W. Jones & J. Adams (Eds.), *Handbook of interpersonal commitment and relationship stability* (pp. 411–424). New York: Plenum.

Stanley, S. M., & Markman, H. J. (1992). Assessing commitment in personal relationships. *Journal of Marriage and the Family, 54*, 595–608.

Stanley, S. M., & Markman, H. J. (1997). *Marriage in the nineties: A nationwide random phone survey.* Denver, CO: PREP.

Stanley, S. M., & Markman, H. J. (1998). Acting on what we know: The hope of prevention. In *Strategies to strengthen marriage: What we know, what we need to know.* Washington, DC: Family Impact Seminar.

Stanley, S. M., Markman, H. J., Prado, L. M., Olmos-Gallo, P. A., Tonelli, L., St. Peters, M., Leber, B. D., Bobulinski, M., Cordova, A., & Whitton, S. (in press). *Community-based premarital prevention: Clergy and lay leaders on the front lines.*

Stanley, S. M., Markman, H. J., St. Peters, M., & Leber, D. (1995). Strengthening marriages and preventing divorce: New directions in prevention research. *Family Relations, 44*, 392–401.

Stanley, S. M., Trathen, D., McCain, S., & Bryan, M. (1998). *A lasting promise: A Christian guide to fighting for your marriage.* San Francisco: Jossey-Bass.

Van Lange, P.A.M., Agnew, C. R., Harinck, F., & Steemers, G.E.M. (1997). From game theory to real life: How social value orientation affects willingness to sacrifice in ongoing close relationships. *Journal of Personality and Social Psychology, 73*, 1330–1344.

Wallerstein, J., & Blakeslee, S. (1995). *The good marriage.* Boston: Houghton Mifflin.

Whitehead, B. D. (1997). *The divorce culture.* New York: Knopf.

Whitton, S., Stanley, S., & Markman, H. (under review). *Sacrifice in romantic relationships: An exploration of relevant research and theory.*

Finding a Counselor
When You Need One

There are so many potential therapists and counselors to choose from in most areas that it's hard for many couples to know how to find the best help. How do you find a good couples therapist out of all the psychologists, marital therapists, professional counselors, psychiatrists, and social workers who are listed in the Yellow Pages?

The best way to find a couples therapist is to try to get names from a source you trust—a friend, a physician, a clergy person. If all else fails, you can write to us for referrals of people in your area who have been trained in the PREP approach, if there are any. If you want to do that, send a self-addressed, stamped envelope to us at:

PREP, Inc.
P.O. Box 102530
Denver, CO 80250-2530
Or visit our website: www.prepinc.com

Or you can write:

The American Association of Marriage
and Family Therapists
1100—17th Street N.W., 10th floor
Washington, DC 20136

Ask them to send you a list of certified marriage and family therapists in your area. You can also call your state's marriage and family therapy association, psychological association, or social work association. There might even be a trustworthy radio talk show psychologist or therapist in your area. These individuals are likely to know of some of the best resources in your community because they have to be prepared to refer a lot of people for help.

Getting two or more names is a good idea. Then be an active consumer: call them up and ask about their training, experience, approach, fees, license, and billing policies. If you really like the approach taken in this book, you might ask for a therapist who specializes in what is called the cognitive-behavioral approach. You can and should ask a potential therapist directly about their approach or techniques used in therapy, and anything else that's important to you—such as religious or cultural background, viewpoints on codependency issues, or experience with very specific issues such as the effects on marriage of having a seriously ill child. You get the idea. Again, you are the consumer; if you don't like the answers to your questions, move on and try another person.

It is critical for you to ask therapists if they specialize in working with couples or if, in contrast, they mostly do individual therapy. Many individual-oriented therapists will gladly do marital therapy, but that doesn't mean they are skilled at it. There are members of all the professions listed above who specialize in marital or couples work. We recommend that you choose a therapist whose areas of specialization match your need.

If you begin to see a therapist, keep the same issues in mind. If, after a few sessions, you don't feel that this person can help you, you may be right. You are going to spend a lot of money with a therapist, so don't persist very long with someone with whom you are not comfortable.

It is probably most important to get a sense of the connection you may have with the potential therapist and of whether you feel you have a good "fit." As is true of all types of therapy, one of the best predictors of success in couples therapy is the quality of the relationship you have with the therapist. Do you think this is someone you can trust and respect?

Last, what if you want to get professional help, but your spouse isn't interested? Here's what psychologist and colleague Andrea Van Steenhouse often suggests on her radio call-in show. Say something like this to your partner: "I've been concerned about some of the issues in our relationship, and I think we could benefit from some help. I've made an appointment with a therapist for Wednesday at 4 P.M. I'd really like you to come with me. I want to do this together. But if you don't want to, I want to let you know that I plan to go anyway. I want to do what I can to get this situation turned around for both our sakes." This kind of strategy shows your positive intent. It also shows how serious you are about getting help. It may not work, but then again, it just might. It takes some courage to get help when you need it; if you need help, we hope you will seek it.

Some of our colleagues have developed new approaches to relationship therapy that focus on the willing partner. If your partner chooses not to participate in therapy, you may choose to seek a therapist experienced in one-partner approaches.

SOME THOUGHTS ON DOMESTIC VIOLENCE

Because PREP (and therefore this book) deals with communication and conflict between partners, questions about domestic violence arise at times. Domestic violence is a very complex topic, and not the subject of this book. Nevertheless, we have a few key points we would like to stress on the matter:

- Neither PREP nor this book is a treatment program for domestic violence.

- There are some couples who can reduce their chances of becoming physically aggressive by learning techniques such as those taught here. Those would be couples who are at risk for physical violence as a result of difficulty with handling conflict well together—rather than couples who are in situations where a controlling male is using aggression to dominate or control his partner.

- Domestic violence of any sort is unacceptable and wrong and dangerous.

- There is an alarming level of domestic violence (at various levels) taking place in families in our society.

- No matter what the nature of the violence, when males strike females, rather than the other way around, there is every reason to believe that females are both in greater danger and will likely suffer more long lasting and negative aftereffects. Of course, many females strike males, too, and that is just as unacceptable and occasionally as lethal.

- *In the presence of any kind of domestic violence, the preeminent concern should be safety.* That means that people should seek whatever level of services are necessary to ensure that neither partner is in danger. That could mean seeking counsel from a therapist or a pastor *who has experience in this area,* or going to a community shelter for battered women in cases where the woman is very fearful and in significant danger.

- We recommend that those who work with couples be aware of the complex issues around domestic violence and also be fully aware of local resources for help in dealing with domestic violence in ways that can increase safety (for example, law enforcement access, shelters).

For further reading about domestic violence issues, we recommend the book *Current Controversies on Family Violence* (1993), edited by Richard Gelles and Donileen Loseke, and published by Sage Publications.

Resources and Training

The authors of this book have a variety of resources available. Further, we conduct workshops both for couples and for those who work with couples. We have included the following section for those of you who may wish to go further, either as a couple or as someone who works to help couples make great marriages.

THE PREP® APPROACH

Books

In addition to this book, we have the following titles in this series. Each represents the same basic approach for helping couples build their marriages, but each is adapted and developed for a special purpose. All are published by Jossey-Bass.

Fighting for Your Marriage (1994), by Markman, Stanley, and Blumberg, is the original book in this series.

A Lasting Promise: A Christian Guide to Fighting for Your Marriage (1998), by Stanley, Trathen, McCain, and Bryan.

Becoming Parents: How to Strengthen Your Marriage as Your Family Grows (1999), by Jordan, Stanley, and Markman.

Fighting for Your Jewish Marriage (2000), by Crohn, Markman, Blumberg, and Levine.

Audiotapes and Videos

Fighting for *Your Marriage* audiotapes and videos are available from PREP Educational Products, Inc. Please call (303) 759-9931 or write to us at PREP, Inc., P.O. Box 102530, Denver, CO 80250-2530, to order. The books listed can be ordered from PREP, Jossey-Bass, or from any bookstore. Books or tapes can be ordered from Jossey-Bass by calling (415) 433-1740.

Workshops

We conduct workshops for mental health professionals, clergy, lay leaders, and other marriage educators who desire to be more fully exposed to the PREP approach. For information about these "instructor" workshops, please call (303) 759-9931 or write to us at the address above. We will be glad to give you information about seminars or products to help you in your own relationship or in your work with other couples.

We also have a list of people who have been trained in this approach and who either conduct workshops for couples or do counseling using aspects of this model. To obtain that list, you can either write to us at the address below and request the referral list, or you can visit our website.

You can write to us at:

PREP
P.O. Box 102530
Denver, CO 80250-2530
E-mail: PREPinc@aol.com
Website: www.prepinc.com

MARRIAGE ALIVE INTERNATIONAL
Bringing marriages and families to life!

Marriage Alive International (MAI) was founded by David and Claudia Arp and is a 501(c)3 not-for-profit educational organization dedicated to developing resources for building healthy relationships. Through seminars, books, and video curricula, Marriage Alive seeks to teach relational skills for successful living. MAI provides programs and resources for both the church and community. Resources include the following:

Video Curricula

10 Great Dates to Revitalize Your Marriage. Spark romance with memory-making evenings built on key marriage-enriching themes. Videos include ten fun date launches based on the Arps' book *10 Great Dates*.

The Second Half of Marriage. This ten-session small-group resource is based on the book *The Second Half of Marriage* and will help couples surmount the challenges of the empty nest years.

Marriage Books by David and Claudia Arp

The Second Half of Marriage (with study guide), HarperCollins/Zondervan, 1996

10 Great Dates (with tear-out dates), HarperCollins/Zondervan, 1997

Love Life for Parents, HarperCollins/Zondervan, 1998

52 Dates for You and Your Mate, Thomas Nelson, 1993

Marriage Moments (thirty-one-day devotional guide), Vine Books, 1998

Quiet Whispers from God's Heart for Couples (inspirational couple devotions), J Countryman, 1999

Seminars

The Second Half of Marriage: Facing the Challenges of the Empty Nest Years. Based on a national survey of long-term marriages and on the award-winning book *The Second Half of Marriage*, in this seminar the Arps reveal eight challenges that all long-term marriages face, and give practical strategies for surmounting each.

Marriage Alive: Bringing New Life to Your Relationship. This seminar offers a fun-filled approach to building a thriving marriage. Some of the topics include making your marriage a priority, finding unity in diversity, learning to talk even when you disagree, cultivating spiritual intimacy, and having an intentional marriage.

To schedule the Arps for a seminar or other speaking engagement, contact Alive Communications at (719) 260-7080.

To order books, videos, or other Marriage Alive resources, or for more information, write:

Marriage Alive
P.O. Box 31408
Knoxville, TN 37930
Phone: (888) 690-6667
E-mail: mailine97@aol.com
Website: www.marriagealive.com

Survey Results and Problem Rankings

Three hundred seventy-four people responded to the Arps' Second Half of Marriage survey. Couples completed the Issues Inventory (found on page 20 in this book) by ranking a list of issues from 0 (not a problem at all) to 10 (a severe problem). The table below lists the top seven issues and the average score given by respondents.

Issues	Average Score
Conflict	3.99
Communication	3.88
Sex	3.61
Health	3.45
Fun	3.28
Recreation	3.15
Money	3.00

As you can see, the highest score given was approximately a four, indicating a mild to moderate level of concern with these issues. The range of scores given went from 1 to 10 however, demonstrating that some couples felt these issues were unimportant, while others felt they were severe problems. If your scores on the inventory are significantly higher than these average scores, that would be a reason to think you might need to concentrate on those issues, perhaps using the skills described in this book.

When the list of issues was put through a statistical analysis, called factor analysis, four clear groupings emerged. Couples saw the issues in the inventory as falling into one of these four categories:

1. How we get along (communication, conflict, friendship)
2. Our physical relationship (sex, fun, health)
3. Dealing with others (family, friends, in-laws)
4. Financial issues (money, retirement, career)

These groupings indicate where empty nest couples are focusing their attention. In particular, the first two categories, which encompass the quality of marriage a couple has, dominated the list of problems couples at this stage of life were worried about.

The Authors

Claudia Arp and David Arp, MSW, a husband-wife team, are founders and directors of Marriage Alive International, a groundbreaking program providing marriage- and family-building resources and training for the church and community. The Arps are popular speakers, seminar leaders, and columnists, and are the authors of numerous books and video curricula, including *10 Great Dates* and *The Second Half of Marriage*, winner of the Gold Medallion Award. Frequent contributors to print and broadcast media, the Arps have appeared as empty nest experts on the *Today Show* (NBC), *This Morning* (CBS), and *CrossTalk* (MSNBC). Their nationally syndicated radio program, *The Family Workshop*, is heard daily on more than two hundred stations. David and Claudia have been married for over thirty-five years and live in Knoxville, Tennessee. They have three married sons and five grandchildren.

Scott M. Stanley, Ph.D., is codirector of the Center for Marital and Family Studies at the University of Denver and president of PREP Educational Products, Inc. He has published widely—both research reports and writings for couples. He is internationally known for his work on the PREP approach for reducing the risks of marital distress and divorce, as well as for his research and theory on marital commitment. Stanley coauthored the best-selling book, videos, and audiotapes titled *Fighting for Your Marriage*. He is also the coauthor of *A Lasting Promise* and *Becoming Parents*, and author of *The Heart of Commitment*. He contributes extensively to both print and broadcast media as an expert on marriage.

Howard J. Markman, Ph.D., is a professor of psychology, the director of the Center for Marital and Family Studies at the University of Denver in Colorado, and president of PREP, Inc. He is widely published in academic journals and internationally known for his work on the prediction and prevention of marital distress and divorce. He has often appeared in broadcast and print media, including segments about PREP on *20/20*, *Oprah*, and *48 Hours*. Along with his colleagues, he has coauthored the books *We Can Work It Out: Making Sense of Marital Conflict*, *Fighting for Your Marriage*, *Becoming Parents*, and other works.

Susan L. Blumberg, Ph.D., is a licensed clinical psychologist in private practice in Denver, Colorado, working with children, families, and couples. She presents regularly on topics related to communication and conflict management skills to both professional and public audiences. She leads PREP workshops for couples and works with families and businesses interested in improving communication skills. Dr. Blumberg has coauthored the best-selling book, videos, and audiotapes titled *Fighting for Your Marriage*.

Index

306.81
F

Fighting for your
   empty nest
   marriage.

3391002114 0430

$25.00
02/13/2001

DATE			